Mallarmé and Debussy

Unheard Music, Unseen Text

ELIZABETH McCOMBIE

CLARENDON PRESS · OXFORD

OXFORD
UNIVERSITY PRESS

Great Clarendon Street, Oxford OX2 6DP

Oxford University Press is a department of the University of Oxford.
It furthers the University's objective of excellence in research, scholarship,
and education by publishing worldwide in

Oxford New York

Auckland Cape Town Dar es Salaam Hong Kong Karachi
Kuala Lumpur Madrid Melbourne Mexico City Nairobi
New Delhi Shanghai Taipei Toronto

With offices in

Argentina Austria Brazil Chile Czech Republic France Greece
Guatemala Hungary Italy Japan South Korea Poland Portugal
Singapore Switzerland Thailand Turkey Ukraine Vietnam

Oxford is a registered trade mark of Oxford University Press
in the UK and in certain other countries

Published in the United States
by Oxford University Press Inc., New York

British Library Cataloguing in Publication Data

Data available

Library of Congress Cataloging in Publication Data

Data available

ISBN 0-19-926637-9

3 5 7 9 10 8 6 4 2

Typeset in Baskerville by
Cambrian Typesetters, Frimley, Surrey

Printed in Great Britain
on acid-free paper by
Antony Rowe Ltd.,
Chippenham, Wiltshire

for my GRANDMOTHER, ANNE GIBBON

ACKNOWLEDGEMENTS

This book was written during my research fellowship at St John's College, Oxford; I am particularly grateful for the college's support. I should like here to record my gratitude to several people and institutions who have helped me in various and important ways to produce this study. Malcolm Bowie inspiringly and generously supervised my work on Mallarmé, Debussy, and the music–literature interdiscipline for the doctoral thesis from which this book grew. Many thanks are due to the Arts and Humanities Research Board and Wolfson and Somerville Colleges for funding, scholarships, and other financial support. My thanks, too, go to Roger Pensom, Adrianne Tooke, Ingrid Wassenaar, Clive Scott, Peter Franklin, Ann Jefferson, and Wes Williams for their suggestions and advice. I owe much to Roger Pearson, who introduced me to Mallarmé; to Mary Moore, for giving me my voice; and, finally, to my husband Duncan, who has patiently read and discussed my work with me and has not tired of giving great support and encouragement.

I would like to thank the following for permission to reproduce published material: G. Henle Verlag (Example 1.1); Schott Music International (Examples 2.1, 2.4); Durand (Examples 2.2, 2.3, 2.5–2.12, 3.6–3.15); Edition Peters (Examples 4.1–4.8).

E.M.

CONTENTS

NOTE ON EDITIONS AND REFERENCES

Of the full texts analysed here, Mallarmé's verse and selected correspondence can be found in the new *Œuvres complètes*, edited by Bertrand Marchal for the Bibliothèque de la Pléiade (Paris: Gallimard, 1998), of which only the first volume has so far been published. The critical prose can be found in the first *Œuvres complètes*, edited by Henri Mondor and G. Jean-Aubry for the Bibliothèque de la Pléiade (Paris: Gallimard, 1945). Full details of editions of all works, including scores of works by Debussy, can be found in the bibliography.

The following abbreviations are used in the footnotes:

OC (M)   *Œuvres complètes*, ed. Henri Mondor and G. Jean-Aubry, Bibliothèque de la Pléiade (Paris: Gallimard, 1945)
OC   *Œuvres complètes*, ed. Bertrand Marchal, Bibliothèque de la Pléiade (Paris: Gallimard, 1998)

PROLOGUE

> Debussy is the Mallarmé of music, not because he has set *L'Après-midi d'un faune* to sound, but because the music has all the qualities of the poem and none, for instance, of Verlaine. . . . Mallarmé has a beauty of his own, calculated, new, alluring; and Debussy is not less original, aloof, deliberately an artist.
>
> (Arthur Symons, from his article in the *Saturday Review*, 8 Feb. 1908)

Mallarmé (1842–98) and Debussy (1862–1916) have achieved lasting international fame. Both are renowned as radical innovators of their arts and have monumental status in and across their respective fields, due, not least, to the remarkable waves of artistic influence created by their work. The modernity of their art is still striking today, even when put next to composers such as Webern, Schoenberg, and Boulez, and poets like Claudel and Eluard.

Mallarmé and Debussy's work represents an intensely fertile moment of crossover in the histories of music and literature. They lived at a time of particular mutual awareness between music and letters. Mallarmé stands out from his Symbolist contemporaries by being an extraordinary listener. His observations and aesthetic theories about music inform his poetics at the most fundamental level and a performative musico-poetic vocabulary is woven into his critical prose. In spite of this, Mallarmé is not thought of most commonly as a 'musical' poet, whereas Debussy, who frequented Mallarmé's *Mardis* (weekly Tuesday gatherings of artists), is a notoriously 'literary' composer. Debussy understood that contemporary poetry was home to some of the most imaginative creative minds, who were producing exciting new sounds, senses, and rhythms, and he chose to work at his own art on that site. Paul Dukas corroborates this:

Dès le début de sa vie d'artiste, il s'était ardemment mêlé au mouvement littéraire d'alors. Verlaine, Mallarmé, Laforgue nous apportaient des tons nouveaux, des sonorités nouvelles. Ils projetaient sur les mots des lueurs qu'on n'avait encore jamais vues; ils usaient de procédés inconnus des poètes leurs devanciers; ils faisaient rendre à la matière verbale des effets dont on ne soupçonnait pas, avant eux, la subtilité ou la force; par dessus tout, ils concevaient le vers ou la prose comme des musiciens; ils leur donnaient les soins de musiciens et comme des musiciens encore, combinaient les images et leur correspondance sonore. La plus forte influence qu'ait subie Debussy est celle des littérateurs. Non pas celle des musiciens.[1]

Debussy's saturation in literature was so deep and diverse that it must affect the way in which we hear and appreciate his music. As both Mallarmé and

[1] Quoted in Robert Brussel, 'Claude Debussy et Paul Dukas', *La Revue musicale*, 7 (1926), 101.

Debussy were operating in a similar cultural and aesthetic milieu there are natural overlaps between their work: they lived in very similar worlds. But this is not to suggest that the interesting links between them exist solely because of the bridges they themselves built, or by virtue of their shared nationality. At a theoretical level these two artists often had a very different conception of what they were trying to achieve. Moreover, listening to Debussy and reading Mallarmé can be very different experiences. Whilst Mallarmé is radically disruptive of poetic codes, asking almost the impossible of his reader, Debussy, although profoundly challenging musical conventions (including tonality itself), makes endless effort to weld his motivic elements seamlessly in a horizontal flow so that the joins, although audible, do not jolt the listener. Debussy's acoustic sense of the piano often leads him to favour resonance and sonority over the character of single notes. Nuance and colour of timbre predominate in his writing over clarity of form and there often appears to be no finality in his music.[2] At times he is awkward, unexpected, ironic, childlike. His style is mischievously paradoxical in its improbable partnerships of the tough and the effortless.

Compositional procedures such as these might seem a long way from the angular disjunction and multivalent simultaneity of Mallarmé's verse, and indeed at times they are, but there is also a startlingly resonant interplay in their work. In both artists we experience multiple temporalities, shifting perspectives, double focuses, instabilities, and the melting of one form into another, all of which effects are produced in dialogue between the two expressive systems. The phenomenon of simultaneous asymmetry and overlap, made clear by the Mallarmé–Debussy axis, is not isolated to this example: it merely illustrates the nature of the problems that exist in any act of musico-poetic comparison.

In spite of the fact that the intertextual and interdisciplinary have been very prominent areas of critical investigation in recent years, most notably in the domain of visual art and literature, the interplay between Mallarmé and Debussy and indeed the relationship between music and poetry more generally, which as a source of debate reaches back to the Pythagorean tradition, has yet to be put under any real pressure from comparative critics. In both disciplines, writing about the meetings of text and music has largely been beset by a naive mimetic model of the inter-art relationship. This may be due to the fact that inhabiting and engaging with the middle ground between music and literature is such a precarious business. The natural asymmetry

---

[2] Debussy writes in a letter to Durand (Mar. 1908): 'J'essaie de faire autre chose, en quelque sorte des réalités—ce que les imbéciles appellent "impressionnisme".' E. Lockspeiser, in *Debussy: His Life and Mind*, 2 vols. (London: Cassell & Co., 1962–5), ii. 18, writes that his music is 'based not on a succession of themes but on the relative values of sounds themselves'. The string quartet and 'Jeux de vagues' from *La Mer* (1903–5) are more classical in form, whereas the *Préludes* are built on the interplay of contrast and association of register, sonority, and figures.

between the two kinds of artistic occupation makes the act of comparison difficult: the units of composition do not correspond, their modes of reception (reading and listening) differ widely, and their greater and lesser degrees of performativity are to be negotiated.

When a piece of music and poem are placed side by side there is overlap between the dynamic energy and patterns of reading and listening of each. Text and piece when performed or read aloud are similar in that both take place within strict time limits and often according to a set of conventions constraining them within an allotted space. In both, the nature of the welding of content and form means the two cannot be dissociated. In a poem the reader has time to glance back and forth at will, in a similar way to the score-reader. In a performed musical work, however, the listener is at the mercy of the score and the performer, allowed no autonomy in choosing the order in or speed at which to listen, as with a recital of poetry. The *décalage* that already exists in music between the way timbre and sounds are interpreted and heard in performance, and the 'phonology' of the score, becomes even larger and more multiple when music is put in the same matrix as literature.

Yet there is no critical language or method, at present, for sufficiently unravelling the overlap or articulating the asymmetries. Music is often left to lurk nervously in the background in literary criticism, and a proper understanding of literature is rarely used to illuminate musical commentaries.

Tentative steps in the direction of inter-media criticism have been made, with mixed success. By distancing itself in the 1980s and 1990s from the formalism and positivism of traditional analysis and from Schenkerian analysis, a 'new musicology' has emerged, whose explicit programme is to bring musicology into contact with the social science, culture, and gender studies available to other disciplines, including literature.[3]

The advent of 'new musicology' has had a considerable effect on word and music studies, not least in opening it up to literary theoretical approaches. Lawrence Kramer has contributed some of the most promising preparatory work in this field so far. In his three major studies, *Music and Poetry: The Nineteenth Century and After* (1984), *Music as Cultural Practice, 1800–1900* (1990), and *Classical Music and Postmodern Knowledge* (1995), he aims to develop a musicological discourse, which he calls 'cultural practice', that fully integrates up-to-date cultural studies and critical theory with music analysis.[4] In this view music is no longer taken as a formal, autonomous object, but as an entity or activity that shapes the cultural identity of listeners. Kramer has generated

---

[3] See, for example, Susan McClary, *Feminine Endings: Music, Gender and Sexuality* (Minneapolis: University of Minnesota Press, 1991) and Carolyn Abbate, *Unsung Voices: Opera and Musical Narrative in the Nineteenth Century* (Princeton: Princeton University Press, 1991).

[4] (Berkeley and Los Angeles: University of California Press, 1984); (Berkeley and Los Angeles: University of California Press, 1990); and (Berkeley and Los Angeles: University of California Press, 1995) respectively.

and employed an imaginative vocabulary of inter-art discourse in many areas of music–text convergence with some success, most notably in lied interpretation and musical narratology.

Charles Rosen (who distances himself from, and is often sharply critical of, 'new musicology') is particularly open to using literature and philosophy as interpretative keys for unlocking music. His analysis of Schumann's *Dichterliebe* in *The Romantic Generation* (1996), for example, is based around the form of the literary fragment.[5] Noting that, by contrast with the centripetal movement towards a kernel of meaning in La Rochefoucauld, in Chamfort's maxims 'words often lose their definition as thought gains in precision', he continues by extending the idea to music, clearly positioning the literary phenomenon so as to elucidate the musical thought:

The words in this observation begin to expand as if with some kind of inward pressure: the direction is centrifugal. As we puzzle out the thought, the individual words— 'learn', 'forget', 'guess'—begin to move to the margins of their meaning, to connote more than they denote. This expansive movement attains its greatest power with the Romantic Fragment, and it entailed a renunciation of classical focus.[6]

Enlisting literature as a co-worker is a powerful facet of Rosen's work, although the brevity of his comparisons, in the case of the fragments for example, leaves the impression that if the literary analysis were pushed further many more fascinating parallels could be uncovered.

Much of the best work in this growing field has been published in a series of collaborative volumes edited by Steven Scher and others, in the series 'Word and Music Studies'. These volumes contain the work of literary critics and musicologists whose scholarly concern is to find new ways (some terminological and some typological) of theorizing and articulating the many and varied levels of the relationship between music and literature. Essays in *Music and Text: Critical Inquiries* (1992) contribute some useful early explorations into this interdisciplinary area, focusing upon it from diverse angles such as the use of literary theory as a model for music criticism, genre theories in literature and music, and the conjunction of cultural and historical approaches in interpretative practice.[7] Thomas Grey revisits metaphorical modes in nineteenth-century music criticism, exploring concepts of 'inter-art', particularly analogies between music and architecture, through contemporary writers and philosophers;[8] Antony Newcomb draws on Peter Brooks's *Reading for the Plot* to

---

[5] *The Romantic Generation* (London: Harper Collins, 1996).

[6] Ibid. 50.

[7] Ed. Steven Scher (Cambridge: Cambridge University Press, 1992). Other volumes in the series include Walter Bernhart et al. (eds.), *Word and Music Studies: Defining the Field* (Amsterdam: Rodopi, 1999); Walter Bernhart and Werner Wolf (eds.), *Word and Music Studies: Essays on the Song Cycle and Defining the Field* (Amsterdam: Rodopi, 2001).

[8] 'Metaphorical Modes in Nineteenth-Century Music Criticism: Image, Narrative, and Idea', in Scher (ed.), *Music and Text*, 93–117.

propose narrative paradigms for interpreting Mahler;[9] Marshall Brown asks
if there are useful organizational symmetries between plot structure and musical closure.[10] Susan Bernstein's recent book *Virtuosity of the Nineteenth Century:*
Performing Music and Language in Heine, Liszt and Baudelaire (1998) examines
Romantic conceptions and problematizations of music and the relationship of
the arts through nineteenth-century theories of *correspondance*.[11] Organizing
her study of Heine and Baudelaire around the central figure of Liszt, whose
role as metaphor in certain poetic and journalistic modes she examines,
Bernstein very effectively pursues the conflicts and tensions created by identity and non-identity between music and language at this time.

   Although these studies have provided some initial lift-off in this area there
is a long way to go. None gives sufficient space to analyses of *each* art in order
to make the appropriately complex and detailed demands upon the text and
music that are necessary to unravelling the intricate patterns of the overlap. I
will not rehearse the gestures made by Kramer, Rosen, et al. here, but will
explore the possibility of pushing the kind of analytical cooperation glimpsed
in these writers further, to articulate an area of artistic experience still largely
inaccessible to criticism: the meeting ground or interface between music and
poetry as it is instantiated in Mallarmé and Debussy.

   Kramer asks if 'a discipline that could situate the two arts in a coherent
and significant context' is possible. 'If so,' he continues, 'it would have to be a
discipline that could embrace both arts without merely assimilating one to the
other, without scanting the idiosyncrasy of either, without losing sight of
particulars.'[12] This book grew, in part, out of a frustration with the frequently
woolly and devalued critical use of potentially very fruitful musical terms and
metaphors (such as 'sonata form', 'counterpoint', and 'leitmotif') in literary
studies and with the reluctance of musicology to engage fully with connected
literatures in its interpretative practice. What motivates the study is the need
for a more thoughtful and carefully examined reinsertion of music into the
literary critical sphere and vice versa. This book searches for a much-needed
mobile textual approach that is able to reconstruct the particular force of the
intermediate ground and its underlying dialogue of slippages and collusions,
while at the same time insisting on the independence of the arts.

   My comparative approach is suggested by the textual operation of music in
Mallarmé's *œuvre*, in which textual–musical tension is a continuous impulse on
a specific and detailed level. The Introduction discusses the complex prism of
the music–literature overlap, positions it in relation to various interdisciplinary
critical and theoretical stances, delineates a category of the 'intermediary' for

[9] 'Narrative Archetypes and Mahler's Ninth Symphony', *Music and Text*, 118–36.
[10] 'Origins of Modernism: Musical Structures and Narrative Forms', ibid. 75–92.
[11] (Stanford, Calif.: Stanford University Press, 1998).
[12] *Music and Poetry*, p. vii.

further investigation and scrutiny, and suggests a possible method for its articulation. Chapter I re-examines the special place occupied by the concept of
music and musical vocabulary in Mallarmé's critical prose. The chapter
culminates in a reading of *La Musique et les Lettres* through its performative
musico-textual structures, which reflects the extent and originality of
Mallarmé's preoccupation with the text–music relation and is used as an
example of a precise point of textual–musical intersection. Following this
example, the overlap between music and poetry, or the 'intermediary', is
explored using the tools of analysis appropriate to each art; analyses of pieces
by Debussy and poems by Mallarmé act as frameworks for each other. Each
subsequent chapter places the relationship under differently pressured types
of scrutiny, passing the argument of the book through a kaleidoscopically
changing set of parameters and coordinates, the tracking system for which is
designed and defined almost as the analysis progresses.

The specific dynamics of the association and dissociation of music and text
are captured in a series of figures, or conceptual motifs, which are listed in a
Glossary at the end of this book. The figures are chosen to act as pressure points
expandable into enactments of the intermediary, informed by each art and able
to accommodate and express them both. It will become clear that although a
specific relationship is in question here the implications are far-reaching for
other points of contact and crossover in European music and literature.

The textual exploration of the 'intermediary' in this study, focused as it is
through the particular set of aesthetic relationships set up by Mallarmé and
Debussy, is meant neither as a contribution to systematic musicology nor
purely as a literary study about music as it relates to literature. Rather it is
intended as an illuminating adjunct to those disciplines, working at their interface to find new ways of negotiating and usefully expressing the many and
varied levels of the relationship between music and literature, that they might
be encouraged into full critical view. The musical analysis used in the book is
based more on the experience of performance and listening, and on a
hermeneutics of recognition, than on traditional analysis. This is due, in part,
to the evasive nature of Debussy's music, as will become clear. In addition, the
language of the poetic and musical analyses aims to be both accessible to the
non-specialist and informative to the specialist.

There are few critical precedents for this kind of work in Mallarmé or
Debussy studies. Given the wealth of material it is odd that reading music in
Mallarmé has not yet been given proper attention. So far no work has been
devoted entirely to the nature of the relation since Suzanne Bernard's
Mallarmé et la musique (1959), which remains very firmly within the domain of
the Mallarmé text and makes no specific outward-looking references to actual
pieces of music or composers.[13] The result is to render rather meaningless the

---

[13] (Paris: Nizet, 1959).

musical forms posited as models of Mallarmé's growth into a truly 'musical'
poet. Mary Breatnach's study of Mallarmé and Boulez provides useful
surveys, although it does not attempt to formulate a rigorous analytical
language of the intermediary.[14]

Naturally any study of Mallarmé works in the shadow of the groundwork
laid by many great Mallarmé critics. In particular, Jean-Pierre Richard's articulation of Mallarméan poetics in *L'Univers imaginaire de Mallarmé* through
networks of forms, structures, rhythms, dynamic essences, and interwoven
motifs has been influential in shaping my understanding of the overlap. In his
discussion of 'Le Mystère dans les lettres' Richard's vision of the overlay of
textual shape and music is extremely insightful. He writes: 'Ces merveilleuses
analyses structurales, où Mallarmé traite la ligne mélodique comme une véritable phrase écrite, aboutissent toutes à fêter une éclatante apparition.'[15]
Malcolm Bowie's rigorously demanding analyses of the syntactical and metrical make-up of the Mallarmé text and his exploration of the potential of the
minute textual detail in *Mallarmé and the Art of Being Difficult* have also been
greatly facilitating in this project.[16]

Of the many books on Debussy, surprisingly few examine his music
together with his literary world in anything other than a loosely descriptive
fashion. Biography often proves more enticing to the critic, perhaps because
there appears to be some degree of indecision within musicology itself over
how to write about Debussy. Edward Lockspeiser's biography of Debussy has
been seminal in drawing critical attention to the ambiguous elements in the
music, and in particular for bringing Debussy in line with artists other than
Impressionist painters.[17] He discusses the influence on Debussy's mental
world of Hokusai, Turner, Edgar Allan Poe, and Proust, for example. On the
whole, however, Debussy criticism has not yet looked in as much detail as it
could at the nature and extent of the cross-fertilization between Debussy and

---

[14] *Boulez and Mallarmé: A Study in Poetic Influence* (Aldershot: Scolar, 1996).

[15] (Paris: Seuil, 1961), 397.

[16] (Cambridge: Cambridge University Press, 1978). During the writing of this book there has been
an explosion of renewed critical interest in Mallarmé, prompted in part by the centenary of his death
in 1998. It is not the ambition of the book to write an exhaustive survey of Mallarmé criticism, nor has
it been within its scope to absorb all of the recent material. It does seem appropriate, however, to
acknowledge here some of the more important developments for Mallarmé studies, and for this book.
The first volume of Bertrand Marchal's admirably precise and informative edition brings together in
one collection much that has only recently been made accessible for the first time, thanks principally
to work, following Henri Mondor's lead, by Gordon Millan, Carl Paul Barbier, Lloyd Austin, and
Marchal himself. In addition, two excellent volumes have appeared as a result of the 1998 'Colloque
de la Sorbonne': the first a set of critical essays edited by André Guyaux (*Stéphane Mallarmé: Colloque de
la Sorbonne* (Paris: Presses de l'Université de Paris-Sorbonne, 1998)) the second a much-needed collection of documents by Mallarmé's immediate circle of critics, edited by Marchal (*Stéphane Mallarmé:
Mémoire de la critique* (Paris: Presses de l'Université de Paris-Sorbonne, 1998)). Both these and the collection of essays entitled *Meetings with Mallarmé in Contemporary French Culture*, edited by Michael Temple
(Exeter: University of Exeter Press, 1998), inject fresh, sometimes daring criticism into the field and
are of great critical value.   [17] *Debussy: His Life and Mind.*

the poets. Many simply gloss Mallarmé's poems if they refer to them at all. Lockspeiser's work shows up the lack of an adequate critical language for penetrating Debussy's music and, indeed, the lack of commentary on its relation with other arts. Jean Barraqué, a French composer in the post-war period, is a rich and rewarding writer on Debussy and perhaps comes closest to a literary perspective on his music.[18] The problem largely remains, however, in spite of much fresh and exciting criticism to have appeared since the wave of publications in the 1960s to mark the centenary of the composer's birth.[19]

This book rereads some Mallarmé texts and poems in the light of his claims for music in poetics, and also reaches beyond the closure familiar in Mallarmé studies to realize fully the liberating potential of his work for this interdisciplinary field more generally considered. It suggests, in turn, ways in which literary studies can work fruitfully in conjunction with musical ones. In addition, it is hoped that the wider modernist and inter-art aesthetic problems addressed will be of interest to the more general reader.

In Mallarmé's lecture, language takes on musical properties through its new performative immediacy, and music takes on the property so often denied to it, by breathing through the greater self-discursiveness of letters. Literature, at a certain stage of self-consciousness, can illuminate music; something within literature resonates with the experience of listening. The illumination and resonance is at present obscured to each discipline by the lack of a powerful and precise enough critical language with which to articulate it. One excitement of *La Musique et les Lettres* lies in watching a *rapprochement* take place. The art of the *rapprochement* does not lie in the forming of grounds on which to produce a perfect union of the arts. Rather it consists in bringing them into the same arena and watching the sparks fly from the jarring and scraping caused by their asymmetry. In the world of the 'intermediary' at times a union of the arts seems a distinct possibility; at others the two seem impossibly far removed.

---

[18] *Debussy* (Paris: Seuil, 1962).

[19] Many critics since, of course, have moved this area of Debussy studies forward in several ways. Roy Howat, for example, has written on numerological proportion and the golden mean in *Debussy in Proportion: A Musical Analysis* (Cambridge: Cambridge University Press, 1983). Margaret Cobb's *The Poetic Debussy*, 2nd edn. (Rochester, Minn: University of Rochester Press, 1994) has brought literary sources into focus in Debussy scholarship; Robert Orledge has illuminated Debussy's unfinished theatre projects in *Debussy and the Theatre* (Cambridge: Cambridge University Press, 1982). A recent volume edited by Richard Langham Smith, *Debussy Studies* (Cambridge: Cambridge University Press, 1997), provides a variety of fresh source-study, biographical, and interdisciplinary approaches as a useful complement to purely analytical ones. (This is intended as a representative, rather than a comprehensive list.)

INTRODUCTION:
SEARCHING FOR THE INTERMEDIARY

1 The meeting ground

Music and poetry have appeared together in many forms down the ages, from Greek tragedy to the medieval French *chanson*, Baudelaire to Wallace Stevens. Ronsard's *Amours* were written specifically to be set to music. Whilst music was viewed in Ronsard's time as an imitative poor second cousin to a literature of ideas, philosophers since, as divergent as Rousseau, Schopenhauer, Nietzsche, and Adorno, have made higher claims for it. The nature of the relationship of the word to music has changed over time in reciprocity with linguistic, musical, and semiotic theories.[1]

The independent histories and criticisms of music and literature together provide the stage upon which the desire for supremacy over the other art conflicts with the desire for its imitation. Meetings of music and literature can take many different explicit forms, shaped by the varying degrees of sensitivity and indifference from one to the other: text and music inhabit each other in song; textless music intentionally refers to, excludes, or rewrites text. These meetings can take place from a limitless variety of perspectives, such as parodic imitation, violent rejection, and embedded or overt allusion.[2]

---

[1] In the Pythagorean model music, expressed in mathematical laws of proportion, was the ordering principle of the universe and, by extension, of epistemology and ontology. From the earliest times interpretations of music have been articulated through implicit notions about language and being. Music and the quantified, pitched word in poetry were considered as a unity by the ancient Greeks in the term *mousike*. In 18th-century France new enquiries into the nature and origin of language included music. Most famously Rousseau calls in *Essai sur l'origine des langues où il est parlé de la mélodie et de l'imitation musicale* (1781) for the original unity between poetry and melody to be restored. Setting his face against Rameau's mathematically grounded theory of harmony, Rousseau refigures music in the image of language, declaring it the language of the heart and thereby transforming the perception of music as transcendental into that of a language expressive of a hidden interior. (*Écrits sur la musique, la langue et le théâtre*, ed. Bernard Gagnebin and Marcel Raymond, Bibliothèque de la Pléiade (Paris: Gallimard, 1995), v. 375–429 (pp. 381, 410)). (I cannot give a comprehensive historical account here, merely highlight some obvious ways in which the conceptualization of the relationship between word and sound has changed.)

[2] Liszt significantly redramatizes Petrarch's sonnet with fantastical flourishes in *Sonetto 104 del Petrarca* (*Années de pèlerinage*, book II, 1848), for example, and Schoenberg redramatizes it in violently jerky repetitive movements in his *Serenade*, Op. 24 (1920–3). The force of Schumann's musical imagination can render Heine's poetic text an insignificant sketch in the margin in the *Dichterliebe*. See, for example, 'Aus meinen Tränen spriessen', where the bareness of harmony underpinning the voice in the piano contradicts the depiction in the words of a choir of nightingales: 'Und meine Seufzer werden, ein Nachtigallen chor.' The acoustic drama conveys the emotional paradoxes brilliantly, either following the text or diverging from it, at times taking centre stage altogether, e.g. bars 5–8 (*Songs with Piano* (Leipzig: Breitkopf & Härtel, 1914)).

The relationship of these arts had reached fever pitch in France in the latter half of the nineteenth century with Wagner, whose controversial theory of the *Gesamtkunstwerk* provoked an uncomfortable, defensive response in Symbolist circles. Wagner's influence challenged writers to reclaim language as the supremely expressive medium to rival the power of music. Huysmans mingled colours, tastes, and sensations freely with music in *A rebours*, for example, making play to the inherent poetic content in music and musical content in poetry. René Ghil and Stuart Merrill tried harnessing the colours and emotions of music to specific nuances of language in a systematized way. Ghil in particular, hailed by Merrill as 'maître de la musique du Verbe', made a pseudo-scientific attempt to 'instrumentalize' the verb and orchestrate the vowel in his *Traité du verbe* (1886).

Mallarmé distances himself from the *Gesamtkunstwerk* in 'Richard Wagner. Rêverie d'un poète français', accusing him, albeit in admiring tones, of over-simplified juxtaposition of the two arts:[3] 'Quoique philosophiquement elle ne fasse là encore que se juxtaposer, la Musique … pénètre et enveloppe le Drame de par l'éblouissante volonté et s'y allie: pas d'ingénuité ou de profondeur qu'avec un éveil enthousiaste elle ne prodigue dans ce dessin, sauf que son principe même, à la Musique, s'échappe.' Mallarmé admires Wagner as a creative artist for having married 'le drame personnel et la musique idéale' and for striking upon such a popular formula, but sees his relationship of music to the drama to be far from a true philosophical marriage.[4]

The representation of passions in Wagner was quite different from any heard in opera before. As archetypal psychosexual situations are discussed on stage the orchestra grapples with what appear to be inchoate feelings below levels of conscious awareness, in a newly foregrounded shifting chromatic harmonic language developed from the melodic-harmonic fragments of the leitmotif. The leitmotif technique revolutionized form in post-Wagnerian music (and arguably in literature), instilling radical temporal change into musical conventions while keeping them tethered to through-composed elements. The blend of psychological motivation as ordering principle with musical ideas challenges the autonomy and organizational function of musical conventions. The vestiges of the leitmotif as structuring principle remain in Debussy's avoidance of linear, goal-orientated progressions in favour of static, circular patterns, and in his preference for modal and whole-tone constructions. The influence of the leitmotif can be perceived in *Pelléas et Mélisande*, and indeed later in *Jeux*, with their stretched and compressed psychological time, the saturated density and motivic working out of the musical language in quasi-dream sequences and themes of foreboding.[5]

---

[3] Written in 1885 for E. Dujardin, editor of *La Revue wagnérienne* (*OC* (M), 541–6).

[4] Ibid. 543.

[5] Although Debussy eventually rejected Wagner, he did assimilate and transform Wagner in his own manner. Features of his style such as realism, closeness to speech of song, and the use of shifting triads and extended chords in *Pelléas*, for example, owe much to *Parsifal*.

Other music of the nineteenth century, especially with Beethoven's Ninth Symphony (1824) and the development of programme music, frequently evoked literary paradigms, although these often bore little resemblance to their musical manifestations. Modes of lyricism, fantasy, and the grotesque from literature fed and were transposed by the musical imaginations of Schumann, Berlioz, and Liszt, to name only some of the most famous. Hugo, Banville, Baudelaire, and Rimbaud placed great value on the rhythm of dramatic breaks in sense produced from the affective tension between scansion and accent in poetry. For Verlaine, the euphony of phonetic patterning and calculated rhythmic irregularity invested poetry with 'musicality':

> De la musique avant toute chose,
> Et pour cela préférer l'Impair
> Plus vague et plus soluble dans l'air,
> Sans rien en lui qui pèse ou qui pose.[6]

What Verlaine perceives as the musical quality of verse seems to be a kind of unhindered weightlessness produced by the *vers impair*. Achieving such an exquisite, directionless hanging effect is to be the principal aim of the poet, he says. It is through *l'impair*, which divests verse of the traditional vectors of poetic organization, that verse can draw attention first and foremost to its rhythmic and sonorous qualities. Some of the ballast and anchors of regular prosody are loosened; rhythm and sound can float in a new ethereal space. If the semantic force of words in verse takes second place to rhythm and sound, language is behaving more musically than linguistically.

Of course, Debussy's music is saturated with literary reference. His early work includes settings of Verlaine's *Fêtes galantes* in 1882 and of Mallarmé's *Apparition* in 1884 and he would go on to set poems by several other poets, including Louÿs and Villon. He wrote *Cinq poèmes de Charles Baudelaire* from 1887 to 1889 and, having revised the *Fêtes galantes* in 1892, composed three 'Ariettes oubliées' from Verlaine's *Romances sans paroles* (1903). Lifelong opera projects never to be completed included *Le Diable dans le beffroi* and *La Chute de la maison Usher*, in which Debussy exhibits his fascination with Poe's death-drama, as well as a taste for the perverse. But it is not only in song settings that the literary influence is clear. In *En blanc et noir* (1915), a very late work for two pianos, fragments of text from Villon's *Ballade contre les ennemis de la France*, coupled with a dedication to Lieutenant Jacques Charlot, 'tué à l'ennemi', are quoted in the score of the second piece, filling the music with connotative association. Quotations and misquotations from 'La Marseillaise' and J. S. Bach's setting of the chorale *Ein feste Burg ist unser Gott* are interwoven with echoes of reveille calls, adding ironic and subversive dimensions to the musical texture through

---

[6] 'Art poétique', *Œuvres complètes*, ed. Y. G. Le Dantec and Jacques Borel, Bibliothèque de la Pléiade (Paris: Gallimard, 1962), 326.

its interplay with the implied texts. Debussy's final encounter with Mallarmé in the *Trois poèmes de Stéphane Mallarmé* (1913), in which musical textures are strongly reminiscent of Mallarmé's broken handling of syntax, is one of the least explored.[7]

The intense atmosphere of interchange between music and letters was at the forefront of Mallarmé's mind when he was invited in 1893 to give his celebrated address to the Taylorian Institution in Oxford. Indeed when delivered in 1894 the lecture, entitled *La Musique et les Lettres*, formed part of an intriguing cluster of artistic events. While Mallarmé was steeped in the new sound world to be heard at the Wagner concerts, Debussy, having seen the premiere of Maeterlinck's *Pelléas et Mélisande* in 1892 with Mallarmé, was using the play as the libretto for his new opera from 1893 to 1895.

Around 1890 Mallarmé, impressed by the recently published *Cinq poèmes de Charles Baudelaire*, had asked Debussy whether he would collaborate in a theatrical production of *L'Après-midi d'un faune*. Between 1892 and 1894 Debussy worked on the *Prélude à l'Après-midi d'un faune*, announced in 1893, according to Orledge, 'as *Prélude, interlude et paraphrase finale pour l'après-midi d'un faune* for performance in Brussels at the Libre Esthétique of Octave Maus, possibly in conjunction with a dramatic reading of Mallarmé's eclogue'.[8] It is easy to see why Debussy was attracted to this project, given Mallarmé's revolutionary poem and hallowed status in Parisian artistic circles at the time. The extraordinary use of suggestion, unfamiliar syntax, and the implicitly theatrical structure in the Mallarmé poem to achieve such eroticism had laid down a kind of aesthetic manifesto to other artists. There was a new sensual quality of suggestiveness in the world of Mallarmé's *Faune*, which had not yet been heard in music in quite the same way.

The nature of this particular 'collaboration' makes it clear, however, that the two artists thought they were doing very different things. Mallarmé's reaction to the piece, as Debussy records it, seems distinctly lukewarm: 'Mallarmé vint chez moi, l'air fatidique et orné d'un plaid écossais. Après avoir écouté, il resta silencieux pendant un long moment, et me dit: "Je ne m'attendais pas à quelque chose pareil! Cette musique prolonge l'émotion de mon poème et en situe le décor plus passionnément que la couleur." '[9] Debussy's rather bathetic depiction of the poet, who seems to bear the responsibility of destiny on his shoulders whilst sporting a rather ordinary shawl, suggests his suspicion that Mallarmé's comment was not as friendly as it might have been. Rather than offer a compliment, Mallarmé seems to be expressing with some surprise how similar his poem has remained.

The bases for comparison between Mallarmé and Debussy, then, are fertile

---

[7] See Chapter 4 for further discussion of these songs.

[8] Orledge, *Debussy and the Theatre*, 155.

[9] Letter to Georges Jean-Aubry, 25 Mar. 1910, *Correspondance (1884–1918)*, ed. François Lesure (Paris: Collections Savoirs, 1993), 265.

and various, but most unstable and asymmetrical. The difficulty of comparing lies in finding an approach that deals with the instability and asymmetry of the overlap between the different arts. A comparative approach needs to account in a non-reductive manner for the web of similarities and differences created at the interface between the different building blocks, the notes and the phonemes, of each art.

When two works, musical and poetic, are brought side by side, a great friction is created between the two. The friction exists more or less in the background of our everyday hearing and reading of the works, but is currently obscured from critical view, since there is no adequate vocabulary for releasing and exposing it. The question now is how to set about the task of mapping the similarities and differences that make up the intermediate terrain. The next section of this chapter will explore the nature and extent of the asymmetric interface further, examine some of the critical attempts already made at unlocking it, and suggest the kind of discourse to be developed if a more successful articulation of the middle ground is to be found. Of course, the kinds of overlap I am exploring are not found in Mallarmé and Debussy alone, nor do they exist simply because of the special terms of those artists' relationship. Examples of music in poetry and poetry in music fill our reading and listening at every turn, and have long been a subject of discussion for artists in both disciplines.

2 Music in poetry and poetry in music

Valéry insists on the creative power of words in the hands of a poet's sonorous imagination, in pleasant contrast with the more limited, monolinear sound produced by the cello:

Le seul timbre du violoncelle exerce chez bien des personnes une véritable domination viscérale. Il y a des mots dont la fréquence chez un auteur nous révèle qu'ils sont en lui tout autrement doués de résonance, et par conséquent, de puissance positivement créatrice. . . . Ces considérations nous serviront à éclairer un peu la constitution de la poésie, qui est assez mystérieuse. Il est étrange que l'on s'évertue à former un discours qui doive observer des conditions simultanées parfaitement hétéroclites: musicales, rationnelles, significatives, suggestives, et qui exigent une liaison suivie ou entretenue entre un rythme et une syntaxe, entre le son et le sens. Ces parties sont sans relation concevables entre elles. Il nous faut donner l'illusion de leur intimité profonde.[10]

For Valéry, musical elements in poetry occur in words whose repetition lends them a new, unfamiliar resonance or poeticized sonority. They form part of the web of poetic signification ('une liaison suivie ou entretenue entre un

---

[10] *Introduction à la poétique*, 6th edn. (Paris: Gallimard, 1938), 54.

rythme et une syntaxe'). He points out how bizarre the virtuoso critical act of juggling each element ('musicales, rationnelles, significatives, suggestives') is, the act that holds each strand on the same poeticized level (although it also illustrates the power and breadth of the poetic field). Two questions arise: what is lost by fitting the musical elements of poetry neatly into one 'poetic' category and, if we do so, what happens when they appear to exceed its limits? It might be more enlightening to think of phonetic sonorities in poetry not simply and narrowly as poeticized music, but as being shared with musical properties, and as overstepping the limits of one art into the terrain of the other.

Where a poem is passed through various composers' hands, such as in Liszt's and Schoenberg's reworking of Petrarch's sonnet number 104, for example, deliberate distance is put between the two expressive artistic systems. It seems evident in these cases that the relationship is best understood in terms of disjunction and difference. Even in a situation where one artwork does not set out to rewrite or align itself with another, it may be that this expressive difference could still be present in tacit form.

There are obvious problems with placing music and poetry on the starting blocks together without considering the asymmetrical semiotic relations between them. In music meaning is non-predicative: connotations are displaced and unlocalized.[11] Tacit connotations, such as the stability, disruption, and restabilization implicit in the traditional sonata form, rest on explicit combinatory structures, which can be charged with expectancy and tension by the progression of keys.[12] In poetry this balance is inverted. Poetic meaning is displayed in a limitless set of possibilities for play within explicit associative relationships such as tropes, displacements, allusions, associations, phonetic patterning, and irony, which are not foregrounded in combinatory structures. The structures in poetry act as support; they can enhance meaning but not carry it alone when emptied of semantic content. Meaning in poetry can, of course, have a further structure of its own. The play is manifested in different rhythms or sonorities but cannot be reductively equated to metrical, phonetic, or syntactical properties.

This being the case, an interpretative language for the interface between music and poetry needs the power to treat the differing emphases in the connotative and combinatory structures equally, and to recognize their respective tacit and explicit features. It needs to go beyond simply allowing a symmetrical match between, for example, the structural features of a poem and a piece, to find distortion as well as reflection interesting, asymmetry as well as symmetry.

---

[11] This idea is explored by Lawrence Kramer in *Music and Poetry*, 6.

[12] The term 'connotation' is used in Barthes's sense of 'des sons qui ne sont ni dans le dictionnaire, ni dans la grammaire de la langue' (*S/Z* (Paris: Seuil, 1970), 15).

The distinctive joint feature of music and poetry is that the formal apparatus of each is based on the rhythmic apprehension of time, and on the periodic division of or resistance to temporal continuity. Both arts turn time into form, which unfolds within the intensified framing effect of a definite beginning and definite ending. While reading (silently reciting) or listening (an inner 'performance') several levels of period define the shaped unfolding of form, from the immediate level (phrase group or phrase structure) to the level of the whole musical or poetic work. Each level, it could be said (if both reading and listening are idealized as uninterrupted activities or performances), exists as some combination of accumulation and release in the texture over the course of the work. Thought of in these terms, the shared temporal and dynamic qualities of poetry and music are highlighted.

Yet there is also a tension between local and overarching levels of listening. In 'Aesthetic Decomposition: Music, Identity, and Time', Joanna Hodge argues that the difference between the conception of time and of the transcendence of time in music, which has a striking equivalent in the relation to time experienced by human beings, is set out and experienced in the practice of musical analysis:

> To grasp a piece of music as a single structure, it is necessary both to grasp its temporal structure and to suspend the fragmentation which extension through time tends to impose on the process thus extended. . . . Aesthetics can become (again) the study of the relation between understandings of spatio-temporal frameworks and the objects contained within those frameworks, as set out by Kant at the beginning of *The Critique of Pure Reason*.
>
> There is an oscillation in the status of artworks between an immanent materiality and a transcendence of spatio-temporal specificity required to grasp that work as a single entity.[13]

Thus, in spite of having temporal and dynamic qualities in common, each art brings the other up against its own limit. Reading can be a far less time-bound activity, since the reader has some degree of control over the recitation, than listening, in which a performance is imposed on a listener. The score analyst, however, is aware of different temporal constraints and conflicts from the listener. In addition, the heightened but less meaning-driven performativity of music, whose 'text' vacates the written score in its instantiation in interpretation, contrasts with latent performativity in the literary text, in which meaning is more explicit. Differing degrees of performativity, in the works themselves and in their reception, both connect and separate music and poetry.

---

[13] In Michael Krausz (ed.), *The Interpretation of Music: Philosophical Essays* (Oxford: Oxford University Press, 1988), 256–7.

3 Critical connection

The language we use to talk about music and poetry is fraught with difficulty. One problem in the language of musicology is the pull between purely formal elements of analysis, and the use of 'extra-musical' language for descriptive purposes. This language is made unstable by the constant problem of how to speak meaningfully of music's meaning without being considered hopelessly subjective. The question of how to talk about music is torn between leaving musical discourse as purely musical and the tale's being told in other ways than by the music itself. If not rigidly formalist to the point of desiccation, then critical accounts of music have, at times, rested on implied or indeed explicit naive mimetic 'readings' of music: the 'theme' of the text dictates what the listener 'looks for'. Anton Schindler, Beethoven's biographer in 1840, once asked him (so he claims) what the D minor Piano Sonata 'meant', and Beethoven told him to read *The Tempest*.[14] As a reporter Schindler has been generally discredited, but the *Tempest* tag has not met the same fate. In the hands of a serious musician-critic like Donald Tovey the idea of *The Tempest* is not imposed as a model. In 1931 Tovey tells pianists in *A Companion to Beethoven's Pianoforte Sonatas* that 'it will do you no harm to think of Miranda at bars 31–38 of the slow movement'.[15] Although still rather prescriptive, he does at least allow a place in listening for divergent elements of fantasy.

Conversely, language with which to describe and discuss can more easily be found in the literary discipline, but this language has no satisfactory means of articulating critically its urge towards or away from music. Readers of poetry are well used to listening for what could loosely be termed 'musical' elements in poetry, such as a richly revealing assonance which colours meaning, for example. Rhythmic patterns in syntax and metre, either regular or syncopated, may support or oppose a particular semantic significance. Musical figures of speech are often used by critics to describe an effect or something sensed in verse beyond the limits of critical language. All too frequently music stands in for the inexplicable. Such a tendency stems in part from the fact that music has traditionally acted as a metaphysical metaphor, allowing the passage back and forth between matter and ideality, but also from the persistent Romantic commonplace definition of music as the ineffable art.[16] Music is also frequently found in text and criticism functioning as a metaphorical language through which text can be defined or can define itself. Stendhal's famous metaphor for reading the novel, in *Vie de Henry Brulard*, likens the novel

---

[14] In *Beethoven As I Knew Him* (London: Dover, 1996), 406.

[15] Rev. edn. (London: Associated Board of the Royal Schools of Music, 1998), 121.

[16] Music grew in importance in the 19th century as a site of expressivity to rival lyric poetry, especially under the widespread influence of Schopenhauer, for whom music is the only art to have direct access to the metaphysical, providing an immediate copy of 'the Will'.

to the bow and the reader to the body of the violin which produces the musical sounds: 'Un roman est comme un archet, la caisse du violon qui rend les
sons c'est l'âme du lecteur.'[17] The metaphor exploits the clear visual aspect,
the visceral performative force and implied, but unheard, sonority of playing
the violin. Enhanced by the intangibility of its musical content, the metaphor
exceeds the power of direct language; in a sense it describes a phenomenon
(reading) produced by language, but closed to self-expression in that same
medium. In effect, the undecidability of the musical metaphor leaves open the
question of whether it is the reader or the author who operates the bow.

Some ready-made musical terms, which have already been adopted by
literary criticism for articulating certain discourses and modes, could potentially be used here. Since Bakhtin's introduction of the concept of
'polyphony', for example, the term has become part of a ready currency of
the discourse on literary structures and fabrics.[18] Terms like 'counterpoint',
'staccato', and 'legato' have been offered more recently as part of an available
corpus of literary critical terms through which to access hitherto unexplored
textual effects.[19] Such terms could conceivably be stretched to articulate the
inter-art terrain as well. Other musical structural concepts, such as repetition,
key, and cadence, are sometimes employed and could also be made more
rigorous devices for the description of shared features of music and poetry.[20]

In *After Babel* George Steiner uses the vocabulary of key progression as an
analogy for the 'development' of *Madame Bovary*: 'The text shifts from "key"
to "key" with intense rapidity.'[21] He goes on to discuss the 'cadence', 'sonority', and 'tonality' of Flaubert's style. This is rather like comparing elements
of the large-scale 'drama' in a Bach fugue, such as harmonic anticipation,
suspense, and climax, to features of the detective novel genre. Although not
particularly accurate or productive as an analogy, the use of such musical
terms is valuable in this discussion for showing the potential a critical vocabulary of the intermediate ground could have and for identifying an area that
is worth looking at in more rigorous detail.

As tempting as such terms might seem, however, the possible mileage to be
gained from this semi-tapped source is only limited for the purposes of this
study. At the moment we lack the exact means even to paraphrase, let alone
formalize, the shared properties of the two arts. Although there is a strong

---

[17] *Œuvres intimes*, ed. V. del Litto, Bibliothèque de la Pléiade, 2 vols. (Paris: Gallimard, 1981–2), ii. 699.

[18] See, for example, Ann Jefferson's powerful application of the term 'polyphony' to articulate the levels and strands of readerly process and narrative game in Stendhal, in *Reading Realism in Stendhal* (Cambridge: Cambridge University Press, 1988).

[19] See in particular Malcolm Bowie's *Psychoanalysis and the Future of Theory* (Oxford: Blackwell, 1993).

[20] A future study could build, for example, on the potential left by Ruwet's extensive study of the structural uses of repetition in Western music. From amongst the undiscovered resources of musical terminology I would suggest, by extension, 'ostinato', a term I will employ only in passing in this book, as rich in possibilities for mapping the overlap.   [21] 392–3.

case for tightening up the critical use of such terms for literary study, the problem with using them might be that they are already too ingrained in the commonplace metalanguage of music analysis. Their use could turn the gaze too heavily towards the literary, ignoring the new demands the literary can make on the appreciation of music. Instead, a structure is required whose conceptual centre is neither of the verbal nor of the musical sign system.

In *After Babel*, Steiner observes that since the units or terms for comparison are not equivalent, a degree of translation between the disciplines is necessary for the sake of mutual intelligibility. Steiner aims to re-establish the value of the uncertain art of translation.[22] He argues that his concept of translation is an extreme example of the process of communication and reception inherent in any act of speech:

In translation the dialectic of unison and plurality is dramatically at work. In one sense, each act of translation is an endeavour to abolish multiplicity and to bring different world pictures back into perfect congruence. In another sense, it is an attempt to reinvent the shape of meaning. . . . Thus translation is no specialized, secondary activity at the 'interface' between languages. It is the constant, necessary exemplification of the dialectical, at once the welding and divisive nature of speech.[23]

The tension in the dialectic of translation, as Steiner envisages it, also informs the activity of articulating the common ground between music and poetry: 'The composer who sets a text to music is engaged in the same sequence of intuitive and technical motions which obtain in translation proper. His initial trust in the significance of the verbal sign system is followed by interpretative appropriation, a transfer into the musical matrix.'[24] The activity of the composer who translates into the musical matrix is comparable to that of the critic of the music–literature interface, caught on the edge of the dialectic between the multiple sensed and real differences between each medium, and the desire to communicate their congruence. But rather than constantly translating from one 'language'—music is a language in that it has its own 'grammar', 'syntax', and 'vocabulary'—into another, I shall propose areas of middle ground in which to talk about the properties of each in a way that is intelligible to each.

Steiner's notion of 'translation' does not refer to an attempt to find a symmetry, a precise mirroring between two semantic systems, but looks towards an articulation of the channel of complex structures and patterns which run between music and poetry. Steiner identifies the need for a language of the overlap: 'The contrastive tonalities, the differing idiomatic habits, the distinct associative contexts, which generate resistance and affinity between two different languages, are intensified and complicated in the interpenetration of language with music.'[25] He identifies this middle ground of

[22] 2nd edn. (Oxford: Oxford University Press, 1992).   [23] Ibid. 246.
[24] Ibid. 437.   [25] Ibid. 445.

conflicting gestures of resistance and affinity as 'an integral but intermediary genre, for which we lack a defining term'.[26] Integral since the unnamed genre consists in the independent meeting and meshing of music and language, yet at the same time intermediary: hovering between the two, independent from but essentially part of them both. If the fabric and contours of the intermediate and integral, or, if Steiner is to be coined, the 'intermediary', ground were mapped, perhaps almost topographically, according to the demands of each particular case, then three-dimensional asymmetric spaces in which the meetings of music and poetry take varied forms—convergences and divergences, rewritings, manipulated representations and collusions, embedded imitations—could be postulated.

It is vital for literary and for musical study that we acknowledge properly the extent of their interpenetration, largely ignored by most criticism, allowing an entirely new area of critical understanding to be forged and unleashed. To do this we need to explore beyond music in literature as a convenient analogy that fails to locate its opposite term, and start to unpack the relationship at the level of its intricate structure. At the moment we lack the exact means even to paraphrase, let alone formalize, the shared properties of the two arts. The units or terms for comparison are not the same, so that a degree of translation between the disciplines is necessary.

Some, like Suzanne Bernard in *Mallarmé et la musique* (1959), have explored the potential of existing musical forms to categorize structural likeness. But this approach can have only mixed success. Categories of form are of limited use in identifying a specific common ground between music and poetry since they themselves are open to the differing perceptions of composer and writer. Take, for example, the fugue. Pierre Boulez, who has a preference for forms capable of transformation, writes of the Bach fugue: 'Je crois que les œuvres de J.-S. Bach sont le grand modèle. En particulier la manière dont il arrive à façonner toute une forme à partir de très peu de chose, très peu d'idée. . . . Plus Bach va, plus il va profondément dans le sens de son texte pour l'épanouir.'[27] But how different the work based on this model of fugue would be from the fugue that Milan Kundera envisages for the structure of his novel *La Plaisanterie* (1998). He writes: 'Le fil déchiré de cet amour court tout au long du récit, éveille d'autres thèmes qui se détruisent, se répondent comme les thèmes d'une fugue.'[28] An awareness of general structural similarities without a consideration of their temporal natures can only inform and not specifically alter our hearing of music or our reading of text. Being able, for example, to recognize that reading the Beat poets is like listening to jazz improvisation does not in itself provide the necessary tools for taking the comparison further.

---

[26] Ibid.

[27] *Par volonté et par hasard* (Paris: Seuil, 1975), 15.

[28] *La Quinzaine littéraire*, 749 (1998), 10.

Barthes's notion of 'intertexte' offers a powerful model of polyphonic space in which the tensions of the music–text interplay could perhaps be staged. 'Tout texte est un intertexte,' he writes in *Texte (théorie du)*, 'd'autres textes sont présents en lui, à des niveaux variables.'[29] The notion of intertext is closely linked to 'l'interdisciplinaire', which he discusses in *Le Bruissement de la langue* as a prelude to defining 'texte': 'On dirait en effet que *l'interdisciplinaire* . . . ne peut s'accomplir par la simple confrontation de savoirs spéciaux . . . Il commence effectivement . . . lorsque la solidarité des anciennes disciplines se défait, peut-être même violemment à travers les secousses de la mode, au profit d'un objet nouveau, d'un langage nouveau.'[30] The post-structuralist willingness to abandon disciplinary confines is particularly liberating for inter-disciplinary enquiry.

For Barthes, text need no longer be purely literary, as he writes in *Texte (théorie du)*: 'Toutes les pratiques signifiantes peuvent engendrer du texte: la pratique picturale, la pratique musicale, la pratique filmique, etc. Les œuvres, dans certains cas, préparent elles-mêmes la subversion des genres.'[31] Although metaphorically powerful, the concept of 'l'interdisciplinaire' as such is, however, of limited use since the space it describes demands limitation and definition rather than to exist as somewhat ill-disciplined flux. The vital element missing for the purposes of serious interdisciplinary study is the actual analysis of works of poetry and music.

In the search for models by which music criticism could extend itself, semi-otics, amongst many other theories, provided new and compelling inroads into what was becoming, for musicologists, the science of 'music–text'. In *S/Z* Barthes makes an extended analogy between the text and the musical score:

L'espace du texte (lisible) est au tout point comparable à une partition musicale (classique). Le découpage du syntagme (dans son mouvement progressif) correspond au découpage du flot sonore en mesures (l'un est à peine plus arbitraire que l'autre). Ce qui éclate, ce qui fulgure, ce qui souligne et impressionne, ce sont les sèmes, les citations culturelles et les symboles, analogues, par leur timbre fort, la valeur de leur discontinu, aux cuivres et aux percussions. Ce qui chante, ce qui file, se meut, par accidents, arabesques et retards dirigés, le long d'un devenir intelligible (telle la mélodie confiée souvent aux bois), c'est la suite des énigmes, leur dévoilement suspendu, leur résolution retardée: le développement d'une énigme est bien celui d'une fugue.[32]

By viewing 'text' (literary or musical) as the mobile intersection of a plurality of forces and codes, linguistic, literary, and historical, lines of commentary are allowed to interweave and reflect upon each other 'polyphonically', appear-ing to overcome the barriers between two analytical languages. A well-known

---

[29] *Texte (théorie du)*, *Œuvres complètes*, ed. Éric Marty, 2 vols. (Paris: Seuil, 1994), ii. 1686.
[30] 2nd edn. (Paris: Seuil, 1984), 69.   [31] *Texte (théorie du)*, ii. 1686. See n. 29.
[32] *S/Z*, 35–6.

semiotic principle holds that language is a subset of a total 'semiotic' class, only one among a multitude of graphic, acoustic, and tactile symbolic mechanisms of communication, which includes music.

Music semiotics was born in the 1950s and has taken many forms. Using linguistics as a way of bringing music and language into the same field of analysis, Nicolas Ruwet's study of repetition as the basis of Western musical form in *Langage, musique, poésie* has been important in drawing to attention, in particular, the structural significance of repetition in Debussy's works.[33] Jean-Jacques Nattiez developed Ruwet's theory of 'paradigmatic analysis' in *Fondements d'une sémiologie de la musique*, a rigorously 'scientific' approach that could be accused of losing sight of discernible meaning in music.[34] Nattiez writes in 'The Contribution of Musical Semiotics to the Semiotic Discussion in General': 'The goal of a musical semiotics is to inventory the types and modalities of symbolic reference to which the music gives rise and to elaborate an appropriate methodology to describe their symbolic functioning.'[35] Although the desire for scientificity and the yearning to assimilate music to language has, at times, made for severely rigid taxonomic frameworks, there is still plenty of mileage left in musical semiotics.

Traditional aesthetics and philosophies of music do not, generally speaking, provide a language with which to talk about specific artworks.[36] However, Theodor Adorno has some provocative and stimulating insights about music and literature, full of intermediary overtones. Perhaps because he comes from the German tradition Adorno takes the music–literature dynamic utterly for granted. In one of his 'Short Commentaries on Proust', for example, he is quick to compare the author to 'great musicians of Proust's era, like Alban Berg, [who] knew that living totality is achieved only through rank vegetal proliferation'.[37] In these juxtapositions Adorno prises open the inward-lookingness of disciplines to expose the intermediary. Such juxtapositions bristle with tantalizing potential for further unravelling. As with Mallarmé's aesthetic writing, Adorno's way of writing about music mimetically traces the cracks and fissures of the work itself. He terms this feature of his style and thought 'constellation', in which the Mallarméan echoes are far from coincidental. Each concept takes on meaning in relation to other concepts, interacting constantly, thereby revealing integrative features in writing that simultaneously

---

33 *Langage, musique, poésie*, 2nd edn. (Paris: Seuil, 1972), 70–99.

34 *Fondements d'une sémiologie de la musique* (Paris: Union Générale d'Éditions, 1975).

35 In Thomas A. Sebeok (ed.), *A Perfusion of Signs* (Bloomington: Indiana University Press, 1977), 121–42.

36 Susanne Langer's theory of art in *Feeling and Form* (New York: Scribner's, 1953) states that all works of art have some single feature in common: 'Art is the creation of forms symbolic of human feeling' (40). Music is 'a tonal analogue of emotive life' (15), a theory anticipated by Schopenhauer's theory of musical representation, which posits human emotions as object. Both theories depend more on a global philosophical system than on a detailed study of music.

37 *Notes to Literature*, 2 vols. (New York: Columbia University, 1992), i. 174.

emphasize fragmentation. The idea of 'constellation' enacts the dialectical friction between the two disciplines, allowing them to be held in productive tension. Ironically, although Adorno's work has provided some clues to a rigorous analytical method for the intermediary, it is limited by offering very little discussion of specific features of works and by selecting its material very desultorily, often disregarding history. The leap to the intermediary remains only a seductive possibility.

It could be postulated, following Barthes in the passage quoted earlier from *S/Z* (see n. 32), as a way of talking about the intermediary ground between poem and piece, that the process of listening to the intricate textural patterns of voicing and modulation of a fugue by Bach, for example, resembles the act of reading. This would be an idea close to Mallarmé's thinking. In his 'Notes' from 1895 he writes:

Le Vers et tout écrit au fond par cela qu'issu de la parole doit se montrer à même de subir l'épreuve orale ou d'affronter la diction comme un mode de présentation extérieur et pour trouver haut dans la foule son écho plausible, au lieu qu'effective-ment il a lieu au delà du silence que traversent se raréfiant en musiques mentales ses éléments, et affecte notre sens subtil ou de rêve.[38]

'Le Vers' in its pure form (away from its public exterior in 'la parole') is a mental music that inhabits a realm in our inner consciousness 'beyond' silence. Adorno expresses a similar idea: that music and language occupy shared material structural forms that reflect a commonality beyond the mate-rial. In 'Music and Language: A Fragment' he writes:

Music resembles a language in the sense that it is a temporal sequence of articulated sounds which are more than just sounds. They say something, often something human. . . . The succession of sounds is like logic: it can be right or wrong. But what has been said cannot be detached from the music. The resemblance to language extends from significant sounds, right down to the single sound; the notes as thresh-old of merest presence, the pure vehicle of expression. The analogy goes beyond the organised connection of sounds and extends materially to structures.[39]

This seems to suggest an approach that would understand the intermediary ground between music and poetry as a process of expanding time and space; a shared temporality based on shared structural features invested with forms of expectancy and desire.

As we saw earlier, time and the temporality of form are the factors common to both music and poetry. Kramer identifies this as a point for comparison: [They are] 'the two arts most saturated by time, the arts most dependent on giving a tangible contour and a distinctive texture to the lived present. In contrast to the teasing, disjunctive movement of narrative fiction,

---

[38] *OC* (M), 855.
[39] *Quasi una fantasia: Essays on Modern Music*, trans. Rodney Livingstone (London: Verso, 1992), 1.

the movement of music and poetry becomes compelling not by fastening value on the outcome of imaginary events, but by enveloping the reader or listener in a kind of polyphony of periodic forms.'[40] But how can the contours and textures of these polyphonic, periodic forms, which mould the intermediary ground without necessarily coinciding, be expressed precisely and usefully? How can they be translated to material forms?

Ideally, a layer of conceptual motifs, neutral yet common to both arts, could be found to articulate as precisely as possible the new figures laid bare by the material of the intermediary. The process I envisage for the comparative act might loosely be described in terms of the picture Steiner paints of translation: 'Translation is a teleological imperative, a stubborn searching out of all the apertures, translucencies, sluice-gates through which the divided streams of human speech pursue their destined return to the sea.'[41] These striking visual metaphors, 'apertures, translucencies', and 'sluice-gates', indicate that the intervening space of the overlap might have a topography expressible in the coordinates of specific three-dimensional figures that articulate the temporal dynamic of the intermediary.

Unravelling the intermediary is a somewhat paradoxical process that involves a benign hermeneutic circle: there cannot be a whole picture of the intermediary without the specific content of the analysis, nor can there be any specific content without the whole picture. The next chapter will look at the unique way in which Mallarmé conceives of and theorizes the musico-poetic relationship in his critical prose, before specific works are discussed in Chapter 2. In particular, specific three-dimensional, ornamental figures at work in the Mallarmé text articulate and enact the shared temporal dynamics of music and poetry and offer a specific point of textual–musical intersection as a comparative model.

40 *Music and Poetry*, 7.   41 *After Babel*, 256–7.

MUSIC IN MALLARMÉ:
A MUSICO-POETIC AESTHETIC

1 Rhythms of sound and sense

1.1 'LA FACE ALTERNATIVE'

Mallarmé's comments about music appear in fragments dotted throughout the critical prose. They occur in a tantalizing array of guises, as wide-ranging as the elusive metaphorical style of 'Richard Wagner. Rêverie d'un poète français'[1] and the hybrid genre of traditional prose poem-cum-review article in 'Crayonné au théâtre'.[2] The climax of Gordon Millan's biography of Mallarmé arrives the moment after the poet's death, when Geneviève and 'Mère' find a book on Beethoven and Wagner open on his desk. This is proof to Millan of the profound commitment behind *La Musique et les Lettres* to the idea that 'literature could and should rise to the challenge thrown down by contemporary music'.[3] The suggestion here is that Mallarmé's entire literary effort stemmed from the desire to set the record straight with Wagner and can be read as such. It might be more important to look at the subsequent influences on the musical world of Mallarmé's challenges to intelligibility. The response made by composers and writers to Mallarmé's literary model has been wide and varied. Most directly, Pierre Boulez has used the concept of 'le Livre' to inform the compositional technique of *Pli selon pli*.[4] The challenges thrown down by Mallarmé to music and literature and to other artistic spheres and fields of knowledge are still in the process of being discovered.

Still unanswered is the question of how Mallarmé's thinking on music should affect our reading of him. The extent to which he implemented music in his own *ars poetica* is often underestimated. Just what lies behind 'la face alternative' is an eloquent, complex, and profound working-out of the overlap between poetry and music, whose ramifications have changed the course of literary and musical history and can still be felt today.

---

[1] *OC* (M), 541–6.   [2] Ibid. 293–351.

[3] G. Millan, *Mallarmé: A Throw of the Dice: The Life of Stéphane Mallarmé* (London: Secker & Warburg, 1994), 318.

[4] For a detailed discussion of this relationship see Breatnach, *Boulez and Mallarmé: A Study in Poetic Influence.*

1.2 THE RHYTHM OF READING

In response to the invitation from Charles Bonnier to speak in Oxford, Mallarmé writes in characteristically elusive style:

Tous ces jours-ci *la Walkyrie* et le *Pelléas et Mélisande* de Maeterlinck et je ne sais quoi d'imprévu qui souffle dans l'air ont retardé ma réponse. Je ne voudrais cependant pas, tant l'offre d'hospitalité ajoutée par Mr York Powell est exquise et me touche, attendre pour vous prier de le remercier de grand cœur, que j'aie définitivement trouvé, sinon le sujet, je ne sors guère du mien, mais l'intitulé de la conférence. Sera-ce *les Lettres et la Musique?*[5]

His immersion in Wagner and Maeterlinck leads him, in 'Planches et feuillets' (1893), to make two claims about *Pelléas*: 'Autre, l'art de M. Maeterlinck qui, aussi, inséra le théâtre au livre! . . . *Pelléas et Mélisande* sur une scène exhale, de feuillets, le délice. Préciser? Ces tableaux, brefs, suprêmes: quoi que ce soit a été rejeté de préparatoire et machinal, en vue que paraisse, extrait, ce qui chez un spectateur se dégage de la représentation, l'essentiel.'[6] Mallarmé admires the apparently translucent or hidden dramatic machinery in the play that allows the audience to experience the essential drama, which takes place outside the realm of material representation (the 'planches'). Maeterlinck has, for Mallarmé, brought drama closer to the abstract, ultimate artistic form of reading, referred to metaphorically as the book ('le Livre', the 'feuillets'), whose imaginative process Mallarmé sees as the real source of the drama.[7] Theatrical scenes become mental process through silent reading, which is dramatic enactment in its purest form. It is this process that Maeterlinck, by writing brief, dreamlike tableaux, has made the fibre and structure of his play, according to Mallarmé, whose remarks beguilingly borrow the stock tones of the critical review but are subtly infused with his own emerging aesthetic manifesto.

The breathtaking part of the argument, and most important for our purposes, has yet to come: 'Silencieusement presque et abstraitement au point que dans cet art, où tout devient musique dans le sens propre, la partie d'un instrument même pensif, violon, nuirait, par inutilité.'[8] The silent, dramatic performance through the pages of the book becomes pure music. In other words, the dramatic paradigm is caught up in the idealized process of reading whereas music (only 'dans le sens propre') is able both to be inserted into the all-encompassing 'livre' and to replace or accompany it, apparently, as a

---

5 Letter of 20 May 1893 (*OC* (M), 1608).   6 In 'Crayonné au théâtre' (ibid. 329–30).
7 See P. McGuinness, ' "Shakespeare ou Maeterlinck": Mallarmé Reading Theatre', in Michael Freeman et al. (eds.), *The Process of Art: Studies in Nineteenth-Century French Literature, Music and Painting in Honour of Alan Raitt* (Oxford: Clarendon Press, 1998), 82–100, where he deals with the tension between reading and performance in Symbolist theories of theatre at greater length.
8 *OC* (M), 330.

term for the global artistic act.[9] Any instrument of an orchestra, rather than mediate the otherwise inexpressible inner emotion as Wagner envisaged it, merely contaminates art with its materiality. Put another way: 'Musique, certes, que l'instrumentation d'un orchestre tend à reproduire seulement et à feindre.'[10]

If these at first seem to be grand but vague claims, Mallarmé's letter to Valéry of 5 May 1891 shows without doubt that there is more to them than first meets the eye: 'Il faut pour concevoir la littérature, et qu'elle ait une raison, aboutir à cette "haute symphonie" que nul ne fera peut-être; mais elle a hanté mêmes les plus inconscients et ses traits principaux marquent, vulgaires ou subtils, toute œuvre écrite. La musique proprement dite, que nous devons piller, démarquer, si la nôtre propre, tue, est insuffisante, suggère tel poème.'[11] His advice to the younger poet is to pillage and plagiarize the actual music he hears to achieve a symphony, the supreme orchestral form, now 'haute': a 'poème' that exists in all works even if the poets are unaware of it. Of course, we have only to think of Gautier's 'Symphonie en blanc majeur' to see that at least one of Mallarmé's predecessors made a highly self-conscious attempt at imitating the symphonic.[12] But here we have something different. Mallarmé explicitly states the need to embrace the stuff of real music rather than indulge in the imposition of hasty metaphor appropriated from musical discourse, which results in a blurring rather than a cross-fertilization of the two arts. Mallarmé's symphony is based on what he hears at concerts, as we are told in 'Crise de vers': 'Le moderne des météores, la symphonie, au gré ou à l'insu du musicien, approche la pensée; qui ne se réclame plus seulement de l'expression courante. . . . Certainement, je ne m'assieds jamais aux gradins des concerts, sans percevoir parmi l'obscure sublimité telle ébauche de quelqu'un des poëmes immanents à l'humanité ou leur original état, d'autant plus compréhensible que tu.'[13] Sketched in behind the motivic lines of the symphony, which come close in structure to those of thought ('approche la pensée'), are the outlines of poems immanent in human experience.

A better idea of how such music-in-poetry (and vice versa) might work in the more practical terms of the work's construction can be gained from Mallarmé's review earlier in 'Planches et feuillets' of Édouard Dujardin's *La Fin d'Antonia* (1893). From this it is clear that Mallarmé conceives of and appreciates a work in terms of the structural rhythm it produces: 'Je ne saurais dire mieux des personnages sinon qu'ils dessinent les uns relativement aux

[9] G. Millan recounts the tale told by Henri de Régnier of Mallarmé's ideal performance of 'le Livre'. This would involve his wandering onto a stage as if by accident and acting surprised to discover no piano there. At this point he would take out 'le Livre' instead and read (*Mallarmé: A Throw of the Dice*, 318).   [10] 'Solennité', *OC* (M), 334.
[11] *OC*, 805–6.   [12] *Émaux et camées*, ed. Adolphe Boschot (Paris: Garnier, 1954), 21–3.
[13] *OC* (M), 365–7.

autres à leur insu, en une sorte de danse, le pas où se compose la marche de l'œuvre. Très mélodiquement, en toute suavité; mus par l'orchestre intime de leur diction.'[14] The relational network built between the characters forms the punctuating rhythm of the work 'en une sorte de danse'. The adverb 'mélodiquement' evokes metaphorically the rhythm and structure of the relational pattern by aligning it with the note-to-note configuration of a melody, executed by the 'orchestre' of the characters' delivery, and offers an audacious challenge to Wagnerism. But the heart of the musical rhythm that Mallarmé so admires in the work lies in the fluidity of the verse, which could even sound like prose to the untrained ear: 'Le vers, où sera-t-il? pas en rapport toujours avec l'artifice des blancs ou comme marque le livret: tout tronçon n'en procure un, par lui-même; et, dans la multiple répétition de son jeu seulement, je saisis l'ensemble métrique nécessaire.'[15] Mallarmé composes a metrical framework by allowing the sequences of repetition and series forged by the auditory, semantic, and visual elements of language itself to be his material for construction, rather than be guided by a more conventional and artificial relationship of language to the space and shape of the page. The ensuing rhythm of verse, or metrical pulse, creates a fluid and palpitating texture: 'Ce tissu transformable et ondoyant pour que, sur tel point, afflue le luxe essentiel à la versification où, par places, il s'espace et se dissémine, précieusement convient à l'expression verbale en scène ... Voici les rimes dardées sur de brèves tiges, accourir, se répondre, tourbillonner, coup sur coup, en commandant par une insistance à part et exclusive l'attention à tel motif de sentiment, qui devient nœud capital.'[16] Here is a brilliant picture of Mallarmé's three-dimensional imagining of verse. The urgent search for vocabulary to convey his sense impression takes shape through the device of enumeration, a favourite technique. This creates in the syntactical composition of the sentence the quality of the verse being described. Commas frame each verb, aerating the sentence and sending a shiver of fragility through the line as the being-performed poetic experiences arrive scattered, transformed into infinitives: rhymes thrusting up from their short stalks, rushing up, replying to one another, whirling and spinning at speed. We get a better sense from the varying pace of the line of the conflicting poetic dynamics that Mallarmé describes, earlier in this passage, by 'il s'espace et se dissémine'.

All this is an eloquent warning of the danger of reductionist Wagnerian criticism: 'Aisément, on parlera d'un recours à la facture wagnérienne; plutôt tout peut se limiter chez nous ... je me plais à rester sur cette explication qui désigne un cas rythmique mémorable.'[17] Indeed, rhythm will be the common basis for the cross-hatched artistic paradigms which constitute 'le Livre', the supreme music expressed through the configurations of verse:

---

[14] Ibid. 326.   [15] Ibid. 327.   [16] Ibid.   [17] Ibid. 327–8.

Oui, en tant qu'un opéra sans accompagnement ni chant, mais parlé; maintenant le livre essaiera de suffire, pour entr'ouvrir la scène intérieure et en chuchoter les échos. Un ensemble versifié convie à une idéale représentation: des motifs d'exaltation ou de songe s'y nouent entre eux et se détachent, par une ordonnance et leur individualité. Telle portion incline dans un rythme ou mouvement de pensée, à quoi s'oppose tel contradictoire dessin: l'un et l'autre, pour aboutir et cessant où interviendrait plus qu'à demi comme sirènes confondues par la croupe avec le feuillage et les rinceaux d'une arabesque, la figure, que demeure l'idée.[18]

A piece of verse provides from its own elements an ideal representation (in the sense that it represents the 'idée') with no need of actual musical accoutrements. This is because verse is composed of motifs—the musical term for melodic phrase or fragment is converted into a literary one—elation and dream, which mingle and interweave at certain points in the work and diverge at others according to the overall organizing framework of the piece and their individual behaviour within it. The interweaving motifs, the source of the structural rhythm of the whole, map mental patterns ('un rythme ou mouvement de pensée'), strands pulling against one another or coming together ('à quoi s'oppose tel contradictoire dessin') like the motifs of a symphony, whose movement Mallarmé brings to life in an ornamental figure: 'comme sirènes confondues par la croupe avec le feuillage et les rinceaux d'une arabesque, la figure, que demeure l'idée.'

If the key to the music-in-poetry of 'le Livre' lies in rhythm then this rhythm is executed by the punctuation of a three-dimensional space formed by the relational movements of contrasting motifs which conflict and agree, converge and diverge. But how can this be translated into purely poetic terms, into silent music residing in the interplay of words on a page? And how can this undulating rhythmic texture be notated or articulated?

I.3 THE KEYBOARD OF VERSE

Although for the most part Mallarmé has reservations about the writers of *vers libre*, he admires the fluidity they achieve within traditional poetic parameters through their musical instincts: 'Si, d'un côté, les Parnassiens ont été, en effet, les absolus serviteurs du vers, y sacrifiant jusqu'à leur personnalité, les jeunes gens ont tiré directement leur instinct *des musiques*, comme s'il n'y avait rien eu auparavant; mais ils ne font qu'espacer le raidissement, la construction parnassienne, et, selon moi, les deux efforts peuvent se compléter.'[19] A co-presence of rigid framework and disseminated line, the one holding the other in check and at tension in the poetic space, would seem to fit the requirements

---

[18] *OC* (M), 328.
[19] *Réponse à une enquête de Jules Huret sur l'évolution littéraire, OC* (M), 868 (my italics).

of 'une ordonnance et leur individualité' (see section 1.2). As further illustration, Mallarmé turns once more to a musical example that shows evidence of acute powers of listening: 'D'ailleurs en musique la même transformation s'est produite: aux mélodies d'autrefois très dessinées succède une infinité de mélodies brisées qui enrichissent le tissu sans qu'on sente la cadence aussi fortement marquée.'[20] The shifting, fragmented, multi-layered melodic texture ('une infinité de mélodies brisées') that Mallarmé describes is a far cry from the symmetrical, harmonically compliant melody of the Classical convention found in a Mozart aria or a Haydn string quartet, which obeys laws of unity, balance, repetition, and linearity, and more akin to the style that would take shape in Debussy's *Prélude à l'Après-midi d'un faune*. Etched behind the musical model in this passage is the shadow of the desired literary one: it is a complexly interwoven surface of motifs not far behind which, through their notable absence or half-presence, formal *points de repère* of convention lurk in the texture. For example, 'cadence', a musical term for (semi-)closure and literary term for metrical beat, is connoted in semantically asymmetric simultaneity by this passage. As such, 'cadence' implies a formal gesture that pulls against the predominant direction taken by the unconstrained, improvised individuality of the line. The two parts of the comparison converge by the end of the sentence in the description of their shared structural rhythm, which is expressed in this common term. It is as if the syllogistic outcome has been pre-empted and fed back as a disturbing tension into the balanced binarism of the initial statement.[21]

In the alexandrine 'mélodies brisées' unleash new possibilities of sound and of rhythm:

Les fidèles à l'alexandrin, notre hexamètre, desserrent intérieurement ce mécanisme rigide et puéril de sa mesure; l'oreille, affranchie d'un compteur factice, connaît une jouissance à discerner, seule, toutes les combinaisons possibles, entre eux, de douze timbres. . . . Le poëte d'un tact aigu qui considère cet alexandrin toujours comme le joyau définitif, mais à ne sortir, épée, fleur, que peu et selon quelque motif prémédité, y touche comme pudiquement ou se joue à l'entour, il en octroie de voisins accords, avant de le donner superbe et nu: laissant son doigté défaillir contre la onzième syllabe ou se propager jusqu'une treizième maintes fois.[22]

Individual syllables become independently active elements in the line so that each can be heard in relation to the others. Released from the artificial metrical uniformity of fixed caesuras and regular groupings, with limited possibilities for variation, verse can produce fresh colours and timbres. The ear is not simply impressed by the unusual sonorities but by the rhythmic changes in metre. The syllables in a poetic line are like independent notes 'played' by the poet in startling combinations.

[20] Ibid. 867.
[21] We will see similar foreshortening effects in *Un coup de Dés jamais n'abolira le Hasard*.
[22] 'Crise de vers', *OC* (M), 362.

Fragment by fragment, a metaphorical picture of the keyboard of verse is drawn, a simple, powerful metaphor that works in far more extended ways than the musical grammar of René Ghil or Stendhal's violin[23] to generate a quite precise working method, both poetically and musically. The poet has 'un tact aigu' with which he touches and plays the syllables in a tantalizing prelude to the emergent alexandrine. The surrounding material is literally accompaniment,[24] although not in the sense of a Classical Alberti bass since the main subject or alexandrine is only glimpsed. Rather the accompaniment to the alexandrine consists of nuances, reflections, suggestions, and echoes ('de voisins accords') as shadows around it.[25] The treatment of the timing and pace of the alexandrine has a keen musical sense of line behind it. Using his precise fingering technique to move over and manipulate the syllables of the alexandrine to the best musical effect the poet lingers over the eleventh syllable leaving it to hover in delicious suspense as it stops short of its expected point of repose. At other times he will stretch the phrase unexpectedly to a thirteenth syllable. Such 'infractions volontaires ou de savantes dissonances' are successful because 'la réminiscence du vers strict hante ces jeux à côté et leur confère un profit'.[26] Syllables are not subject to random forces but play in relation to a fixed boundary like Brownian motion between smoke particles in a confined space. The image of the instrument in Mallarmé's prose, whether it be the 'latent clavier'[27] or the individual 'souffle' of the flute playing against the 'grandes orgues du mètre officiel',[28] signifies this new-found autonomy. In place of the actual instruments of the orchestra, poetry can be played like an instrument in its own 'haute symphonie'.

1.4 TWO-WAY TERMS

As *Crise de vers* progresses, expressions of the common ground of music and poetry become more direct and concise. Elements of musical language act as two-way terms which can switch in and out of each art or allow both to be

---

[23] See Introduction, sections 1 and 3.

[24] Mallarmé calls them such: 'M. Henri de Régnier excelle à ses accompagnements' (*OC* (M), 362).

[25] For a similar idea see *Réponse à une enquête*, 870, where Mallarmé acknowledges the importance of Verlaine's 'vers fluide' and 'dissonances voulues' for his own work: 'Plus tard, vers 1875, mon *Après-midi d'un faune* . . . fit hurler le Parnasse entier. . . . J'y essayais, en effet, de mettre, à côté de l'alexandrin dans toute sa tenue, une sorte de jeu pianoté autour, comme qui dirait un accompagnement musical fait par le poëte lui-même et ne permettant le vers officiel de sortir que dans les grandes occasions.' That Mallarmé should have made this observation in such a way as to echo so resonantly the later upheavals that were to occur in tonality is extraordinary. He could not have known that Schoenberg and his pupils Berg and Webern would challenge the key system of tonality by developing a twelve-tone system, to include each semitone of the scale in a tone row, different permutations of which would be developed through a piece in a wandering, unfamiliar harmonic texture with none of the familiar anchors.

[26] 'Crise de vers', *OC* (M), 362.

[27] Ibid.

[28] *Réponse à une enquête*, 866.

caught up alongside each other by the action of metaphor, now assuming rather than explaining the comparison: 'Selon moi jaillit tard une condition vraie ou la possibilité, de s'exprimer non seulement, mais de *se moduler*, à son gré.'[29] The essence or behaviour of each art is characterized in one shared word given special significance in the literary field because of the motion lent to it by the musical connotation of 'se moduler', which does much more work than 's'exprimer'. 'Se moduler' contains a powerful vector of movement up and down a vertical spectrum: the action of modulating (of passing from key to key to change mood or to create surprises) and the horizontal vector of inter-art parallel. This is not simple analogy since the technical language fits the actual workings of each art. If poetry were to modulate in the manner of music it would require an impressive flexibility.

Further two-way terms follow:

Parler n'a trait à la réalité des choses que commercialement: en littérature, cela se contente d'y faire une allusion ou de distraire leur qualité qu'incorpera quelque idée.

À cette condition s'élance *le chant*, qu'une joie allégée.

Cette visée, je la dis *Transposition*—Structure, une autre.[30]

Mallarmé's well-known aim is to free linguistic objects from their ordinary, contingent relations to material objects: not '*Nommer* un objet' but 'le *suggérer*, voilà le rêve'.[31] Rather than refer to an external, received reality the mystery of the symbol is evoked by allusion, from which springs 'le chant' (the musicalized term for 'parler') in a process of sublimation captured by another go-between term, 'Transposition' (in music meaning the changing of written notes to sound in another key when played). This is an ideally crystalline language for Mallarmé: one that expresses its own method of construction as well as depicting the action of a phenomenon much larger than itself, thereby incorporating two artistic paradigms into reading.[32] In his famous letter to Edmund Gosse (10 January 1893) there is extraordinary substance to his claim to be making music. Mallarmé is developing in his critical prose a prototypical shared language for the two arts and one that performs their common ground poetically:

Il y a, entre toutes, une phrase où vous écartez tous voiles et désignez la chose avec une clairvoyance de diamant, la voici: 'His aim . . . is to use words in such harmonious combination as will suggest to the reader a mood or a condition *which is not mentioned*

---

[29] *OC* (M), 363 (my italics).   [30] Ibid. 366 (my italics).

[31] *Réponse à une enquête*, 869.

[32] Relationality and transposition into 'le chant' gives a verse that is bursting with vital energy. Lexical items escape ('s'évade') to the magical 'au-delà' when placed in a texture organized on a principle of the free disposition and disjunction of its elements: 'Toute la langue, ajustée à la métrique, y recouvrant ses coupes vitales, s'évade, selon une libre disjonction aux milles éléments simples'; finding a structural equivalent in music: 'et, je l'indiquerai, pas sans similitude avec la multiplicité des cris d'une orchestration, qui reste verbale' (*OC* (M), 361).

in the text, but is none the less paramount in the poet's mind at the moment of composition.' Tout est là. Je fais de la Musique, et appelle ainsi non celle qu'on peut tirer du rapprochement euphonique des mots, cette première condition va de soi; mais l'audelà magiquement produit par certaines dispositions de la parole, où celle-ci ne reste qu'à l'état de communication matérielle avec le lecteur, comme les touches du piano. Vraiment entre les lignes et au dessus du regard cela se passe en toute pureté, sans l'entremise des cordes à boyaux et des pistons comme à l'orchestre, qui est déjà industriel; mais c'est la même chose que l'orchestre, sauf que littérairement ou silencieusement. Les poëtes de tous les temps n'ont jamais fait autrement et il est aujourd'hui, voilà tout, amusant d'en avoir conscience. Employez musique dans le sens grec, au fond signifiant Idée ou rythme entre les rapports.[33]

Mallarmé's music is not based simply on the sonorous euphony of words placed together in poetry, but rather on the superior, calculated relations created by 'certaines dispositions de la parole' which give rise to a magical 'audelà'. The 'rythmes entre les rapports' are the rhythms figured by the relationship of the words on the page, which 'dans le sens grec' of *mousike* (where the quantified and pitched words in poetry were considered to be music) are inextricably coupled with music.

I.5 CONFIGURING (NON-)REPRESENTATIONS: ARTISTIC AFFINITIES

Implicit in Mallarmé's aesthetic conception of the poetic, therefore, is an alignment of terms and vectors common to the structural rhythm of each art.[34] But the 'rhythmic' alignment of structures is more extended and complex than a simple matching of the fragmented structural manifestation of music's non-semantic signifying elements—timbre, pitch, metre, tempo, melody, and harmony—to a similarly fractured but directly signifying, more overtly semantic, poetic partner. In other words, music is not conceived of as a mere shadow of poetry, which is similarly structured while possessing an additional semantic layer of signification. Rather, the extraordinary subtlety of Mallarmé's vision of the interrelation of the arts lies in the alignment he makes, built through the shared structural rhythm, of the sense-making and representational properties belonging to each.

Whether the asymmetrical relation between music and language, caused by their differing signifying capacities, has been viewed as a point in their favour or not has depended on the period in philosophical history. For

---

[33] *OC*, 807. For details of the Gosse article to which Mallarmé refers, see *Correspondance complète*, ed. H. Mondor and J.-P. Richard (vol. i), H. Mondor and L. J. Austin (vols. ii–xi), 11 vols. (Paris: Gallimard, 1959–85), vi. 26.

[34] As we saw in the Introduction, Adorno understands the 'musical' in both language and music as sharing a temporality: 'Music resembles a language in the sense that it is a temporal sequence of articulated sounds which are more than just sounds,' *Quasi una fantasia*, 1.

Schopenhauer, for example, the superiority of the art of music lay in its direct emotional significance, free from the corrupting influence of words. But Mallarmé does not want to strip music of its representational and semantic power in this oversimplified manner. Unlike in Wagner, the role of music for Mallarmé is not to provide language with an emotional immediacy or suggestiveness. Instead, the hermeneutic gaps in music are shared by language. Mallarmé refuses to locate poetic origins in the imagination or in a conventional poetic unconscious. Instead, his view of poetic alterity attributes the austere beauty of the ideal work to the word, leading to the separation of the author and the work: 'L'œuvre pure implique la disparition élocutoire du poète, qui cède l'initiative aux mots, par le heurt de leur inégalité mobilisés; ils s'allument de reflets réciproques comme une virtuelle traînée de feux sur des pierreries.'[35] In this way the action of words is close to the expressive system of music, whose identity lies in the relation between its constituent parts, rather than in an outside signified. The rhythm of impersonality weaves a lacework of meaning, over which the poet presides, connecting the strands in a web. Mallarmé famously uses the web image in a letter to Aubanel:

J'ai voulu te dire simplement que je venais de jeter le plan de mon Œuvre entier, après avoir trouvé la clef de moi-même—clef de voûte, ou centre, si tu veux, pour ne pas brouiller de métaphores—centre de moi-même, où je me tiens comme une araignée sacrée, sur les principaux fils déjà sortis de mon esprit, et à l'aide desquels je tisserai *aux points de rencontre* de merveilleuses dentelles, que je devine, et qui existent déjà dans le sein de la Beauté.[36]

This web of words and of signification, whose 'rythmes entre les rapports' form a 'dentelle' from its points of intersection, evokes as an image an overlapping net which holds equally the potential to signify and not to signify. Gaps, silences, or non-'rapports' are present wherever intersecting threads create meaning. Presence is counterbalanced with absence. 'Dentelle' metaphorically designates and rhythmically calibrates a pattern of co-presences: the presence of nothingness or of referential failure in conjunction with the presence of a semantic construction formed by overlapping signifiers.

This linguistic model of signification could conceivably be used as a plausible model for modes of signification in music contemporary to Mallarmé. Although music does not have a direct capacity for conveying conceptual meaning, and as such is often open to uncontrolled subjective-interpretative abuse, it does have certain mechanisms for meaning embedded in its own structure. This is something that Mallarmé's self-reflexive *ars poetica* emulates. Interrupting the flow of music can add either comedy, irony, or despair to a piece. Ultimately, it is the psychological climate of the piece that determines whether such suspensions in the flow will be bathetic or eerie, amusing or

---

[35] 'Crise de vers', *OC* (M), 366.　　　[36] 28 July 1866 (*OC*, 704–5).

strange in effect. For example, Alfred Brendel notes that 'two of Haydn's hall-marks, his sudden rests and fermatas in unexpected places, and his repetitions of the same soft chord, or note, over several bars' can have a different impact depending on the character of the piece.[37] Certain stock cadential progressions can suggest particular shapes of listening independently of their context. A perfect cadence, which shifts within the key from the dominant chord (the fifth of the scale), to the tonic (the first or home note of the scale), indicates complete closure to the ear. The key has been brought back home with a feel-ing of resolution. An imperfect cadence is the inverse cadential device, moving from the tonic to the dominant, leaving the key open and unresolved, awaiting further development. These mechanisms for closure and suspension shape the narrative of a piece. At the end of a conventional first movement of a sonata, for example, the return of the opening motif of the exposition, in the recapit-ulation, can create a point of relief. The turbulent uncertainty and openness of the development is over. Now the listener, who hears repeated material in or moving towards the home key, feels safely in the home straight.

Adorno writes in 'Music and Language: A Fragment' that there are points in music that give 'magisterial confirmation of something that has not been explicitly stated. In supreme moments of great music, and they are often the most violent moments—one instance is the recapitulation in the first move-ment of Beethoven's Ninth Symphony—this intention becomes eloquently unambiguous by the sheer power of its context.'[38] The meaning of music in this case is given through the disclosure of a concealed but desired symmetry, the making explicit of something suggested through the arrival of the long expected, to give the listener the pleasure of hearing resolution and comple-tion. The pleasure lies in the violence of the transitional event.

In late nineteenth-century music moments of signposting or recognition occur more intermittently, giving the piece a structural rhythm formed by passages of non-meaning punctuated by moments where meaning emerges. The epiphany at the end of Mahler's Second Symphony ('The Resurrection') is so resounding because of the depths of danger explored before it, in long, wandering, fragmented passages that sound garish and provisional. Out of the tail-chasing obscurity, sound that gives no clear signposts, emerges newly intensified *clarté*. Meaning in music is both revealed and concealed, suggested but never totally unveiled, according to the context's own logic.

Similarly intermittent patterns of musical meaning are reflected in Mallarmé's poetry. The 'reflets', 'fils', or 'rapports' of the 'dentelle' capture the fluctuation of meaning and non-meaning, the hermeneutic gap in musi-cal signification. In a letter to François Coppée this intention is made clear: 'Les mots—qui déjà sont assez eux pour ne plus recevoir d'impression du

---

[37] *Music Sounded Out* (London: Robson Books, 1990), 25.
[38] *Quasi una fantasia*, 4.

dehors—se reflètent les uns sur les autres jusqu'à paraître ne plus avoir leur couleur propre, mais n'être que les transitions d'une gamme.'[39] But there is here a further sense in which poetry operates to a musical model of meaning. Words acting in the service of allusion and suggestion are 'transposed' into a network of reciprocal relations that appear to be the notes of a musical scale. From the mutually reflecting words, a new essence or pure sense arises whose principal quality is a stepwise movement of sonority. Words that are removed from the world of objects associated with ordinary reference share the non-representative quality of music: 'Je dis: une fleur! et, hors l'oubli où ma voix relègue aucun contour, en tant que quelque chose d'autre que les calices sus, *musicalement* se lève, idée même et suave, l'absente de tous bouquets.'[40] The poet excises a word from the indifferent text of the world ('l'oubli'), prising it loose from both verbal clichés and the attributes of the objects it names ('en tant que quelque chose d'autres que les calices sus'). The word assumes a new and singular existence as a pure musical form ('l'absente de tous bouquets'), associated in the following passage with a higher metaphysical realm:[41] 'La musique nous offre un exemple. Ouvrons à la légère Mozart, Beethoven ou Wagner, jetons sur la première page de leur œuvre un œil indifférent, nous sommes pris d'un religieux étonnement à la vue de ces processions macabres de signes sévères, chastes, inconnus.'[42] Poetry shrouded in a veil of obscured meaning imitates the mystery in music. This suggestive power of transposition is also founded on the dialectic of presence and absence. The word points at once to a thrilling nothingness, 'le néant', and the pure generative power of language itself when the author 'disappears'.

Such is the status of the rhyme word 'ptyx' in 'Ses purs ongles'.[43] Cut free from immediate semantic reference this word asserts first and foremost its status as pure rhyming sonority. The absence of the 'ptyx' from the poet-narrator's room leaves a space that is filled by a sonorous material presence in the word itself. (Rhyme used for arbitrary ornamental effect has been abolished.) Language freed from denotation has 'matter' independently of the sign yet at the same time, as Kristeva points out, the word experienced as word creates an immediate consciousness of the absence of identity existing between object and sign.[44] In a note Mallarmé writes: 'Le moment de la

---

[39] 5 Dec. 1866 (*OC*, 709).   [40] 'Crise de vers', *OC* (M), 368 (my italics).

[41] Mallarmé's need to reach an objective world through words free of authorial mediation, acting autonomously upon one another, stemmed from his own deep religious crisis, after which he fought reluctantly to find the closest non-human system to the divine he could. In his struggle for meaning not contingent upon the chance encounters of the human world, his efforts to fix an objective order came constantly up against his fears that outside the material presence of the world there was nothingness, 'le néant'. It was perhaps in music that Mallarmé found a coherent system that mapped worldly and human thought processes as objectively, as mysteriously, and as spiritually as possible, without acknowledging the notion of God.   [42] 'Hérésies artistiques', *OC* (M), 257.

[43] *OC*, 37.

[44] 'The Ethics of Linguistics', in David Lodge (ed.), *Modern Criticism and Theory: A Reader* (New York: Longman, 1988), 230–9 (236). Kristeva is quoting Freud's *Totem and Taboo*.

Notion d'un objet est donc le moment de la réflexion de son présent pur en lui-même ou sa pureté présente.'[45] The true representation of an object, the 'Notion', is achieved when the 'son' (sound) is reflected in and of itself. In 'Ses purs ongles' 'un **or**' is picked up in 'lic**or**ne' and 'déc**or**' and in its mirror reflection 'mi**ro**ir'. Sound is literally born ('sonnet', 'son né') in and of the poem ('sonore', 's'honore').[46] As a symbol of pure self-reflection (the rhyme 'yx' contains the figure of its own chiasmus, 'x'), the 'ptyx' has been found by Émile Noulet, amongst others, to signify 'pli' or a conch shell (which creates a 'creux' within its own casing), an emblem of the dialectic of presence and absence that is inherent in the pure word object at the pinnacle of 'transposition'.[47]

Thus in the evocation or 'suggestion' of an object vectors of presence, absence, and transposition are all there: 'Évoquer, dans une ombre exprès, l'objet tu, par des mots allusifs, jamais directs, se réduisant à du silence égal, comporte tentative proche de créer.'[48] To represent an object is to suggest an object position without filling it. In reading the sonorous and visual signifier of the object is displaced and the object mobilized in space. Georges Poulet illustrates a similar spatial mobilization with an image from *Igitur*: 'Dans une chambre vide, sur une table, un livre attend son lecteur.'[49] Poulet the reader notes the transposition from the material status of the book to the mental realm of ideas and images as he leafs through the pages:

Où est le livre que je tenais dans la main? Il y est encore, et, dans le même moment, il n'y est plus, il n'est nulle part. Cet objet entièrement objet, cette chose en papier comme il y a des choses en métal ou en porcelaine, cet objet n'est plus, ou, du moins, il est comme s'il n'était plus, tant que je lis le livre. Car le livre a cessé d'être une réalité matérielle. Il s'est mué en une suite de signes, qui se mettent à exister pour leur compte.[50]

The 'transposition' of an object into a 'notion pure' whose existence is at once affirmed and denied is captured in the disappearing and re-emerging smoke rings from the slow-burning cigar in 'Toute l'âme résumée':

> Toute l'âme résumée
> Quand lente nous l'expirons
> Dans plusieurs ronds de fumée
> Abolie en d'autres ronds[51]

---

[45] *Igitur, Divagations, Un coup de dés*, ed. Yves Bonnefoy (Paris: Gallimard, 1976), 382. Mallarmé also writes famously to Cazalis after his 'crise': 'Je viens de passer une année effrayante: ma Pensée s'est pensée et est arrivée à une Conception pure' (14 May 1866, *OC*, 713).

[46] I am grateful to Roger Pearson for illuminating some of these plays on words for me.

[47] Jean-Pierre Richard notes that, in Mallarmé, 'réfléchir intellectuellement, c'est déjà se replier' (*L'Univers imaginaire*, 177). Derrida works with a similar aspect of the symbol of the 'pli': 'Le pli ne lui survient pas du dehors, il est à la fois son dehors et son dedans'. (*La Dissémination* (Paris: Seuil, 1972), 290). See Chapter 4, section 4.11.   [48] 'Magie', *OC* (M), 400.

[49] *La Conscience critique* (Paris: José Corti, 1971), 275.   [50] Ibid. 277.

[51] ll. 1–4, *OC*, 73.

As a smoke ring is formed and disappears time has passed, but the space the ring leaves in the air is filled by another ring, cancelling out the last but replicating it. Time appears to stand still. The smoke ring is both present and absent.[52]

In the 'Ouverture d' "Hérodiade" ' ['Ouverture ancienne'] the simultaneous presentation and cancellation of an image and the multiplication of interpretative possibilities surrounding certain words creates an overdetermination of signification:

> Abolie, et son aile affreuse dans les larmes
> Du bassin, aboli, qui mire les alarmes,
> De l'or nu fustigeant l'espace cramoisi,
> Une Aurore a, plumage héraldique, choisi
> Notre tour cinéraire et sacrificatrice[53]

This passage creates points of immobility through magnetic pulls of attraction and repulsion. The semantic space opened up by the initial act of repression or abolishing ('Abolie') is drowned again by its pursuit of a partner. The feminine 'Abolie' finds its mirroring reflection in the masculine version in line 2. The repetition both fills the emptiness created by the opening, in a matching sonority that has the effect of a double negative, and reiterates the sense of emptiness in a string of negative statements. Finding a masculine equivalent amounts to a reciprocal cancelling-out, yet the partnership gives birth to an overload of reflections in the line-final rhymes ('cramoisi', 'choisi'). 'aile' is 'Abolie' with its centre removed and its internal elements juggled. Sound patterns offer the promise of possible thematic centres, refuges from the pull between volume and emptiness. Yet to follow the path suggested by the phonetic patterning is to be misled. They are loci of stabilizing and destabilizing reflection, pools of verbal heterogeneity. The abolished pool is and is not reflecting 'les **a**' of '**a**boli(e)' ('dans les larmes', 'mire les **a**-larmes'). The associative pattern set up by /a/ is coupled with a search to make sense of the syntactical relation between '**A**bolie' and '**A**urore'. Dawn is abolished in the crimson space and yet its crimson may still be reflected in the pool. The hesitancy over the status of dawn is embodied in the word itself, aurally overdetermined, self-reproductive and self-cancelling [ɔRɔR]. Orthographically however, the stars are inscribed in the material word of dawn, filled with gold (*aurifier*): '**au**r**o**re'.

The rhythm of the 'fils sacrés' of signification, a reflection of the patterns of the 'Idée', occurs at the level of the representation of objects transposed into 'notions pures'. Objects do and then do not fill the in-between of the presence–absence dialectic, hovering as they do in ontological uncertainty

---

[52] Note that a similar dialectic is explored through the image of interlace in 'Une dentelle s'abolit', *OC*, 42.   [53] ll. 1–5, ibid. 137.

between the ideal realm and the physical, generative concreteness of the word signifier.

1.6 RHYTHMS OF SOUND AND SENSE:
MEANING AND NON-MEANING

In his *Cahiers* Valéry describes a fluctuation inherent in the condition of verse as 'cette hésitation prolongée entre le son et le sens'.[54] Sound and sense are two musical, meaning-carrying elements simultaneously interwoven in verse between which the reader is pulled. As the fabric of the poem is woven, elements of pure sound ('son présent') gain meaning from within the logic of the poem's structure. Mallarmé breaks away from the line of verse, which contains nothing beneath the purely decorative sonority of its surface, in the arresting declamation: 'Aboli bibelot d'inanité sonore';[55] and replaces it with an assonance- and alliteration-driven celebration of pure sound and the sheer materiality of the word ('lampadophore', line 2, for example). Referential meaning is obscured in favour of sound, which is pushed into the foreground. Reading such verse requires a constant switching between waves of pure sonority and of sense that emanate from the multi-contoured texture of the verse surface. Mallarmé evokes a similar fluctuation between sound and sense in 'Crise de vers': 'Le vers qui de plusieurs vocables refait un mot total, neuf, étranger à la langue et comme incantatoire, achève cet isolement de la parole: niant, d'un trait souverain, le hasard demeuré aux termes malgré l'artifice de leur retrempe alterné en le sens et la sonorité, et vous cause cette surprise de n'avoir ouï jamais tel fragment ordinaire d'élocution.'[56] The mysterious sonorous aura arising from the unusual juxtaposition of the words disorientates the ear: words dipped in and out of sound and sense prevent it from picking out immediately familiar meanings.

Mallarmé conceptualizes the tensions in the poetic texture between moments of clarity and obscurity, sound and sense, syllabic independence and a constraining metrical framework, and the converging and diverging strands of motifs. This texture is the product of an examination of the inner workings of music and poetry, a search for the roots of the shared inheritance that underlies the barely recognized overlap, and an attempt to redress the balance in the relationship so that the rhythmicity, temporality, and shapes of each art inform the other. Such writing extends the individual possibilities of each in a web of mutual enrichment and brings to the surface a complex relation previously hidden from even acute perception. Mallarmé never suggests that music and literature perform the same function or are the same art, but that

---

[54] Valéry writes this in 1912. *Cahiers* (Paris: CNRS, 1957–61), iv. 782.
[55] 'Ses purs ongles', *OC*, 37, l. 6.   [56] *OC* (M), 368.

they offer, in differing intensities, manifestations of 'le Livre', the essence of creativity. The patterns of 'vers' discussed above enact this essence in a manner specific but also common to music and poetry.

The interplay in 'Ses purs ongles' between sound and sense, inside which the reader struggles to grasp meaning for a second until, as pure sound takes over, sense fades and slips out of reach again, is a potent poetic depiction of metaphysical struggle—poetic because of poetry's supremacy in Mallarmé's system for configuring the silent architecture of the 'Idée', the overarching and embracing network and ultimate expression of the Unity of all arts.

The rhythmic intermittence of meaning in music resonates with Mallarmé's picture of alternating sound and sense in *vers*. The pull between meaning and non-meaning lies behind Mallarmé's artistic enterprises and at the source of his sense, despite all surface differences, of the proximity of music and poetry.

2 *La Musique et les Lettres*

1.7 THE THYRSUS, OR 'SELON UN THYRSE PLUS COMPLEXE'

Reading Mallarmé in the light of his claims for music, in what I shall call a musical way, allows a real insight into his self-enacting prose. One of Mallarmé's most famous claims for music and poetry is made in the lecture *La Musique et les Lettres*, 'que la Musique et les Lettres sont la face alternative ici élargie vers l'obscur; scintillante là, avec certitude, d'un phénomène, le seul, je l'appelai, l'Idée'.[57] Making music a proper consideration, that is to say, has a certain part in and effect on the text, opens up ways of reading his late prose not available before. I shall propose a reading that takes Mallarmé at his word and examines the joint architecture of music and verse as it structures the prose through the cross-rhythms of sound, metre (rhythm), and syntax.[58]

This address is the crowning statement of the relation of music and letters and the culmination of Mallarmé's thought on music and poetry. It is a prose that illustrates his theory in practice to the most extreme degree, an ultimately

---

[57] Ibid. 649.

[58] *La Musique et les Lettres* has many other frames of reference, of course. My work has profited in particular from the following readings of the lecture: Mary Lewis Shaw, *Performance in the Texts of Mallarmé: The Passage from Art to Ritual* (Pennsylvania: Pennsylvania State University Press, 1993); Rachel Killick, 'Mallarmé's Rooms: The Poet's Place in "La Musique et les Lettres" ', *French Studies*, 51/2 (1997), 155–68; *Mallarmé et la prose*, ed. Henri Scepi (Poitiers: UFR Langues Littératures, 1998). This work aims to go some way towards improving the situation noted by Winifred Nowottny, who complains in *The Language Poets Use* that 'the critical language available for the discussion of rhythm is so unsatisfactory' (London: The Athlone Press, 1962), 17. There is still much to be done in this area of poetic criticism.

self-enacting aesthetic manifesto written into the manner in which it says rather than into what it says. This statement near the beginning of the lecture suggests the way in which we are to read:

En raison que le vers est tout, dès qu'on écrit. Style, versification, s'il y a cadence et c'est pourquoi toute prose d'écrivain fastueux, soustraite à ce laisser-aller en usage, ornementale, vaut en tant qu'un vers rompu, jouant avec ses timbres et encore les rimes dissimulées: selon un thyrse plus complexe. Bien l'épanouissement de ce qui naguères obtint le titre de *poème en prose*.[59]

Here we have an extraordinary set of claims. There is verse as soon as there is rhythm. Rhythm is a question of style and cadence belonging to any prose in the hands of a fastidious writer. Moreover, there is no difference between prose and verse, just tighter and looser rhythms. We could be forgiven for thinking that Mallarmé's conflated notion of rhythm and style is a rather loose, although attractive, definition of verse. I have shown earlier how in fact 'rythme' in Mallarmé's writing can be a precise term both in describing verse and as a shared characteristic to describe the common ground occupied by music and poetry. In this passage from *La Musique et les Lettres* it is clear that the notion of rhythm is potentially a very exacting one.

Prose is as good as a 'vers rompu'. The poet is digging down or breaking through (*rompre*) the lyrical topsoil to the bedrock, the raw materials of versification, with an exhausting and moving, almost physical, effort to reach the kernel of verse, in a bid for greater manipulation and control of its constituent parts in order to release its essence. New timbres and rhymes emanate from within the 'vers rompu'. Although music is not made explicit in this passage, the behaviour of the verse-prose described has the characteristics of the music-verse examples I have already highlighted. The 'vers rompu' newly incorporates silence into the line to give space and air, a quality Mallarmé admires in the younger poets: 'A cause que de vraies œuvres ont jailli, indépendamment d'un débat de forme et, ne les reconnût-on, la qualité du *silence*, qui les remplacerait, à l'entour d'un instrument surmené, est précieuse.'[60] The liberation of new sounds and rhythms from within the guiding metre of the alexandrine, which holds the jostling of the mobilized elements of the line fragilely and tentatively together in their 'libre disjonction', is here intimately linked with the harnessing of music by Mallarmé's poetic system. Silence is a quality as important and expressive in music as sound, something that, as we saw earlier, Mallarmé has heard in the 'mélodies

---

[59] *OC* (M), 644. This is reiterated in the interview with Jules Huret: 'Le vers est partout dans la langue où il y a rythme, partout, excepté dans les affiches et à la quatrième page des journaux. Dans le genre appelé prose, il y a des vers, quelquefois admirables, de tous rythmes. Mais, en vérité, il n'y a pas de prose: il y a l'alphabet et puis des vers plus ou moins serrés: plus ou moins diffus. Toutes les fois qu'il y a effort au style, il y a versification' (*OC* (M), 867).

[60] Ibid. 644 (my italics).

brisées' and transferred to verse (see section 1.3). Out of the literal rupture of certain lines by syntax come 'timbres et encore les rimes dissimulées' from whose overall rhythm a new metre is born: 'Très strict, numérique, direct, à jeux conjoints, le mètre, antérieur, subsiste; auprès.'[61] The metrical rhythm is founded on the patterns of sound and silence ('retrempe alterné en le sens et la sonorité', see section 1.6) that punctuate and compose the sentences, which qualify as verse because of their style and cadence.

All these strands seem to converge on the figure of the thyrsus, a summarizing enactment of the textual patterns in simultaneous three-dimensionality. Inserting a figure into the text at this point gives a single, expandable, textual pressure point in the search for the extra-linguistic power to provide a physical—visual, sensual, and dynamic—experience of the integration of music and verse. The thyrsus configures the poetic activity, following the movement upwards through space of the foliage entwined around the Bacchic staff: it is an elegant, performative vision of the fragile balance between containment and frenzy.[62] The rigid linearity against which the florid departures are sensed has the same structural frame as the firmness of traditional metrical form pulling against the more individual voice of the ruptured line, which is syntactically mobile and plays syllable off against syllable, word against individual word. The figure holds within it vectors which express the intermittent patterns of the line, which is 'transformable, ondoyant', produced by the structural interweave of music and verse. Music and poetry are held in precarious simultaneity by a figure whose space allows their cohabitation.

1.8 'CETTE MENTALE POURSUITE'

'Tout l'acte disponible, à jamais et seulement, reste de saisir les rapports, entre temps, rares ou multipliés; d'après quelque état intérieur et que l'on veuille à son gré étendre, simplifier le monde.'[63] According to Mallarmé, the aim of all creative acts is to seize the links between times or temporalities, according to their inner natures. In this sentence 'entre temps' sits between the noun and another predicate, becoming an illustration of betweenness which needs to be bridged in the act of 'saisir'. It is in this act that all disciplines, all domains of thought, are linked: 'L'observance qu'un architecte, un légiste, un médecin pour parfaire la construction ou la découverte, les élève au discours: bref, que tout ce qui émane de l'esprit, se réintègre. Généralement, n'importe les matières.'[64] The poet's task is to find templates to fit between such disciplines.

---

[61] Ibid. 644.

[62] Mallarmé will have known Baudelaire's prose poem 'Le Thyrse', which explores the ornamental properties of the thyrsus in a homage to Liszt, master of the 'ligne arabesque' (*Petits Poèmes en prose*, ed. H. Lemaître (Paris: Classiques Garnier, 1980), 162–6). [63] *OC* (M), 647.

[64] Ibid. 645.

The practitioner of each profession listed expresses his expertise when building or discovering something through language, in which all activities of the mind converge. So the poet, by finding the underlying relationship between domains of thought, whether they be few or multiple, can distil an essence from them ('simplifier le monde') by 'une transfiguration en le terme surnaturel'.[65]

Following the description of 'Tout l'acte disponible', but independent from it, is a phrase that presents itself as straightforwardly qualifying but is deceptively complex: 'À l'égal de créer: la notion d'un objet, échappant, qui fait défaut.'[66] Is the all-defining act the same as the act of creation or is creating being defined another way, as the notion of an object that, escaping, creates absence? The reader is forced to move back and forth between sentences, seizing the 'rapports' between definition and counter-definition and gleaning semantic links between the words that are offered, expanded, and redefined almost in one breath. The colon marks the balance point between the two equally weighted parts for comparison, each six syllables in length: 'À l'égal de créer: la notion d'un objet.' Even when the relation of 'la notion d'un objet' to the first part of the sentence and to the preceding paragraph has been juggled with, the whole phrase itself, bifurcated by an isolated lexical item ('échappant'), has to be read twice. The semantic and visual effect of this present participle describing the noun phrase is to appear to escape from the sentence to leave a gap. With the obstacle removed the sentence can be reread as a whole, 'la notion d'un objet qui fait défaut', although semantically it still describes an absence; the equality formed by the pivotal colon is revealed as chimeric. What appears to be a balancing, defining complement is actually the site of an absence. In short, this section of the lecture plays with balances and imbalances in syntactic and semantic rhythm. 'Saisir les rapports' is a precarious business: it is not simply a question of seeking symmetrical relationships, but of understanding the mobile, asymmetrical ones. The act of 'simplifying the world' or refining systems of thought to their essence means causing objects to disappear in favour of their 'notion'. Every act of creating ('Tout l'acte disponible') involves the musical process of removing objects or systems of thought into a higher shared realm in language. It is musical because it releases them from their immediate world of reference into a unified sphere based on 'rapports'.

1.9 'SAISIR LES RAPPORTS'

'Je sais que la Musique ou ce qu'on est convenu de nommer ainsi . . . cache une ambition, la même.'[67] Music, in the sense Mallarmé is proposing, shares

---

[65] *OC* (M), 646.   [66] Ibid. 647.   [67] Ibid. 648.

the same purpose as all-encompassing literature: 'Il y a une minute, des sinueuses et mobiles variations de l'Idée, que l'écrit revendique de fixer, y eut-il, peut-être chez quelques-uns de vous, lieu de confronter à telles phrases une réminiscence de l'orchestre.'[68] Writing traces the changing patterns of the Idea, as we saw above in the letter to Gosse (section 1.4), and, as Mallarmé reminds the audience here, they may have had occasion to hear echoes of orchestral music in such winding, mobile figures. Mallarmé goes on to clarify in a manner that, again, leaves a clue to reading some of the earlier passages: 'où succède à des rentrées en l'ombre, après un remous soucieux, tout à coup l'éruptif multiple sursautement de la clarté, comme les proches irradiations d'un lever de jour: vain si le langage, par la retrempe et l'essor purifiants du chant, n'y confère un sens.'[69] Here the distinct shapes of an aural landscape, not dissimilar to the meaning-producing contrasts in music discussed above, are depicted. Although couched in highly metaphorical terms, a familiar symphonic structure emerges: following a patch of scarce, introverted motifs a backwash or eddy of sound creates an upheaval that leads into a joyous or serene eruption of multiple brightness or clearness.

This passage has profound consequences for the way we read the 'rapports' in Mallarmé from now on. By the end of this half of the lecture he feels able to claim that he has proved his case: 'Alors, on possède, avec justesse, les moyens réciproques du Mystère—oublions la vieille distinction entre la Musique et les Lettres, n'étant que le partage, voulu, pour sa rencontre ultérieure, du cas premier'.[70] The lecture provides the tools required for seeing and realizing the shared properties of music and letters: 'L'une évocatoire de prestiges situés à ce point de l'ouïe et presque de la vision abstrait, devenu l'entendement; qui, spacieux, accorde au feuillet d'imprimerie une portée égale.'[71] Music is gifted with the power (to which he aspires for letters) to evoke completely abstract aural, even almost visual, spatial (or three-dimensional) shapes. We can see how Mallarmé is setting the two arts up in relation to one another in his argument, and in such a way as to mirror or perform the very claims he is making for them. There is a continual, extremely subtle shifting of viewpoint from one to the other. Earlier in the lecture the suggestion was that letters came out on top as the ultimate meaning-giving vehicle for the aesthetic mobilization of the Idea ('le vers est tout, dès qu'on écrit').[72] Here, music and letters are all the time being aligned but kept apart, mapped onto each other but at the same time slightly offset from each other. They are depicted as being separate yet common manifestations of the Idea. In this passage music grants the printed page new qualities of

---

[68] Ibid. 648.   [69] Ibid. 648.

[70] Ibid. 649. See his qualification of the 'Mystère' at the end of the lecture: 'Appelez-la Mystère, ou n'est-ce pas le contexte évolutif de l'Idée' (653).   [71] Ibid. 649.

[72] Ibid. 644.

space ('accorde au feuillet d'imprimerie une portée égale'). The page has an equal 'portée'; that is to say, it can and should have a range or reach of abstract, spatial properties that is similar to that of music. But the claim goes further than this: 'portée' is also the technical term used to denote the musical stave. Rather than just implying that the spatial layout of the page will bear visual resemblance to the scattering of black notes on a stave, Mallarmé is also punning playfully. Encased within the word is a signifer which can equally be applied to music. If this seems far-fetched, one only needs to look as far as *Un coup de Dés* for a radical and ruthless implementation of these ideas. The mixture of *vers libre* and *poème en prose* that will become *Un coup de Dés* is embryonic here, inspired by music: 'Surtout la métrique française, délicate, serait d'emploi intermittent: maintenant, grâce à des repos balbutiants, voici que de nouveau peut s'élever, d'après une intonation parfaite, le vers de toujours, fluide, restauré, avec des compléments peut-être suprêmes.'[73] The new verse is fluid and mobile, with only intermittent occurrences of recognizable metre.

1.10 READING MUSIC IN *LA MUSIQUE ET LES LETTRES*

As we saw earlier, Mallarmé has a new, enlarged sense of rhythmicity and metricality that comes, among other things, from the contrapuntal rhythm of syntax and timbres playing against traditional elements of metre and rhyme. This rhythmicity creates a silent texture in poetry for which Mallarmé calls near the end of this section of the lecture: 'Je réclame la restitution, au silence impartial, pour que l'esprit essaie de se rapatrier, de tout—chocs, glissements, les trajectoires illimités et sûres, tel état opulent aussitôt évasif, une inaptitude délicieuse à finir, ce raccourci, ce trait—l'appareil; moins le tumulte des sonorités, transfusibles encore en du songe.'[74] This passage, however, could not be further from 'silence impartial'. Mallarmé revels in sibilants (which provide a phonological link between sound and silence) and /r/s to create a deliciously rich sonorous fabric that more than fills the silence ('**rest**itu**t**ion', 'silence', 'e**sp**rit', 'e**ss**aie', 'gli**ss**ements', 'ce **r**accour**c**i', and so on). The overspilling list is onomatopoeically enticing: 'chocs', 'glissements', in which the reader can easily discern 'la réminiscence de l'orchestre' (see section 1.9). Brusque syntactical splicing carves silences into the line that are as eloquent as their verbal counterparts. Silences exist in the form of interruptions and frozen moments, each of which is filled by a different sound or sensation. The short gap is contrasted with the infinite stretches suggested in the phrase 'les trajectoires illimités'. 'Tel état opulent aussitôt évasif', a richly overdetermined state, immediately evaporates; the space that follows the comma

---

[73] *OC* (M), 644.   [74] Ibid. 649.

suggests both richness and absence, unlikely partners knitted into the unspoken fabric of the text—unspoken but sustained by the syntax. The gaps between become loaded with more multi-layered semantic suggestion than the words do themselves. Embedded in the rhythmically regular syntactic divisions are quantities that do not fit, that are too large for their 'metrical' category. 'Une inaptitude délicieuse à finir', for example, has a semantic implication that resists the closure of the syntactical group. Such 'inaptitude délicieuse' contains echoes of the lingering thirteenth syllable (see section 1.3).

The air provided by the commas gives a dynamic energy to the page that belongs at once to the text and to music. The shared structural rhythm of music and letters is at work in the nouns, syntax, and metre of the prose even as it prescribes future conditions for itself. Juxtaposed with the request for the return of these shapes and figures to their rightful place in the realm of silence so that the mind can try to find its natural home again ('pour que l'esprit essaie à se rapatrier') is an onslaught of the most violent, guillotining punctuation, hardly in line with the former tone of repatriation. The 'trait' that prepares the list of everything ('de tout') has an almost Domesday feel to it. It signals linguistic anarchy in the midst of an otherwise well-behaved sentence. The list will have no conclusion, closure, or justification; it simply fills the present with a flourish and leaves, with no semantic rationale other than that of enacting its own presence ('ce raccourci, ce trait—l'appareil'). The list of effects explodes into life, each cut off from the other and marking a clipped, isolated movement; the list's sum forms no coherent or stable picture. Each element escapes: jolts, slides, lifts, unlimited trajectories, lines, glissandi, turning points, shocks, augmentations, and foreshortenings. Each contributes to forming a sinuous and mobile texture ('par le heurt de leur inégalité mobilisés', see section 1.4).

For Adorno, the unfinished is a musical property. He draws a distinction between two types of representation of music in literature by opposing the 'truly musical' to the 'musicalized': 'Kafka treated meanings of spoken, intentional language as if they *were* music: parables broken off in mid-phrase. Contrast this with the "musical" language of Rilke and Swinburne—their imitation of musical effects and their remoteness from true musicality.'[75] He identifies the implied, promised, incomplete, and unstated as inherently musical properties and differentiates these in Kafka from the literary fabrication of so-called musical effect in Rilke and Swinburne.

In the passage from *La Musique et les Lettres* above, the movements listed appear to be limitless but are nonetheless enclosed by the surrounding borders formed by punctuation. The stepping of each one outside of the ordinary behaviour of the text has a performativity that closely resembles a musical

[75] *Quasi una fantasia*, 3.

tour de force. More like music, then, than an aesthetic treatise for its immediacy of enactment, the text is a *mise en abyme* of its own signification. It is made all the more potent by its two-pronged excursus into the unexplored and overlapping structures, rhythms, and auditory drama created between music and letters.

1.11 'UNE INAPTITUDE DÉLICIEUSE À FINIR': MUSIC AND CADENCE

What is constructed in this passage, then, is not only a textually performative drama of the shared architecture of the two arts but also a framework ('appareil'), provided figurally, to describe their abstract relation (which at times involves integration and at others mismatch) in general terms. This, in turn, provides a model that can be extended outside the text as a working aesthetic definition of the overlap. The equivalent 'inaptitude délicieuse à finir' in music could be imagined, for example, as the great cadenza in Beethoven's Piano Concerto in C, Op. 15. Alfred Brendel describes it thus:

Cadenzas of classical concertos were allowed, and supposed to be unpredictable. The final trill, however, traditionally leading from the dominant seventh into the tonic and the orchestral tutti, was something that could be relied on, for listeners and orchestral players alike. ... In the marathon cadenza for his own [Beethoven's] C major concerto, the trill is the special target of his mockery. . . . The dominant of C major is reached, the trill has begun. But why has there been a diminuendo that deflated the tension? And why is there no dominant seventh chord?[76]

What Brendel identifies as comic here could in another context be felt as 'délicieuse'. The idea of the challenge to closural expectation is the same.

The bizarre regularity in Mallarmé's prose of the brief spells of sound punctuated by rests and short staccatos (see section 1.10) could in itself be said to have a distinctly musical character if compared with, for example, the first movement of Beethoven's Sonata in G, Op. 31 No. 1 (Example 1.1).

The jerky, syncopated, dotted rhythms of the motif starting at bar 3 in piano, underpinned with staccato octaves on the beat, are juxtaposed with almost a whole bar's rest in bar 5. The pattern, unusual for opening onto a silence (bar 3, end of bars 5 and 7) is repeated three times, each time elongating the two-bar phrase (beginning of bars 5, 7, and so on). The third time is suddenly forte, ending on a pivotal chord, ready to modulate into D major (bar 9). The cadence confirms expectations but the rhythmic pattern does not: the fourth time only staccato quaver chords are heard. In this motif the gaps

---

[76] *Music Sounded Out*, 22.

Example 1.1 Beethoven, Sonata in G, Op. 31 No. 1, 1st movement, bars 1–16

articulate the music as forcefully as the sound. As the rests begin to overspill with G major sonority, so the expectation of change becomes greater. They brutally dislocate each repetition, highlighting the variation of the motif, which each time becomes more saturated with notes in the triad.

Of course, there are enormous differences between the closure of the overarching Beethoven phrase and the fragmented multiplicity of the saturated Mallarmé sentence. However, the overlap between the formal structures of each art is clear. They overstep the limits of their individual primary languages and together perform a common aesthetic function. This might illuminatingly be compared with Jakobson's notion of function. For example, his poetic function works in an 'applied' context in verse, but may be lifted from this applied context and generalized:

I say 'linguistic phenomenon' even though Chatman states that 'the meter exists as a system outside the language.' Yes, meter appears also in the other arts dealing with time sequence. There are many linguistic problems—for instance, syntax—which likewise overstep the limit of language and are common to different semiotic systems. We may speak even about the grammar of traffic signals. There exists a signal code, where a yellow light when combined with green warns that free passage is close to being stopped and when combined with red announces the approaching cessation of the stoppage; such a yellow signal offers a close analogue to the verbal completive aspect. Poetic meter, however, has so many intrinsically linguistic particularities that it is most convenient to describe it from a purely linguistic point of view.[77]

Mnemonics and advertising jingles, to use Jakobson's own examples, use the poetic function but do not assign it the determining role that it has in verse. Thus functions of syntax and metre such as 'cadences' and 'anticadences', as

---

[77] 'Linguistics and Poetics', in David Lodge (ed.), *Modern Criticism and Theory: A Reader*, 32–57 (45).

he calls types of final juncture, overstep the limits of poetry. In Mallarmé the poetic function stretches to include a 'silent' musical one.

I.12 'LA TOTALE ARABESQUE'

Semblable occupation suffit, comparer les aspects et leur nombre tel qu'il frôle notre négligence: y éveillant, pour décor, l'ambiguïté de quelques figures belles, aux intersections. La totale arabesque, qui les relie, a de vertigineuses sautes en effroi que reconnue; et d'anxieux accords. Avertissant par tel écart, au lieu de déconcerter, ou que sa similitude avec elle-même, la soustraie en la confondant.[78]

Intersections occur when a musical and a literary model are mapped, mutually resonate, and inhabit the same structural breathing space. At the intersections (word gaps, commas, or hyphens) a flurry of overdetermined semantic resonance emanates, here termed figurally 'l'ambiguïté de quelques figures belles'. The complete picture, the sum of the contained, conflicting, three-dimensional movements of text and music as they create ruptures and links in the texture, is depicted in the mobile, sinuous, twisting, and self-regenerative ornamental form of the arabesque. The poetic act consists in the relation within ('après quelque état intérieur', see section 1.7) and across ('entre temps', see section 1.7) the punctuating crevices formed by groups of words now self-organizing, now self-disorganizing. From the site of the 'betweenness', 'aux intersections', arises in a counteracting but not equilibrating move, 'l'ambiguïté de quelques figures belles'. Evoked in this passage is a very specific rhythmic pulse composed at once of rupture, the act of seizing 'les rapports' from within, and of the element that escapes from between the sections of coherence and non-coherence, pulling against the horizontality of the 'rapports'. At this point, as with the thyrsus, Mallarmé inserts an ornamental figure to do major work for him, moving the ornament from its usual position in the margin, or as a decorative addition, into the foreground to become meaning-carrying material: 'La totale arabesque, qui les relie, a de vertigineuses sautes en effroi que reconnue; et d'anxieux accords.'

Arabesque is an ancient and tenacious figure that is at times indistinguishable from its own process. In sixteenth-century France *arabesque* simply meant 'Arabian' but came to be associated by the early seventeenth century with Renaissance imitations of classical *rinceaux* inspired by Herculaneum, the ceiling of Raphael's loggias in the Vatican, and the Orient. In decorative art it referred to a strangely mixed, interlacing plant form, a fantastic mural or surface decor composed of flowing lines fancifully intertwined. Arabesque was gradually borrowed by literature and music from the field of architecture and ornamental art. In the nineteenth century it became associated with the

---

[78] *OC* (M), 647–8.

essence of the Romantic imagination and poetry, embodying richness and totality as well as the structure of irony. Rae Beth Gordon writes, on the subject of Gérard de Nerval's *Aurélia*, that 'Romantic poetry as "eternally becoming" allows us to witness the production of the text as it unfolds, changes course, and remains open to further development. Thus the reader follows along the same sinuous, intricate, and seemingly chaotic paths to the vision as does the hero.'[79] The arabesque figures at once the phenomenological mode of expression of the imagination and the overall structure of artfully ordered chaos in poetry.

Revisiting the passage from 'Planches et feuillets' will shed additional light on Mallarmé's conception of the arabesque as figure for the ideal rhythm of 'le Livre':

Un ensemble versifié convie à une idéale représentation: des motifs d'exaltation ou de songe s'y nouent entre eux et se détachent, par une ordonnance et leur individualité. Telle portion incline dans un rythme ou mouvement de pensée, à quoi s'oppose tel contradictoire dessin: l'un et l'autre, pour aboutir et cessant où interviendrait plus qu'à demi comme sirènes confondues par la croupe avec le feuillage et les rinceaux d'une arabesque, la figure, que demeure l'idée.[80]

Motivic strands of exaltation or dream in the ideal representation converge and diverge, in tension ('s'y nouent entre eux et se détachent, par une ordonnance et leur individualité'). This mental structure of through-composition and interruption is again figured through the swirling leaves and foliage of the arabesque, entangled here with sirens' haunches in a more baroque tableau. As a dynamic form of generative expansion, the arabesque figure articulates a space, and non-linear directional energies, that are common to poetry and music.

In *La Musique et les Lettres* the arabesque has quite a specific function in asserting the rhythmicity of the music–poetry overlap, which shall be examined over the next few pages. A uniquely polysemic figure and open-ended proliferating structure, the arabesque obfuscates the relation of its parts, creating ambiguity between the figure and the ground by simultaneously moving back into itself and forking into new arabesque, unfolding out of and shaping itself. The openness and digressive qualities of the arabesque depict movement and freedom whose profusion and variety evoke an energy that appears both to stem from fantasy and to trigger it. This aura of fantasy and undecidability is coupled with the arabesque's rigorous and definite movements. There is in the concept of arabesque an expansive motion from the small scale into an area of great, abstract energy. This expansiveness presents a problem for any language which tries to describe the arabesque as it is manifested in text. The

---

79 *Ornament, Fantasy and Desire in Nineteenth-Century French Literature* (Princeton: Princeton University Press, 1992), 33.   80 *OC* (M), 328.

undecidability the arabesque expresses plays an important part in conveying the intermediary ground between music and poetry, but is in tension with the *mise en abyme* aspect of the arabesque that makes it so precise a figure. To a certain extent the reader's peregrinations within this section of *La Musique et les Lettres*, one in a series of local enquiries into its own figural productions of textual-musical space, are mimetically enacted in the arabesque's sequences of progressions, digressions, and turning points. Discussing the *mise en abyme* without being over-metaphorical and overloading this passage with arabesque-like associations is extremely difficult. Nonetheless, something of the expansive quality of the concept of arabesque is enacted even at the local level of the text, and it is this that I shall endeavour to show here.

In the first syntactical group of the sentence, 'La totale arabesque', the position of the adjective creates an elision between 'totale' and 'arabesque'. This pivot gives a quite different rhythmic balance to the group from if the adjective had followed the noun. Rhythmically the elision arrives at the central point of the group to give the impression of a peak before a curve away in 'arabesque'. The rhythm of the word 'arabesque' ends the group with a tightly articulated flourish, the open vowel sound heightening the impact of the expanding gesture it makes. After the gesture of expansion a clipped, parenthetical syntactical group, only four syllables in length, follows: 'qui les relie'. Simply stated and more matter-of-fact, this subordinate clause clearly brings the grandiloquent flourish (which appeared to need no qualification) back to earth in a gesture of closure. The near-infinity of the curling 'totale arabesque' is made finite, a syntactical segment in part of a longer chain, by its alternation with a smaller segment which curls inward, and pulls the flourish with it. Another syntactical break follows, from which the closing gesture is converted into a rising upwards energy ('figures belles, aux intersections') and the line wings outwards again in 'vertigineuses sautes en un effroi que reconnue'. The effect of 'que' is to perform one such sudden change. The act of recognition at the feminine 'reconnue' is also one of non-recognition that forces the reader to reconsider the role of 'que'. At this point the reader sees that 'reconnue' is dislocated from the syntactical material immediately preceding it and that an overarching leap leads back to 'la totale arabesque' (with which 'reconnue' agrees). The reader performs the bifurcated leap of an arabesque. In this sense 'reconnue' indicates proleptically what will be recognized. This is no mere coincidence, as is suggested by the words attributed to Mallarmé by Maurice Guillemot: 'Il y a à Versailles des boiseries à rinceaux, jolis à faire pleurer; des coquilles, enroulements, courbes, des reprises de motifs. Telle m'apparait d'abord la phrase que je jette sur le papier, en dessin sommaire, que je revois ensuite, que j'épure, que je réduis, que je synthétise.'[81]

---

[81] Maurice Guillemot, *Villégiatures d'artistes* (Paris: Flammarion, 1898), quoted in Henri Mondor's *Vie de Mallarmé*, 14th edn. (Paris: Gallimard, 1941), 506–7.

At the semicolon after 'reconnue' the line effectively forks. One can take the fork that leaps back to the opening or, in a pattern that suggests itself as continual, follow the route after it that curls inwards again to 'et d'anxieux accords'. After the breathtakingly rapid changes ('vertigineuses sautes'), the rhythmic regularity of 'anxieux accords' reinstates a harmonic balance, even if, semantically, discord is implied. The perennial alternation of expansion and contraction, curving and forking of the arabesque is traced by the syntactical, rhythmical, and phonetic crescendos and decrescendos of the line. The line takes effect by tracing the figural pattern of the arabesque ('Avertissant par tel écart, au lieu de déconcerter'), performing its meaning in one action rather than referring to it in two ('ou que sa similitude avec elle-même, la soustraie en la confondant').

The musical framework (the 'Chiffration mélodique tue'), or the precise melodic motivation for the structure (the 'mélodies brisées' themselves), lies silently within the poetic texture: 'Chiffration mélodique tue, de ces motifs qui composent une logique, avec nos fibres. Quelle agonie, aussi, qu'agite la Chimère versant par ses blessures d'or l'évidence de tout être pareil, nulle torsion vaincue ne fausse ni transgresse l'omniprésente Ligne espacée de tout point à tout autre pour instituer l'idée.'[82] The texture both constitutes and is constituted by the numerical, rhythmic presence of a 'chiffration' that is 'mélodique', and so the foremost voice heard in the texture, yet 'tue'. This notion of the relation of number and music recalls the Pythagorean tradition. The 'Ligne espacée' is a pattern of the Idea, which writing has fixed into its internal 'rapports', a basket-weave of elliptically filled silences and sinuous line rigorously reinforced by syntax and metre pulling against one another, at once integral and interdependent (like the two impulses of exaltation and dream in the ideal representation). The silent framework shared with letters also occurs at the very end of 'Le Mystère dans les lettres', expressed in articulating ornamental figures: 'L'air ou chant sous le texte, conduisant la divination d'ici là, y applique son motif en fleuron et cul-de-lampe invisibles.'[83] The melodic subtext drives or shapes the divination 'd'ici là'; the state between the presence of the here-and-now of the signifier and the implied, absent ideal realm (the state of 'betweenness' of objects also). 'L'air ou chant' is a kind of gestalt figure: a rhythm-giving, shaping presence; text-building and written into the text yet simultaneously written out of it; invisible, or visible only in the silences. Absence in the text is confirmed as a presence in the musico-poetic 'motifs', the 'fleuron' ('jewel' or 'floweret', a piece in a crown or a typographical term) and the 'cul-de-lampe' ('tailpiece', a typographical symbol, possibly in the form of an engraving, occupying the bottom of a page or at the end of a chapter, or the strip of ebony to which the strings on an instrument in the violin family are attached at their base). They rise clear of the text

[82] *OC* (M), 648.   [83] Ibid. 387.

as the 'Notion pure', figured articulations of the joint architecture of music and letters.[84] The motif, or melodic cipher, is a through-composed thread in text, creating not only rhythm but also the temporal and directional drive forward that links poetry and music as arts.

It is through the use of these ornamental figures that Mallarmé reaches far beyond the accepted literary, 'musicalized' notion of music as sonority and euphonious phonetic patterning, to write the 'truly musical' as poetry. It is the aim of the next chapter, challenged by the underlying possibilities of Mallarmé's theory and practice of a shared architecture ('la face alternative, ici élargie vers l'obscur'), to bring non-verbal instrumental music and poetry into conjunction. It will attempt to reinvent the interlocutory field between the two and explore the use of figures to make the tacit tensions and dissonances between music and poetry explicit in a precisely articulated fashion.

---

[84] In the 'prospectus pour l'édition originale de L'Après-midi d'un faune' (1873) by publishers Alphonse Derenne, the following appears: 'Cette publication, avec frontispièce, fleurons et cul-de-lampe, offerte aux Bibliophiles, montre, avec les matériaux les plus rares, tout le savoir-faire qui honore la Typographie et l'Édition contemporaine.'

THE POETICS OF DISCONTINUITY:
EXPLOSANTE FIXE AND *ÉCLAT*

In 'Le Mystère dans les lettres' there is an extraordinary passage, displaying the most detailed structural precision, in which Mallarmé sets out a dialectic of listening and reading in music and poetry:

On peut, du reste, commencer d'un éclat triomphal trop brusque pour durer; invitant que se groupe en retards, libérés par l'écho, la surprise.

L'inverse: sont en un reploiement noir soucieux d'attester l'état d'esprit sur un point, foulés et épaissis des doutes pour que sorte une splendeur définitive simple.

Ce procédé, jumeau, intellectuel, notable dans les symphonies, qui le trouvèrent au répertoire de la nature et du ciel.[1]

For Mallarmé the intellectual process is shared ('jumeau') between music and letters: 'notable dans les symphonies', but copied by both from the wider 'répertoire de la nature et du ciel'. In the first structure of the dialectic proposed a triumphal 'éclat' leads to a momentary interjection followed by a backwash of reverberations, 'libérés par l'écho', whose effect is one of surprise. The second structure consists of the inverse movement: hesitations pile up into a stack that collects in a synchronic fold ('foulés et épaissis des doutes'), which is perceived as one concentrated, representative point ('un reploiement noir soucieux d'attester l'état d'esprit sur un point'). This shimmering point of repose is the tip of the iceberg or point of suspense above a contained, hovering, jostling assembly of polyphonic significations ('pour que sorte une splendeur définitive simple').

But what are we to make of these structures? Clearly they have a proposed acoustic, as well as literary, drama to them, but can they be taken seriously as generalizable structures of some use in comparative thinking? Over the course of this chapter I shall be standing back from the models of musico-poetic critical thinking offered by the Mallarmé text, to concentrate on testing by other means the basis of the joint architecture he proposes. Looking at the structural dynamics involved in meetings of non-verbal music and poetic text will serve to show Mallarmé's models, in particular this important one I

[1] *OC* (M), 384–5.

have just discussed from 'Le Mystère dans les lettres', as serious, rigorous tools. I shall begin by considering structural occurrences elsewhere in Mallarmé that might prove fruitful, when brought into alignment with music later, for carrying out this comparative test of the middle ground.

We have seen that readers of Mallarmé are expected to cope with multiple, conflicting, and concurrent temporalities: 'Un ensemble versifié convie à une idéale représentation: des motifs d'exaltation ou de songe s'y nouent entre eux et se détachent, par une ordonnance et leur individualité.'[2] Motifs of exaltation and dream can be crowded into one polyphonic space, co-present and then separate, subject now to a guiding framework and now to themselves alone. Conflicting elements are knitted together in dance, observed closely by Mallarmé in 'Crayonné au théâtre', to create an effect of 'suspens':

Une armature, qui n'est d'aucune femme en particulier, d'où instable, à travers le voile de généralité, attire sur tel fragment révélé de la forme et y boit l'éclair qui le divinise; ou exhale, de retour, par l'ondulation des tissus, flottante, palpitante, éparse cette extase. Oui, le suspens dans la danse, crainte contradictoire ou souhait de voir trop et pas assez, exige un prolongement transparent.[3]

The choreography of dance captures the tension ('suspens'), which hovers in a state of exquisite anticipation ('crainte contradictoire'). The desire to see more but to be tantalized by not seeing enough is obviously to be read as a metaphor for the text that at once reveals and hides its significance. 'Une armature ... éparse cette extase' describes equally the textual blend of controlling framework and elements trying to escape it. Two simultaneous three-dimensional dynamic movements operate beneath or alongside the outlining frame of the vision or 'armature' (the musical term for a key signature). First, fragments or motifs that pierce the surface texture are tight kernels of potential form ('tel fragment révélé de la forme'). Secondly, around the concentrated energy of the fragments is a more dissipated ecstatic counter-energy of material in flight 'ou exhale, de retour par l'ondulation des tissus, flottante, palpitante, éparse cette extase'. The interwoven movements of dance evoke the complex patterns of *vers*. Within the structure of dance and of the sentence, the unstable elements (the 'éclair' of glimpses of the body; the 'extase' of the whirling material) threaten its balance and composure. They distract the spectators' attention (both the *crayonneur*'s and the reader's) by constantly dipping in and out of 'le voile de généralité' of the dance, diverting its course by offering the potential for different dances within dances of varying forms.

Winifred Nowottny analyses the inextricable movements that make up the dance in T. S. Eliot's 'East Coker' and finds their distinctions to have been blurred:

---

[2] 'Crayonné au théâtre', *OC* (M), 328.   [3] Ibid. 311.

It is particularly striking, when one reflects on these patterns and ambiguities, that the object—the dance, or the movement of the dancers—is nominally one object; if analysed, the movement of the dancers turns out to contain two different movements, the circling of the dance and the rising and falling of the dancers' feet. The poet sets himself to blur the distinction, insisting by all his means that these two movements are inextricable from one another and that each is the same as something further and that all the movements in the poem evince the circular pattern.[4]

Similar cross-rhythmical currents occur in the second stanza of 'Billet'.

> Pas les rafales à propos
> De rien comme occuper la rue
> Sujette au noir vol de chapeaux;
> Mais une danseuse apparue
>
> Tourbillon de mousseline ou   5
> Fureur éparses en écumes
> Que soulève par son genou
> Celle même dont nous vécûmes
>
> Pour tout, hormis lui, rebattu
> Spirituelle, ivre, immobile   10
> Foudroyer avec le tutu,
> Sans se faire autrement de bile
>
> Sinon rieur que puisse l'air
> De sa jupe éventer Whistler.[5]

The dancer who appears in line 4 is an analogy for, and intended as a compliment for, the finely honed writing in the journal *The Whirlwind* and the arts in general, in favourable contrast to the merely scurrilous gusts of wind of ordinary journalism ('rafales'), the language of the street.[6] The dancer immediately becomes the 'tourbillon', whose taut energy takes hold of the poem without letting go. Images of frothing whirlpools and stormy waters link the juxtaposed movements set off by the raising of the dancer's knee: 'Tourbillon de mousseline ou | Fureur éparses en écumes | Que soulève par son genou.' Both the glimpsed fragment of body and the simultaneous, effervescent winding, spiralling, and scattering movements, emerge from the texture to offer new tempos of reading, as though they are subject to different controlling frameworks altogether but contained within the overall gestures of the dance.

The movements invoked are types of hesitation acting within the guiding framework of the whole, the perceived telos or general directional flow that

---

[4] *The Language Poets Use*, 178.   [5] *OC*, 34.

[6] Much has been written on this poem, which was commissioned by Whistler for the journal *The Whirlwind* (a literary journal; hence the image of the 'tourbillon' personified in the dancer). See in particular Marchal's notes in *OC*, 34 and Graham Robb's *Unlocking Mallarmé* (New Haven: Yale University Press, 1996), 141–51, for an enlightening reading of the 'syntaxe elle-même tourbillante', as Mallarmé called it.

keeps a tight rein on the frantic energy of the whirling tutu. The blurred, foam-scattering fury strikes down everything in its path, which is, by comparison, 'rebattu | Spirituelle, ivre, immobile'. The excitement, incisiveness, and fizz of art, or of this kind of writing, throws into relief the apathy around it ('hormis lui'). The force of the spinning vortex seems all the more powerful for being expressed through the rhythmically malleable octosyllabic line and the tightly packed *rimes croisées*. In lines 5 and 6, for example, 'Tourbill**o**n/ de mousse**li**n/e o**u** | Fureur épar/ses en écumes' (3+4+1 | 4+4), the coupe after 'Tourbillon' gives a renewed release of energy at the launch of the next measure ('de mousseline'), momentum that is sustained by the syncopated accentual rhythm and the enjambement into 'Fureur' in the next line.[7] At the same time, the forward drive of line 5 into line 6 is held back by the hesitational 'ou', an isolated syllable in the last measure that forms a point of suspension within the enjambement before the furious unleashing of the next line. The foaming fury of 'éparses' and 'écumes' is scattered against the line's syntactical balance and syllabic regularity. The phonetic explosiveness of these words rebels against their phonetic homophony; their articulation against the firmly fixed position of 'écumes' within the powerful stanzaic framework of line-final rhymes and its partnership in a *rime léonine* with 'vécûmes'.

Now that the feverish but contained composite energies in Mallarmé's dancer have been examined, I shall hold them up against some equally complex temporal moments in Debussy's music. At this stage I shall do little work to make connections between the poetry and music. Through the simple proximity of the two it will be clear how different are the individual internal constraints that produce the conflicting temporalities in each, and, by extension, how fraught with difficulty is the task of mapping the rhythms of overlap in their specific encounters.

2.2 CONFLICTING TEMPORALITIES IN DEBUSSY'S *LA MER*

In much of Debussy's music melodic and harmonic hierarchies are broken down, so that within the structure of a piece the theme does not develop along conventional lines but instead in a series of instants. The construction and periodicity of his phrases are fluid within a larger rhythm of repetition across shorter and longer passages of the music. Figures appear in an ever-changing context, lengthened, contracted, or with their accents displaced; repeated or alternated in a fluctuating rhythm of movement and immobility that develops by a process of accumulation. The focus on and between thematic instants

---

[7] Marking convention (used throughout): | = line break, // = caesura; / = *coupe*; **bold** = accented syllable; : = lengthened syllable of *coupe enjambante*; ' = *coupe lyrique*.

within the larger framework results in very supple changes of tempo. Not based on predictable patterns of evolution with fixed consequences for the melody, Debussy's harmonies are extremely unstable and explore regions a long way from the original key, which is usually, in earlier music, such a strong orientating force.[8]

Classical concepts of exposition, development, and recapitulation are still quite strongly evident in *La Mer* (1903–5), particularly in the outer movements, but begin to lose their traditional sense later, in the *Préludes* book I (1910) and book II (1912–13) for example, becoming very distant in the *Études* (1915). In *La Mer* different motifs evolve through compressions and stretchings of tempo in a rhythm of tension and release that runs alongside the tensions caused by the harmonic relations. Melodic hierarchy is dissolved by the ambiguously fluctuating roles of the motifs: one that might appear to have a lesser role can without warning take centre stage or make a bid for equal attention, so that the ear has to flit between two types of activity happening at once, not knowing where to listen. In 'Jeux de vagues', the second movement of *La Mer*, as is generally characteristic of Debussy, rhythm, phrase, dynamics, and tone colour are freed from direct dependence on harmonic motion. Their functions become interwoven and interchanged in an extraordinary manner so that there is, for example, a clear 'rhythm' of tone-colour changes.

The manipulation of tempo and the interpolation of different time signatures in Debussy do not completely destroy overall coherence in the music, but put it under pressure by building and diminishing tension within it. The main tension is that between the evolving motifs: repeated, inverted, played in different pitch, timbral, and rhythmic contexts. The linear development of variation and growth from one motif to the next is cut across by fissures, ellipses, and silences. These create the cross-current of an alternative hearing, a shadow of other temporal pulls that disturbs the smoothness of the flow. The patchwork of sound and silence, density and sparseness, is supported by the additional current of alternation between an enriched and an attenuated harmonic texture. Debussy delights in the supple rhythm of weight and lightness given by moments that soar or hover in suspension that lends his musical language a blend of spontaneity and unpredictability. Boulez, one of Debussy's finest commentators, captures this spontaneity well in *Jalons (pour une décennie)*: 'Une logique surgit, plus souple, plus ambigüe, susceptible de créer des relations qui ne soient plus unilatérales . . . pas absolument prévisibles.'[9]

In 'Jeux de vagues', watery structures, for which Mallarmé shares

---

[8] Clearly these aspects of style, so broadly described, cannot be claimed for Debussy alone, especially with contemporaries including Mahler, Strauss, and Stravinsky in their number. I will discuss some influences on Debussy as the chapter progresses, with the aim of identifying particularly Debussyan elements of vocabulary for comparison and contrast with Mallarmé.

[9] (Paris: Christian Bourgois, 1989), 226.

Debussy's fascination, circulate in surges of powerfully undulating and varying crests and troughs. Turbulent, fleeting, fragmentary figures are interwoven in conflicting movements. Jean Barraqué writes: 'Comme dans l'organisation sérielle, une projection du vertical sur l'horizontal apparaît dans cette œuvre, mais elle est vue dans l'instantanée: concept anti-sériel qui fait naître la musique de ce qui précède immédiatement.'[10] The surges are constantly moving in sequences of anticipation, overspill, and backwash, responsible in part for the restless, overdetermined 'presentness' of the music. Surges that burst out of the texture are counterposed against eddying moments of stasis, at times concurrently, at others juxtaposed. Tension between the static and the mobile creates conflicting surface- and undercurrents in the rhythmic, dynamic, and timbral texture of the piece. A few selected pressure points will serve as illustrations of the eddies and cross-currents here.[11]

A two-bar crescendo, starting from piano, of slow-moving crotchet octaves in the upper strings, against triplets in the wind and hemiolas in the cellos and basses (bars 46–7), builds towards the point shown in Example 2.1 (a) (bar 48), where a sudden surge (from piano to mezzoforte) out of the texture is made by one harp, without any movement underneath it. After a mirroring descent in the second harp, an interpolation marked 'piano' in horns and cellos is heard, again building a crescendo, but in a very static figure (b) (bars 50–1) that only opens out at the end of the two-bar phrase. This sequence is repeated; the horn figure is then extended into a new set of concurrent motifs in bars 54–9. In the well-known passage that follows (shown in Example 2.2), the legato, singing tune in the cor anglais is heard against clipped, staccato semiquaver triplet thirds in the flutes and clarinets. The evolution in the rising and falling texture of the piece is gradual, evoking a heaving body of water composed of separate currents, eddies, and tidal pulls. The ear is required to listen to various kinds of activity with no apparent relation between them, superimposed but surging and relaxing independently.

Violent ruptures of the musical texture in the building of tension, surges, lapses into silence, and re-emergences into life occur alongside the scurrying four-note demi-semiquaver downward scales in the subsequent passage, marked 'Cédez' (Example 2.3; bar 72). First heard in the flute and echoed in the violins, the downward scale figure is neither stable nor dynamic. It appears to lead somewhere but then just turns on the spot, repeated for two bars. The violins echo the flute figure for two beats of the third bar of the section, but the figure is passed back a semitone higher to the flutes for the third beat, accompanied by its inversion in the bassoon (a pattern repeated in

[10] 'La Mer de Debussy, ou la naissance des formes ouvertes', Analyse musicale, 12 (1988), 15–62 (15).

[11] Extracts from La Mer (London: Eulenberg, 1983). These examples are best read in conjunction with a score and recording of the work, since they can only be briefly explained here. The numerical figures shown refer only to the Eulenberg edition. Bar numbers are given for ease of reference to other editions of the score.

Example 2.1 Debussy, La Mer, 2nd movement ('Jeux de vagues'), bars 48–51

Example 2.2 Debussy, La Mer, 2nd movement ('Jeux de vagues'), bars 60–3

Example 2.2 (*cont.*)

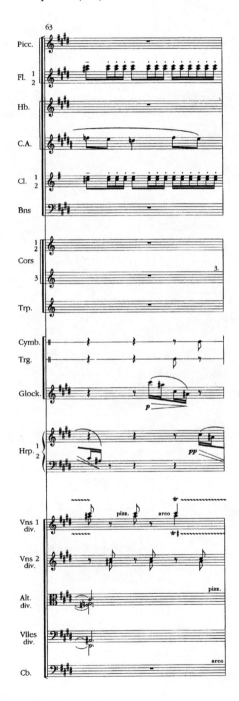

Example 2.3 Debussy, La Mer, 2nd movement ('Jeux de vagues'), bars 72–6

Example 2.3 (*cont.*)

the following bar). These small-scale, symmetrical movements severely weaken the directional motion of the music, forestalling any large-scale harmonic movement beneath them. The whole-tone scale in bassoon directs the ear away from an unambiguous sense of key. This is a 'moment' that appears out of nowhere and is phased into prefigurations of the main theme, which will eventually emerge in the cellos. The extraordinary paralysis of movement, made up of surges checked by stasis and circular patterns, which are born out of nothing and appear to lead nowhere, runs throughout the movement, reaching a climax in a furious unleashing at its end.

This initial comparative analysis shows clearly that the atemporal hesitations in each artist work to very different requirements. In Mallarmé's poem 'Billet' the tension is sustained and unrelenting; unrelenting, that is, until the witty pun of the final couplet that weaves in Whistler's name, deflating the tension and allowing it to escape, finally, into the air. In the poem we are whipped into an instant, almost white-hot frenzy. The depiction of the 'tourbillon' is a tour de force in its own right, a virtuosic flourish almost for its own sake that amounts to little more than a droll memento for Whistler. What remains is the impression of immobile stasis one gains from an object spinning with such speed, as well as the impression of an extreme violence that has dislocated the dancer's body into snapshot fragments. But the metrical framework of the verse measures the 'tourbillon' across the poem in a series of rhythmical thrusts that threaten to vanish into the nothingness, rather than in a series of isolated incidents that allow the nothingness and silence to enter.

In *La Mer* the surfaces presented by rupture, stasis, and hesitation are in a constant flux of thickening and thinning, increasing and decreasing layers of complexity. At times the *découpage* of the texture seems translucent, at others it is threatened by incoherence. Balanced, undulating statements can be upset by isolated, apparently unmotivated moments of disturbance that reveal strange silences in the texture.

The two kinds of ruptured surface generated by the analyses of these works refuse to lie neatly side by side. Neither work is easily placed in one reading or listening frame. The exact experience of the reader or hearer will depend on what other kinds of experience and habituation he or she brings to the works. 'Billet' can be read primarily for its fragmented elements, which pull centrifugally against the centripetal force of the metrical and rhyme frame; but it might equally appear as a smooth, unified blend of movements. Similarly, in the Debussy one could hear an overarching frame of smooth undulation or the friction between superimposed and linked passages of differing rhythm, pitch, and articulation, punctuated by strange silences.

The lie of the intermediary land between the two works could be considered as its topographical geography. The conflict between what I shall term the 'discontinuity' in the individual dramas of each work not only heightens the exciting tension of each, as it stands alone, by simple virtue of comparison, but also opens on to a new drama of the intermediary, which is itself pitted and ruptured. As the tectonic plates of the individual landscapes are lined up alongside each other, there are points of convergence, divergence, overlap, and interstice that form the coordinates of the middle terrain, a strange and undiscovered landscape awaiting exploration.

2.3 STRETCHING THE LINEAR IN MUSIC

Discontinuity in music is far from being the sole preserve of Debussy, of course. Listening to Classical music, for example, involves a set of linear and closural expectations that enfold the continuous momentum of the piece. Non-linear elements may stretch or challenge those expectations, working against or within them. Although the main course of enquiry in this chapter is discontinuity, I shall also be dealing with the powerful machinery of continuity in Debussy and Mallarmé, which plays a crucial part in the way discontinuity works.

As we saw earlier, conventions of Classical form are based on repetition and return to familiar narrative points as indicators of the stage the music has reached in its formal development: the beginning, the development of thematic material, the return to the original material to close. The theme of a piece is its principal organizing structure, a motif that formalizes the process of musical development in certain ways: for example, sonata form might have a two-themed dialectical structure and fugue is built on the entries and sustained polyphony of subject and counter-subject. Certain conventional structures accompany the theme in formalized ways, such as harmonic progressions and modulations to mark key turning points in the melodic narrative, and cadences to indicate varying degrees of repose or closure in an overall rhythm of tension and release.

Alfred Brendel gives an example of some startlingly original convention-stretching in Haydn's late C major Sonata (Hob. XVI:50): 'The teasing avoidance of classical four- or eight-bar patterns, the abortive storm in D minor that peters out almost before it begins, and its laughing and bouncing staccatos contribute towards making it comical.'[12] Unlike in the open and fragmentary structures of Romantic music, the periodic forms and linear motion in Classical music are basically symmetrical, so that departures from the telos are easily heard. Brendel explains this further: 'To become apparent, breaches of order need a framework of order. In other comical contexts, the framework is given by words and their meaning, by human situations and reactions and by the kind of thought that is connected with language. In music, the framework relies on the established musical forms and expectations, and on the

---

[12] *Music Sounded Out*, 18.

logic of purely musical thought.'[13] Breaches of order are as apparent as they are only because the predominant mode of organization is linear and closural.

The multiple and the non-linear are not confined to premodern music, of course. Equally subtle and complex structures fill the listener's time-experience in Renaissance vocal polyphony, for example. An instance of the non-linear heard against a linear framework, an atemporal hesitation, can be found in the first movement of Schubert's String Quartet in G minor, D173 (1815).[14] Between the end of the first subject and the beginning of the second, at bar 33, we remain firmly in the home key of G minor (Example 2.4). At bar 43, however, the melody slips a semitone, and, mirroring the two-bar phrase preceding it, modulates almost without warning into the relative major. A more lengthy, elaborate transition into the development might have been expected here, but instead there is simply a brief pivotal moment, a swift turning of the corner, marked by the F octave acciaccatura, into the new key. This transition section is dramatically swift. Its use of developmental material in a pre-emptive fashion makes its exact destination unclear. Rather than provide a link between the first and second subjects, as might be expected, it draws the listener's ear to a rupture in the sonata structure against which an atemporal slippage takes place. The four bars create a hiatus or suspension in the symmetry. They open a gap and the synapse across it appears at once necessary but ornamental to the whole. Atemporal hesitations, ways of resisting the onwards flow of metrical time in music, are a part of our listening, provoking primordial emotional reactions by surprising our form-structured listening expectations.

In spite of the apparent suppleness with which conventions are used, the Schubert quartet is still firmly grounded in the developmental-variational principles of tonality, with the 'theme' as its organizational centre. This music is, of course, a long way from the content and expressive form of Debussy's music, which constantly exploits the conflicting temporalities between tonal and formal frameworks and free-floating independently organized ones: whole-tone scales, modes, repetition, and variation, among others.

In *Philosophy of Modern Music* (1949) Adorno, in a move typical of his historical foreshortening, traces modern music back to its 'origins' through the eighteenth-century principle of development.[15] Development from Beethoven onwards was, according to Adorno in his selective account, a process that strove towards depriving conventions of their organizational function so as to organize the work freely within itself. In Beethoven, he goes on to say, development was a subjective reflection upon a theme which resulted in a regenerated form: theme and variations. Variation establishes the identity of the

[13] *Music Sounded Out*, 22. See also 56.   [14] (Leipzig: Eulenberg, 1955).
[15] Trans. Anne G. Mitchell and Wesley V. Bloomster (New York: The Seabury Press, 1973), 25–56.

Example 2.4 Schubert, String Quartet in G minor, D173, 1st movement, bars 24–50

thematic material through difference; identity thereby reveals itself as non-identity, since to secure a theme is tantamount to varying it. Music is no longer built simply on the level of repetition but rather on alteration through time, since only through constant alteration does it retain thematic identity.

In Brahms, for Adorno, the transformation of thematic material is executed in such a way as to expel all coincidental moments. No material is unthematic and so an extreme multiplicity of texture develops. The more the musical form becomes based on a developmental principle as distinct from an expository one, the greater the uncertainty. Conventions can still be heard as remnants or shadows in the music amidst the increasing force of what Adorno calls the 'subjective moments of expression [which] liberate themselves from the continuum of time'.[16]

Of course, Adorno's account is not aimed at providing a prehistory of Debussy or French music. His selective, formalist historical view also fails to account for Haydn's radical moments, for example, and risks making Brahms sound like Webern. Nonetheless it illustrates the relativity and self-reflexivity in play when the assumption about Western music, that one event leads to another, is questioned. The idea of continuous development, of constant alteration at every given moment, reaches an extreme point in the concretely unschematic relationships in Debussy, so that often his music appears to organize itself spontaneously. The destruction of conventional tonal and formal musical language, to which Debussy was a major contributor, gave rise to temporal discontinuities that would radically undermine the principles of linear motion.[17] Jonathan Kramer summarizes the extent to which temporal and harmonic boundaries were stretched by post-tonal composers such as Schoenberg, Berg, and Bartók to achieve new dynamic qualities in listening: 'The power of discontinuity is most potent in tonal music, which is the music par excellence of motion and continuity. Harmonically defined goals and linear priorities for voice-leading provide norms of continuity against which discontinuities gain their power. Tonal discontinuities, when pushed to extremes, create new experiences of time—time that is not linear and not one-dimensional.'[18] Debussy sits somewhere between the tonal and post-tonal poles. Classical patterns of contrast and return are only sketched in the background of his music. 'Je me persuade de plus en plus', he writes to Jacques Durand, 'que la musique n'est pas, par son essence, une chose qui puisse se couler dans une forme rigoureuse et tradition-nelle. Elle est de couleur et de temps rythmés.'[19] In Pelléas et Mélisande laws of

[16] *Philosophy of Modern Music*, trans. Mitchell and Bloomster, 55–6.

[17] For Boulez's version of the development of the theme in Western music and for a fuller picture than the one given here, see *Jalons (pour une décennie)*, 171. Specifically on the theme in Debussy, he writes: 'Elle a résumé l'instant, s'opposant ainsi à une rhétorique convenue du développement.'

[18] 'Moment Form in Twentieth-Century Music', *Musical Quarterly*, 64/2 (1978), 177–94 (177). See also *The Time of Music* (New York: Schirmer Books, 1988).

[19] 3 Sept. 1907 (*Correspondance 1884–1918*, 231).

tonal motion and expectation are very faint, because of the sustained chords, chromaticism, extended false resolutions, and endless beginnings to phrases that are announced hundreds of times. Temporal discontinuities also reach an extreme level in the repeated theme, whose upward swing is constantly interrupted and which never reaches a conclusion. This resistance to closural devices is what Jean Barraqué, frustrated with the limitations of traditional analysis, calls 'forme ouverte':

Debussy créa un nouveau concept formel que l'on peut appeler 'forme ouverte', qui trouvera son plein épanouissement dans *Jeux* et les dernières œuvres: un procédé de développement dans lequel les notions mêmes d'exposition et de développement coexistent en un jaillissement ininterrompu, qui permet à l'œuvre de se propulser en quelque sorte par elle-même, sans le secours d'aucun modèle préétabli.

Une telle conception de l'œuvre d'art frappe évidemment de caducité les moyens de l'analyse traditionnelle. En effet, dans *La Mer*, la technique musicale est réinventée, non dans le détail du langage, mais dans la conception même de l'organisation et du devenir sonore (selon une démarche que l'on pourrait rapprocher de celle de Mallarmé). La musique y devient un monde mystérieux qui, à mesure qu'il évolue, s'invente en lui-même et se détruit.[20]

Barraqué finds parallels between 'la conception même et l'organisation du devenir sonore' in Debussy's music and Mallarmé's linguistic art.

Mallarmé radically upsets conventional models for stanzaic and syntactical structures, all the while leaving their skeletons in place. Around the traditional alexandrine shadows of augmented and diminished versions of the dodeca-syllable suggest themselves. Debussy's compositional technique will also seem very reminiscent of Mallarmé's own poetic manifesto: 'L'acte poétique consiste de voir soudain qu'une idée se fractionne en un nombre de motifs égaux par valeur et à les grouper, ils riment: pour sceau extérieur, leur commune mesure qu'apparente le coup final.'[21] In Mallarmé the fragmented 'idea' is unified (in a 'commune mesure'). The tension between disorganizing and organizing impulses evoked by this passage has something of the mobile quality, the self-reflexive presentness in Debussy. This is the quality Barraqué describes as 'La musique . . . s'invente en lui-même et se détruit' (see section 2.3). The idea of the rhythm of self-generation by the words themselves occurs also in 'Le Mystère dans les lettres': 'Les mots d'eux mêmes, s'exaltent à mainte facette reconnue la plus rare ou valant pour l'esprit, centre de suspens vibratoire.'[22]

The qualities that seem to belong to both Mallarmé and Debussy—namely openness, mobility, and conflicting temporalities—are a good place from which to start considering shared aspects of their languages. But the similar qualities are undercut by dissimilarities and fail to present the whole picture.

---

[20] '*La Mer* de Debussy, ou la naissance des formes ouvertes', 15.
[21] 'Crise de vers', *OC* (M), 365.   [22] Ibid. 386.

In Debussy there is a *moto perpetuo* of ever-altered themes, temporary, fleeting states in loosely tied progressions and a continually forwards-moving under-current, the motion that creates the linear tension with areas of stasis or over-spill. In Mallarmé the oscillating immobility of atemporal hesitation does not have the same function in a large-scale structure of tensions and releases. Hesitation in Mallarmé enacts the intermittence of meaning and non-meaning. Trapped in the uncertainty of the moment all the poet can do is explore the meaning of non-meaning; that is, to make the non-event an event. Sonorous, figural, and rhythmic configurations impose a measure on the otherwise limitless void of non-meaning, 'le néant'. Non-meaning is not necessarily a more real possibility in an art with an overt semantic function, but the possibility of sterility and despair is stark and close in Mallarmé in a way not permitted by Debussy's desire to patch over the cracks. Compressions and resolutions occur with greater frequency and in passages of greater density in Debussy.

Rather than turning to Mallarmé to provide a vocabulary to express the *décalages* between the shared musical and poetic atemporal hesitations at this point, I shall turn instead to the language Boulez uses to describe his own music. Boulez's writing is a rich source that could lead to a more sophisticated classification of the discontinuous.

Boulez has been immersed in and highly influenced by the languages of Mallarmé and Debussy in his career and has often conducted performances of Debussy. He writes: 'Chez Debussy, ce qui m'a intéressé n'est pas son vocabulaire lui-même, mais sa flexibilité, une certaine invention immédiate et justement l'indiscipline locale par rapport à la discipline globale.'[23] Boulez discovered Jacques Scherer's *Le 'Livre' de Mallarmé*[24] as he was composing the Third Piano Sonata, and wrote to Stockhausen on 28 September 1957 that he was

stupéfait et bouleversé par les conclusions qui recoupent exactement tout ce que j'étais en train de chercher dans la troisième sonate. Tout y est! Insensé! Et il a pensé ça en 1890! Cela m'a poussé en avant. C'est une rencontre miraculeuse. Et je retravaille même mes formants car en particulier l'idée d'épaisseur me hante. . . . Lisez ce livre! . . . Nous allons bouleverser toutes les notions de forme et accrocher quelque chose d'extraordinairement important.[25]

In his Second Sonata he explores relationships to traditional forms by writing the first movement in sonata form but replacing the slow second movement with what he calls a 'trope', based on large-scale patterns of variation. His aim is to demolish fugal and canonic forms and to introduce the explosive, disin-tegrating, and dispersive as restricting forms in their own right. It is these ideas on form that seem particularly influenced by Mallarmé:

[23] *Par volonté et par hasard*, 19.
[24] 2nd edn. (Paris: Gallimard, 1977).
[25] Letter on display in 1998 centenary exhibition at the Musée d'Orsay.

Dans une grande forme, en effet, il faut que s'opposent ordre et désordre, sinon la limite extrême de ces deux états, du moins des moments où la perception éprouve un certain nombre d'ambiguïtés avant de pouvoir s'orienter et des moments où elle s'oriente instantanément, sans aucune ambiguïté possible. Pour passer d'un état à un autre, il faut aménager le changement de hiérarchies, faire, par exemple, qu'une caractéristique secondaire devienne la caractéristique principale et *vice versa*.[26]

The shifting ground from disorder to order and vice versa, which draws heavily on Mallarmé and Debussy, is executed with almost scientific precision in many of Boulez's works, some of which I shall discuss in the pages that follow.

2.4 CONCEPTUAL MOTIFS FROM BOULEZ:
ÉCLAT AND *EXPLOSANTE FIXE*

Éclat and *Explosante fixe* are the titles given to two of Boulez's works the compositional principles of which are fascinating and revealing. *Éclat* is a piece for chamber orchestra (1965–71). *Éclat/multiples* (1976) is a revised version of *Éclat* for a larger orchestra and *Explosante fixe* is orchestral and electronic (1972–4). Mobility is achieved in very specific ways in this music. Boulez makes a distinction between two compositional units in the work: 'développant' and 'formant'. These categories are also used in the Third Piano Sonata and based on ideas from Scherer's book on 'le Livre'. The 'formant' is a fixed structure which is allowed no intrusion into the homogeneous structure of the work, but whose place within it may vary. The 'développant' refers to the interference that may occur between musical ideas that are not homogeneous and that can therefore cause discrepancies between different phases of development in the music. Variation between the austerity of some passages and the flexibility of others (achieved by profuse melismata and supple rhythmic structures) gives a permanent flexibility and quasi-improvisatory style that owes much to Debussy. The juxtaposition of 'formant' and 'développant' gives the bare bones of a structure concealed by a fragile, flexible covering.

Using nine resonant instruments in *Éclat*, including piano, vibraphone, harp, cymbalum, and mandolin, Boulez plays with the acoustic phenomena of length and brevity in different registers and at different dynamics on the various instruments. He writes: '*Éclat* se base parfois exclusivement sur ces données tout à fait brutes de la perception matérielle.'[27] The manner of articulation itself becomes the theme of the piece: 'Des articulations d'un type d'événements peut devenir la structure principale . . . la précédente principale étant réduite à un rôle secondaire.'[28] Segments of counterpoint between the resonant instruments (primary) and a viola section (secondary) move in and out of the foreground, the viola sound getting bigger and bigger but the resonant

---

[26] *Jalons (pour une décennie)*, 271.   [27] Ibid. 269.   [28] Ibid. 397.

sound remaining unchanged. The instrumentalists are dependent on a conductor for their coordination but are independent in that they realize the musical figures as they wish: it is an ensemble that breaks apart to find its constituent individualities.

Explosante fixe is composed on a similar principle of juxtaposition. The piece opens with purely electronic music which is transformed in a mounting spiral before dividing between the two media of orchestral and electronic. The eight players are spread out over the whole stage, a formation directly opposite to the traditional notion of chamber music, where players are seated in close proximity. Each part is a solo, but refers indirectly to the others. Parts are heard together or alone in a texture of irregular density. 'La rencontre se place ainsi sur un plan non pas de hasard complet, mais de hasard préparé,' Boulez writes, favouring aleatory principles reminiscent of Mallarmé's.[29]

Through their exegesis in Boulez's prolific critical output *Explosante fixe* and *Éclat* have evolved into concepts in his metalanguage, an aggregate of all the stylistic influences incorporated into his working method in the name of the modern which seem to recognize, articulate, and specify certain types of discontinuity. *Explosante fixe* is a mobile but static turning-in-place which knits together conflicting temporal gestures. *Éclat* suggests a larger, more dramatic discontinuity, surrounded by silence. Boulez explains his choice of title:

D'abord, 'Éclat' veut dire fragment. Le premier éclat est, en effet, une pièce très courte. Il y a aussi le sens 'éclat'—*explosion* et le sens *reflets de lumière*, reflets très fugitifs. Mais tous ces mots ont des sens différents qui s'appliquent aussi bien à la forme de la musique qu'à son expression poétique. J'ai choisi ce mot 'éclat' parce qu'il y a beaucoup de significations.[30]

Over the next few pages I shall undertake some exploratory analysis of selected pieces of Mallarmé's and Debussy's work in order to isolate and define in precise terms the extent and nature of the intermediary ground in a particular case. Following Boulez's lead I shall take the different varieties of discontinuity expressed in the *éclat* and *explosante fixe* and project them backwards on to the works of Mallarmé and Debussy under analysis, using them as conceptual guidelines to navigate the intermediary terrain.

Moving via the motifs borrowed from Boulez in conjunction with this analysis, in order to make the appropriately complex demands of the text and music necessary to revealing the intricate patterns of the intermediate ground, has the aim of providing a mobile framework which will resonate with, but act beyond, the texts and pieces themselves, while being able, at the same time, to accommodate and express them both.

---

[29] *Par volonté et par hasard*, 137–8.   [30] Ibid, 113–14.

2.5 *EXPLOSANTE FIXE* IN DEBUSSY'S *PRÉLUDES*

Clearly when Debussy wrote the *Préludes* he was making a reference to the tradition of Bach, continued by Chopin. Many of the titles Debussy gives the pieces make programmatic suggestions for the music ranging from poetic moods, fairy tales, and mythologies to biographical anecdotes. The way we listen to a *Prélude* is influenced by knowing its title, of course. But listening can equally prove to be a very different experience from the one the title connotes. In form the *Préludes* are musical miniatures, in which can be glimpsed a musical essence that far exceeds the naming possibilities of language. Through its title, each *Prélude* enters a multi-level and sometimes paradoxical realm occupied by the differing connotative power of music and language. The *Préludes* range in style from the extended study of harmonic immobility of 'La cathédrale engloutie' and 'Voiles' to the incessant, restless mobility of 'Les tierces alternées'. I have selected a few examples of extreme temporal complexity for closer examination.[31]

In 'La terrasse des audiences du clair de lune' (book II) the nuances of mobile stasis, depicted in the *explosante fixe*, are amongst some of the subtlest (Example 2.5).

Certain non-tonal harmonic relations govern the fragmented melody in this piece, contributing to a sense that the music is hovering between suspended polarities. The arrival of any sustained motif that could be heard as a theme is postponed until bar 13, when the predominant tonal centre is also firmly established for the first time. Melodic lines emerge and disappear in snatches of scales that extend and suspend tonality. The left-hand pedal C♯, for example, forms the interval of a tritone with the G♮ in the right hand in bar 2. The tritone, or augmented fourth, lies a semitone between a perfect fourth and fifth, making it tonally the most ambiguous interval, as opposed to the fifth, the interval most fundamental to tonality. The beginning and end points of the right-hand chromatic arabesque in bars 1–2 together also form a tritone. The tritone is heard again amidst the F♯ major tonality at bar 16, sounding dissonant and unresolved. (When the figures of the opening are recalled as the piece closes, in bar 37, the symmetrically circling scales are floated over the clear tonal cadences of F♯ major. The weakened directional motion of the running passages conflicts directly with the very clear closural gesture of the cadence.)

A further non-tonal relation is the augmented second (B♭ to C♯) introduced in bar 3, which becomes the basis of a tonal modulation at bar 8, occurring through no movement at all other than chromatically shifting static tied

---

[31] *Œuvres complètes*, ed. François Lesure et al., 8 vols. (Paris: Durand-Costallat, 1985–91), v: *Préludes*, ed. Roy Howat (1985).

Example 2.5 Debussy, *Préludes*, book II, 'La terrasse des audiences du clair de lune', bars 1–21

Example 2.5 (*cont.*)

Example 2.5 (*cont.*)

chords, all marked 'piano'. At this point, the rhythmic ebb and flow of the opening bars appears to have ceased altogether.

In this piece a flow of accumulation and release is created by constantly shifting temporal frames and a succession of brief, kaleidoscopically evolving individual moments. One early example of shifting temporal frames occurs when the arabesque-like flurry of linear and concurrent scales in bar 1 is heard against the stillness of the opening figure.

Bars 10–12 present another example of shifting temporal frames, which is made up of a different interweaving of rhythms and pitch directions. The three pianissimo bars of dotted rhythms and long upwards and downwards runs and arpeggios in B♭ major create only a brief diversion in the patchwork of fragments. They trace a loop of rhythmic and pitch 'ostinato' in which upwards excursions lead swiftly back to their starting point for two bars (10–11), before a glissando (bar 12) leads pre-emptively to the motif in F♯ major (bar 13). The reflexivity of the loop diverts the music from the telos suggested by the preceding modulation (the hesitation in bar 9 on B♭) and enters quite abruptly a new temporal frame, dictated by the duration of the repetition.

In addition, frequent shifts of the metrical focus (between three, six, and nine quavers in a bar), either coinciding with a new phrase (bar 20) or occurring within a phrase (bar 15), contribute to the elusiveness of this music, which nonetheless never loses its sense of overall coherence.

The figure at bar 13 is an ornamental embellishment around D♯. It is a static, circular form containing its own immobile, mirror reflection, yet is a mobile melodic line. It forms a hesitation that disappears as quickly as it arrives. Then the drawn-out process of its disintegration, a slow series of falling fourths, becomes the main material. In this passage non-direction is combined with movement. Immobility is felt as rhythmic duration.

There is an emergent sense that such disintegration is, at the same time, instrumental in the music's development. Each phrase ends but is also continued, refusing complete closure. As a structural principle this inscribes the music in an endlessly self-proliferating present, mobile yet static. Lines interrupt and overlap each other in a texture of stops and starts, which nonetheless has a continuous flow, reminiscent of what Barraqué terms 'points d'aboutissement ou de passage'.[32]

Bars 16–19 repeat the bar 13 figure, oscillating around the fixed pivots of F and $G_{\sharp\sharp}$ and $G_{\flat}$, within the upper and lower $C_{\sharp}$ pedal. What results is a terracing of three distinct static states: the stationary upper and lower $C_{\sharp}$ pedal; the rhythmic and melodic movement around $G_{\sharp}$ (relating to the bar 13 figure) containing the $C_{\sharp}$ to G tritone; and, in the upper line in the left hand, an augmented version of the original bar 13 figure with the melody inverted and longer notes. Each line has its own shape and is distinct, but is tied to the others by its shared motivic material. The lines are momentarily caught in a texture of opposing forces—the inertia of repetition and oscillation, and the movement they imply. This could be called a moment of *explosante fixe* within the fluidity of sudden tempo changes.

Other moments of *explosante fixe* in the *Préludes* can be heard in 'Brouillards' and in ' "Les fées sont d'exquises danseuses" ' (book II). In the first four bars of 'Brouillards' (Example 2.6) two contrasting forms of motion are combined to produce a peculiar sense of stasis. A sequence of triads in the left hand moves in a symmetrical, stepwise, circular motion around the C major triad. Against this movement are heard descending broken chord figures in the right hand, whose starting pitch mirrors the circular, stepwise shapes in the left hand.

At bars 9–15 (Example 2.7) the relation of triad to broken chord in the texture mirrors the opening bar, but now the left-hand triad is fixed in pitch and repeated, creating a greater sense of stasis.

In bar 10 an upper $F_{\sharp}$ pedal note is introduced, suspended over the repeated broken chords and G major triad. Rhythmically, these bars are full of motion, but without any progression in the harmony, the motion is made to stand still. The suspended $F_{\sharp}$ increases the tension of the mobile stasis, further sapping the music of any forwards momentum. Its movement halfway through the six bars produces no change, it is only to descend an octave, moving slowly through the notes of the $F_{\sharp}$ major triad. Music compressed into a moment appears to oppose expansion in linear time.

The topsy-turvy perspectives and double focuses of ' "Les fées sont d'exquises danseuses" ' stem in part from the swift, light, demi-semiquavers of the introductory bars (1–5, Example 2.8), which suggest two keys at once, C major

---

[32] '*La Mer* de Debussy, ou la naissance des formes ouvertes', 16.

Example 2.6 Debussy, *Préludes*, book II, 'Brouillards', bars 1–4

and A♭ major. The repeated demi-semiquaver figure is split within itself by its upwards and downwards movement. Passages working towards certain goals are held in check by their opposing motion.

The interplay of contrast and association is another manifestation of the tension of mobile stasis or *explosante fixe*. Bars 101–16 are circling repetitions of the opening figure, but varied by moving up or down the octave. Contrasts of sonority are achieved by the repetition of mezzo-forte chords at a piano dynamic in the bass, against staccato upwards scales.

Example 2.7 Debussy, *Préludes*, book II, 'Brouillards', bars 9–17

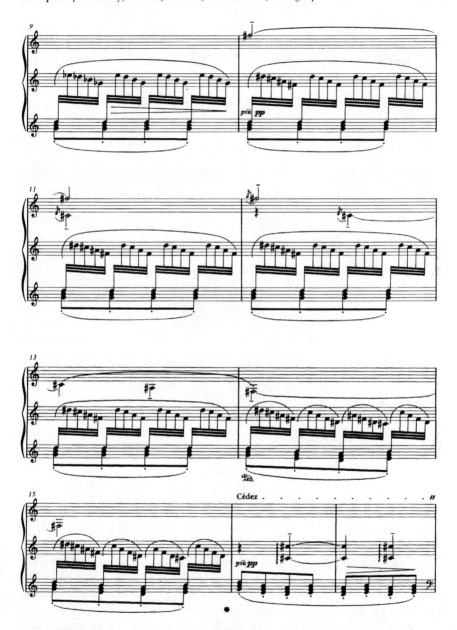

Example 2.8 Debussy, *Préludes*, book II, ' "Les fées sont d'exquises danseuses" ', bars 1–8

In bars 57–63 (Example 2.9) rapid upwards and downwards scales interrupt the progress of the more sedate and coherent motif. The scales become more fragmented at bars 67–72. The forwards momentum of the motor rhythms has pulling against it the awkwardly interrupting motifs of scales. The music is continually testing similarity against difference in spiralling figurations that twist around themselves and around a fixed pitch group, never reaching any desired goal for all their mobility.

There is no let-up until the fragmented ending is added in a whisper with

Example 2.9 Debussy, *Préludes*, book II, ' "Les fées sont d'exquises danseuses" ', bars 51–81

Example 2.9 (cont.)

no warning, the staccato second and third degrees of the scale barely re-
instating the home key.

2.6 *ÉCLAT* IN THE *ÉTUDES*

After the *Préludes* Debussy's musical language becomes more radically
exploratory, particularly in pieces such as 'pour les Quartes', 'pour les notes
répétées', and 'pour les Sonorités opposées' in the *Études*, which investigate
less familiar sound worlds.[33] While the sense of structural return and closure
we saw in the *Préludes* still presides over the *Études*, there is often a more violent
décalage between the instant of rupture and static compression than in the
Préludes. The interstices between different motivic levels create greater silences
and the counterpoint of weight and lightness is more volatile. At times, motifs
interrupt the pulsating texture, to introduce in an instant a totally unexpected,
alien element into the cushion of the ongoing acoustic mass.[34] The moment
of disarticulation is more prominent in an overall effect of greater disorienta-
tion.

In the third *Étude*, 'Pour les quartes', Debussy exploits this volatility to the
full. The hollow-sounding perfect interval of the fourth is the harmonic basis
for the piece, setting it in a bizarre sound world straddled between uncertainty
and certainty (Example 2.10). The piece opens with an undulating passage of
fourths, within which perfect, diminished, and augmented intervals are over-
laid. Still chords follow in bar 5, punctuated by a staccato semiquaver figure,
giving a sense of anticipation in bars 5 and 6. The proleptic ritenuto and a
drop in dynamic to più piano heighten the anticipation.

The dramatic rupture happens in bar 7. The tempo is telescoped into a
stretto section (an accelerando, to almost double time) marked 'martelé'
('hammered') and 'forte'. The violent incursion occurs in the midst of a
pianissimo with no bass accompaniment. This is Debussy at his most subversive and energetic. The stretto bar dives down and up again twice in forte
sextuplets, crescendoing each time, before a third and final burst finally
reaches a bare perfect fourth in bar 8. Here it is held, poised but fading
quickly, followed by slow echoes of perfect fourths in the left hand as it falls to
pianissimo in the next bar. Just as it comes to rest in a silent pause the explosion recurs, an *éclat* from the midst of silence (bar 10).

The pressure of the instantaneous against the larger formal scheme is

[33] *Œuvres complètes*, vi: *Études*, ed. Claude Helffer (1991). Written in 1915 after a wartime fallow
period, these pieces for piano are not simply exercises. They combine the challenge of technical difficulty (for the acquisition of technique in the style of Clementi and Czerny) with the virtuosity of the
musical miniatures by Chopin and Liszt.

[34] One thinks again of Adorno's 'subjective moments of expression [which] liberate themselves
from the continuum of time' (*Philosophy of Modern Music*, 55–6; see Chapter 2, section 2.3).

Example 2.10 Debussy, *Études*, 'pour les Quartes', bars 1–13

maintained, although not with the same intensity, over the whole piece. The pattern of the discontinuous never becomes predictable, so varied are the contexts in which it arises. The stops and starts in the texture mean that each snatched phrase is too short to be developed, and is instead continuously renewed, within the overall continuum of an accelerando and crescendo.

Staccato semiquavers marked 'piano' in the right hand and staccato quavers in the bass marked 'sempre pianissimo' in 53–64 (Example 2.11), for instance, are interrupted by a sforzando chord and momentary crescendo at

Example 2.11 Debussy, *Études*, 'pour les Quartes', bars 53–64

Example 2.11 (*cont.*)

the end of each bar. These bars alternate with a bar of *éclat* (demi-semiquavers marked 'leggiero'). Each *éclat* bar moves up in register within a huge structural crescendo and accelerando to a frenzied unleashing at bars 60–1. The *éclat* interrupts the foreground with such regularity that it becomes the new foreground, filling it with a climactic sense of overspill and excess. The temporal incursions seem finally to have been allowed to take over, until the sudden piano dynamic of bar 62 and an abrupt return of the calm at bar 64.

With the conceptual tools explored here in mind I shall turn to the next part of my analysis, which is devoted to Mallarmé's 'Petit Air I'. I shall leave the *éclat* and *explosante fixe* in the background at present to see what the poem has to offer alone, leaving open the possibility of returning to them when I align poetry and music at a later stage.

2.7 READING MALLARMÉ'S 'PETIT AIR I'

> Quelconque une solitude
> Sans le cygne ni le quai
> Mire sa désuétude
> Au regard que j'abdiquai
>
> Ici de la gloriole   5
> Haute à ne la pas toucher
> Dont maint ciel se bariole
> Avec les ors de coucher
> Mais langoureusement longe
> Comme de blanc linge ôté   10
> Tel fugace oiseau si plonge
> Exultatrice à côté
>
> Dans l'onde toi devenue
> Ta jubilation nue[35]

In 'Petit Air I' the pitted, ruptured texture means we never quite know where to start or how to get a grip in the poetic minefield. The use of the

---

[35] *OC*, 34–5.

Shakespearian sonnet form in this poem draws attention immediately to the final couplet, which stands summatively alone. This couplet asserts the prospect of an imminent dramatic climax and forms a focal point towards which the poem will progress. The *vers impair* of this poem has an essential structural function in the working-out of the mobile semantic hesitations that shape it, a forerunner of the epitome of self-fracturing discourse that will appear in *Un coup de Dés*. The heptasyllabic line is used relatively rarely by Mallarmé; shortened metrical lines and long words mean that the syntax is more disrupted than in more common line forms. A very unpredictable accentual rhythm is derived from the combination of measures of varying lengths in each line.

The opening syntactical proposition of this poem is a fundamentally disarming and disorientating one. Since 'Quelconque' is not elided to the noun, it appears to have been switched from its usual position immediately following the noun to one preceding it. Rhyme dominates the line and guides the reader towards making 'solitude' the subject of the proposition, pushing it into the metrically stressed line-final position. As a result 'Quelconque', which is usually an unstressed addition to denote the insignificance of a noun, now assumes central importance. 'Que' frames the first syntactical group of the poem. Together 'Que' and 'que' refer proleptically by alliteration to 'quai'. At the same time 'Quelconque' points to three alternative shades of dialectical meaning, none of which can be settled on at the early stages of reading. 'Quelconque' could convert the status of a noun to mean either 'something or other'; the 'least' or 'slightest' thing; or something 'poor', 'second-rate', or 'indifferent'. 'Quelconque' hovers between referring to something and to nothing, all the more since the 'quai' is said to be absent in line 2. From the very first instant readerly progress is hindered by the centripetal and centrifugal textual forces exerted.

Line 2 does little to define the solitude; rather it is emptied further of semantic clues, giving an increased sense of unlocatability. The absence of the swan or sign ('cygne' or 'signe') suggests a disjunction between the realm of solitude and that of poetic imagination, or simply that the poet is absent.

Line 3 provides the verb 'Mire' and an object—'sa désuétude'—which allow 'solitude' to assume syntactical sense as subject. The desire for an object has its pull strengthened by the strong closure of the rich rhyme on 'désuétude' at the end of the line. But the closure cannot fix the syntactical pattern that easily, due to the co-presence of various resonant and rhythmical opening gestures. The inordinate length of 'désuétude' in terms of the syllable count of the line, where to make seven syllables each half of the vowel group /ye/ must be articulated, reinforces the impact of the rhyme. Yet so dominating is the rhyme that the phonetic closure can persuasively override the distinction between the subject and object: 'désuétude' is merely a shade or manifestation of 'solitude'. *Rimes croisées* bring this line to rest at an asymmetrical point. It forms a full cadence of overwhelming rhythmic and homophonous convergence with line 1, but sits, at the same time, next to the unfinished cadence of 'quai', which awaits the fourth line to regain its balance. The *rimes croisées* also provide a framework for the forces of attraction and repulsion across the poem. Their tendency is to set lines containing related subject, verb, and object at a distance from one another, so that reading requires a prolonged exercise in scanning and rescanning the syntax, pulling against the powerful rhyming homophony which wants to attract sense towards the right-hand margin.

A similar conflict between imitation and deflection is contained within the verb itself. 'Mire' is either the mimetic medium between subject and object, a reflective dialectic between 'solitude' and 'désuétude'; or it is a reflection that collapses this subject–object structure by making copies of the object. The first meaning is reflected in the rhythmic and visual balance and sound patterning of *dé/su/é/tu/(de)*. But the second meaning is suggested by '*sa* désuétude' (my italics); 'désuétude' belongs to or is part of the 'solitude', from which it can no longer be distinguished.

The line and stanza that follow necessitate a new scansion of the syntax, since the introduction of another reflecting-reflective medium (the 'regard') further complicates the resonances around 'mire', widening the circle of embedded reflections. Each line break creates a hiatus in the sense-making process. Resonances flow across the break, not lost, but added to by the next line. 'Au regard que j'abdiquai' immediately problematizes the status of 'Mire' and of the reflecting-reflected object and agent. The first uncertainty arises when the abstract noun is given an active verb. It could be that the 'désuétude' is an image received by the mirror of the gaze—the gaze reflects the 'désué-tude'—in which case the gaze is an impotent reflecting surface. Alternatively, the 'désuétude' could reflect the gaze, implying that it copies what it sees in the gaze as reflector. Either passive or active, the reflecting surfaces themselves are shifting, not clearly polarized and held apart. The action of 'Mire' is to send out myriad reflections centrifugally, like the polysemic 'Quelconque'. In the first reading, 'désuétude' is projected as part of the accumulative progres-sion of solitude. In the second, solitude has become nested in a set of reflec-tions of the gaze.

In either case, the distracting reflections of 'Mire' are a series of deflections away from or around the source subject, which prepare the gesture of abdi-cation to arrive in line 4. 'Mire' is pulled in upwards and downwards direc-tions simultaneously. The 'Au regard' of line 4 provides an alternative mirroring partner. 'J'abdiquai', rhyming with 'ni le quai' (whose negative particle 'ni' suggests the gesture of abdication in advance), closes the stanza, providing a mirroring closure that gives a sense of equilibrium and resolution at last. But the move to the next stanza immediately upsets the formal drive for closure by throwing up new syntactical possibilities that divert the sense from its already fragilely held frame. It is difficult to read the phrase opening the next stanza, 'Ici de la gloriole', as an independent syntactical unit. The following lines (6, 7, and 8) add subordinate clauses to it, in a structural rhythm that builds one half of a cadence, whose resolution, the main clause, never arrives.

An alternative reading of this section is one that works chiastically across the stanza break, so that lines 4 to 5 become: 'Au regard | de la gloriole | que j'abdiquai | Ici'. The poet-narrator has 'abdicated' his gaze from vainglory, which is now as obsolete as the solitude. The search for tight mirroring oppositions, which shaped the first stanza, is now enlarged, with more terms in play. What seems like a closing gesture, 'que j'abdiquai', invalidating the solitude and pushing the reflecting dialectic aside to take centre stage, is simultaneously opening a challenging set of reflective patterns across the gap of the stanza break.

The surprise use of the past historic tense of *abdiquer* adds a perspective of time and space to the reflections that have, until then, been postulating types of negation. 'Abdiquai' is a turning point from which a dialectical sense of shape and progression starts to grow in the poem. The layout of the metrical accents in line 4 leaves four syllables after the *coupe* to accentuate the ungainly asymmetry of the *vers impair* and to overdetermine the pivotal role of the proposition. The delicate wrangling of the preceding lines is thrown off balance and shifted into a new light. Now we have: 'the solitude, which *formerly* I rejected here as vainglory' (my emphasis). The solitude is obsolete because it reflects a view he has already rejected. The *je* is located in an 'Ici' and the 'regard' continues to exist without an agent, dislocated and mysteriously autonomous, a presence in contrast to the previous patterns of absence. In a similar move, the use of 'gloriole' suggests a change of heart from something previously thought glorious now found to be vainglory.

A pattern of differently compressed or manoeuvred antitheses articulates the poetic space. In the first stanza there is antithesis between polysemic and magnetic forces in the nexus of imitation around 'solitude', 'Mire', and 'désuétude'. Between the first two stanzas the antithesis occurs via a temporal component, 'j'abdiquai', which acts as a pivot. In the word 'gloriole' the antithesis between glory and vainglory is concentrated in a set of centripetal forces. Whilst the first stanza was a rejection of the place without swan or quay, the second is a dismissal as vainglorious of the realm too high to touch. The implication is that the *je* has been in, or has desired, both places; the chiastic relation between the first two stanzas signifies the agony of the separation and the agonizing metaphysical dilemma of being trapped between the two states. There is a process of sublimation suggested in part by the narrative order of the stanzas. The rich assonance of short, long, and nasal phonemes respectively in 'à', 'la', 'pas' (line 6), and 'maint' (line 7) prepares the arrival of the resoundingly rich rhyme 'la gloriole' | 'se bariole'. The powerful resonance makes a semantic association between vainglory and the setting sky's daubing itself with bright colours, as if in a vain parade of beauty. Any romantic nostalgia for the glory of the setting sun is undercut by the preponderant clipped rhythm of monosyllables. The ironic undertones throw into doubt the claim that the sunset ever reflected the dream of glory. The ambiguity poses a question about whether the realm beyond the human can ever be perceived free of human criteria; the very notion of its presence reinforces its relation to the human realm and all its limiting contingency. The blurring of the two poles of experience is achieved through another set of mobile semantic overtones.

The reader has to grapple with these blurrings. The rhyme axis presents another set of alternative readings in the scrambled semantic dish that he or she has been served. The line-final rhyme of lines 6 and 8, 'toucher' | 'coucher', introduces covert sexual connotations into the poem, associating the sunset with bed and caresses. The metrical parallelism suggests a syntactic parallelism, meaning that 'coucher' can be read as a verb as well as a noun. On the other hand, the sky is vainglorious because it is out of reach of the physical. The syntactical distribution of line 6, 'Haute à ne la pas toucher', lends it the air of an imperative or warning. This realm is impalpable, forbidden to the touch. If regarding the sky as vainglorious is interpreted purely as a high-handed gesture, then these rhymes reinforce that reading by implying such abstention from the level of experience, especially physical experience, is frivolous and vain.

The overarching progression of the first two stanzas, then, is from an inert, minimally sketched, watery place of absence, a 'solitude' devoid of 'cygne' or 'quai' (line 2), to the excess of an orgy of sunset colours in the sky ('la gloriole'). In the first stanza the 'regard' supposes the presence of a narrator-voyeur, although we do not know until the second stanza what has been renounced. The eye of the voyeur turns away from the spectacle of the second stanza before it is revealed, to gaze upon the scene in the first, inverting the consecutive narratorial chronology of the stanzas, which led the reader until the last minute to expect a transition from the earthly, watery reality to the heavenly. Instead, the reader has to return to the 'solitude', whose 'désuétude' is mirrored in the empty gaze of the voyeur (lines 3–4). The chiastic mirrorings embedded in the syntactical patterning, outlined above, fill the tentatively settled geographical poles with uncertain paradox. The reflection of 'désuétude' by the narrator's gaze could be evidence of his actual presence in the 'quelconque'. But the loop back to the first stanza that is involved in the rereading needed to place events has the effect of undermining the unfolding of events in time, so that the act of seeing and rejection happens in a separate, atemporal order from the sequential time frame laid down by the sonnet.

In the next stanza, 'Mais', prominently placed at the beginning of line 9, marks the premature end of a metrical group and situates itself as a rhetorical

pivot, preparing the way for a second half of the poem to restore a dialectical balance. But again, no clear separation and progression away from the
preceding material is made because of the return to familiar material (or a
familiar geographical terrain), which has now undergone a transformation
into an erotic realm.

The brevity of 'Mais' is followed by 'langoureusement', whose five syllables
stretch lazily and voluptuously across most of the line space. 'Mais' is followed
in swift succession by 'Comme' and 'Tel', superposed in parallel metrical positions at the beginning of the following lines (10 and 11). The simile causes a
disjunction between 'longe' and its subject 'Tel fugace oiseau', although the
luxuriant rhyme with 'plonge' creates a strong pull across the intervening line.
The logic of transformation and inversion is continued in this stanza, the
absent swan partly reappearing as 'tel fugace oiseau'. The 'quai' suppressed
in line 2 is now powerfully traced by the action of 'longe', attributed to the
bird, along the edge of the water. 'Tel' hovers between acting as indefinite
article and introducing further comparison, in keeping with its parallelism
with 'Comme'. 'Tel . . . oiseau' could be read as metaphor for the woman's
body, since it is in the same metrical position as and in grammatical apposition with the feminine adjective 'Exultatrice'. That 'Tel' is indefinite rather
than comparative, however, becomes clearer by reading on to the last couplet.
Were 'Tel . . . oiseau' a substitution for the woman, 'longe' and 'plonge' would
be in the second person singular to agree with the 'toi' (the woman) of
'Exultatrice'. The voyeur sees or imagines a hallucinatory form, a flash of
whiteness resembling bird or woman. It is unclear who is diving next ('à côté')
to whom and therefore which of the two is likened to 'blanc linge ôté'. The
other rich *rime croisée* of the stanza links 'ôté' to 'côté', balancing the bird's
claim to the simile with the equally plausible possibility, in this half-imagined,
half-seen world, that the 'Exultatrice' is 'Comme de blanc linge ôté', either in
her whiteness, in her birdlike form, or literally, in her nakedness periphrasti-
cally described.

The mobility of the simile befits the instability of the vision, varying itself
naturally as the vision remoulds and reinterprets itself, changing with the
reflected patterns of light. The woman is following the bird along the course
of the water and diving with it, or vice versa. Indeed, whether or not they dive
at all is cast into doubt by the use of another term of dialectical opposition,
'si' (line 11). A hypothetical 'if', temporal 'when', oppositional 'whilst', or hesi-
tational 'whether' presents multiple potential courses of events before the
verb. The action is only furtively glimpsed by the voyeur, whose gaze upon the
scene is still implied, or even imagined. The hesitations and ambiguity provide
an underlay of glimpses of the female body with no reference to the whole
body itself, other than by metaphorical links with a bird and the metonymical
'linge ôté' abandoned at the edge of the water. The diving of the woman,
'Dans l'onde toi', is described only by the extreme pleasure felt by the body

upon contact with the wave. Nakedness appears for full view only in the final line with the ecstatic 'jubilation nue'. This epiphanic use of the final line is a very familiar device in Mallarmé.

In the third and fourth stanzas a rapid succession of events appears in an instantaneous present. In 'Dans l'onde toi devenue | Ta jubilation nue', either the woman becomes diluted in the wave or the wave assumes the form of her 'jubilation nue'. The space of the verse is punctuated with objects and acts (the swimming body, 'linge ôté', and the bird) mixed and caught up in a simultaneous perception. The elements associated with these objects and acts ('linge', 'oiseau', 'onde', 'toi') are set up as interchangeable and can stand in for or alongside one another in the spatial framework. These elements are condensed into one destination: the culmination of the play of oneness against multiplicity is squeezed into the finely honed final couplet. To the last, the erotic pleasure the narrator-voyeur takes in the female body is heightened by the hedonistic 'jubilation' afforded by the simultaneous vision of the scene.

Line 13, 'Dans l'onde toi devenue', is dramatized from the outset by the use of the implied future to recuperate the present. Writing in a course of events behind the static scenes depicted implies an arrival at a future destination, part of the poem's logic of transformation. The narrator turns his attentions from the heavenly spectacle to an empty scene, given only as a bare sketch. He then glimpses the white flash of a sudden dive of body-bird, its form unclear, as she-it swims along until her-its dilution in the bathing wave. The move towards the final event in the couplet, framed as the future in order to recuperate fully the presentness of the moment when it arrives, gives the poem an increasing momentum from the third stanza onwards. The accumulation of counterpart nouns around an undefined subject creates a glissando or crescendo effect towards the climax of the couplet, enabled by the absence of punctuation and the unstable grounding given by the heptasyllabic line. The momentum has a peculiar weight lent to it, however, by the conflicting tempos of the vertical movement. 'Longe' could be a light skidding along the water in time with the glissando. But it is hampered by the tangential movement of 'ôté' and punctuated by the plunge of a dive. The final synthesis in the couplet holds within it an ecstatic blend of the turbulence of watery-human movement, the apex of an evolution, held in a non time-bound, suspended present, freeing itself from the poem's chronology in a glorious exploration of a timeless, reverberating present. Beneath the suspended surface are the kaleidoscopic movements of 'longe', 'ôté', 'fugace', 'plonge', 'Exultatrice' unfurled from the initial rhythmically oxymoronic 'Mais langoureusement'. More vivid in its highly charged, black and white, rhythmic virtuosity, the suggestion of an object in the empty scene gives a display that far outstrips the laboured beauty of the sky, which has only an excess of colour to recommend it.

2.8 MAPPING THE INTERMEDIARY: ALIGNING POEM AND PIECES

When the poetic space of 'Petit Air I', filled with glimpses of elements, objects, and acts of differing temporal status, is set side by side with the moments in the *Préludes* I described earlier, there do seem to be resonances in their rhythmical structures.

The rhythm of grasping and releasing meaning from the scrambled signifying frames in the poem is comparable to the experience of listening to the flow of accumulation and release that is created by the constantly shifting temporal frames in the music. In particular, the interweaving rhythms and pitch directions of the 'ostinato' loop in bars 10–12 of 'La terrasse des audiences du clair de lune' (Example 2.5), which provides a circular temporal diversion from the forwards momentum, share something with the hovering produced by the conflicting movements of swimming and diving in the climax of the poem. Both moments have all the contained eruptive force of an *explosante fixe*. 'Quelconque' in the poem, polysemic yet rooted to the rhyme axis, and the ending (bar 37) of 'La terrasse des audiences du clair de lune', when departing scales wind over clear closural cadences (described after the analysis of Example 2.5), are also characterizable by the *explosante fixe*.

As we have seen, moments of *éclat* occur in the patchwork juxtaposition of the single and multiple elements in the last stanza of the poem. Flashes of the bird or the body dive and dip into the whiteness of the wave ('blanc', 'plonge') and rise 'Exultatrice'. Light and water are juxtaposed, images carved up by the simultaneously unified and multiple identity of the figure dipping in and out of its surface. The figure is either glimpsed or shielded by anonymous whiteness whose brightness lights the scene in intermittent flashes. The eruptions are as irregular and short-lived as fireworks in a display, shifting between kaleidoscopic colour and blankness. The *éclat* captures something of the violence of these moments of dramatic silence and rupture. In Debussy, similar moments give the music its terror, ecstasy, and sheer, vital *élan*. The *éclat* behaves as an instance of Barthesian *jouissance*: a site of loss and disruption, a seam or cut in the text that unsettles and excites the reader-listener. *Éclat* reveals the desire for pleasurably startling gaps in readable discourse or for the disruption of a listened-for line.

The desire of the voyeur to see unity in deliberately plural images is cotemporal with the moment of dissolution, as one being metamorphoses into another, and creates the thrill of the *éclat*. In 'Billet', discussed near the beginning of this chapter, the moments of *éclat* occur in rapid succession, so that the dancer appears to be suspended, as though in midair, providing a euphoric climax to the string of negatives, absences, and evasions that precedes it. At each stage the *éclats*, such as the glimpsed knee, are in tension with the *explosantes fixes* of the spinning tutu. The *explosantes fixes* escape complete grounding, so that as the crescendo builds in a mounting spiral the scene seems to get further and further from the grasp of the reader and of the *je*. *Éclats* pierce the texture, more exquisite because not fully revealed. But the nature of *éclats* can vary from context to context. How different the euphoric 'jubilation' of the climax of 'Petit Air I' is from the violence of the *éclat* found in 'Don du poème':

> Je t'apporte l'enfant d'une nuit d'Idumée!
> Noire, à l'aile saignante et pâle, déplumée,
> Par le verre brûlé d'aromates et d'or,
> Par les carreaux glacés, hélas! mornes encor,
> L'aurore se jeta sur la lampe angélique.   5
> Palmes! et quand elle a montré cette relique
> A ce père essayant un sourire ennemi,
> La solitude bleue et stérile a frémi.
> O la berceuse, avec ta fille et l'innocence
> De vos pieds froids, accueille une horrible naissance: 10
> Et ta voix rappelant viole et clavecin,
> Avec le doigt fané presseras-tu le sein
> Par qui coule en blancheur sibylline la femme
> Pour des lèvres que l'air du vierge azur affame?[36]

'Palmes!' (line 6) follows two other exclamations earlier in the poem (lines 1 and 4) but its solitary, initial position in the line makes its appearance sudden and violent. It is the culmination of a build-up of proleptic sonorous pressure from 't'a**pp**orte', dé**p**lumée', and the repeated line-initial '**P**ar'. 'Palmes!' intrudes initially as a purely sonorous object, a polysemic moment of profound incoherence, refusing unidirectional meaning. Displaced lexical items such as 'L'aurore' (line 5) and 'et quand elle' (line 6) need to be reorganized after the backwash from the doubt-filled incursion has settled.

This isolated incident of dramatic disorganization and reorganization has more of the violence we saw in Debussy's 'Pour les quartes'. Although *éclats* at the climax of 'Petit Air I' are less disabling than this one in 'Don du poème', the work needed in navigating the semantic and metaphysical aporia, through the conflicting syntactical and metrical pathways, leads to a congealed rhythm of grasping and releasing meaning. In 'Don du poème' the *éclat* is sudden and unexpected, but in 'Petit Air I' we expect to not expect from the outset. The aporias almost gain their own regularity and order. The same could be said of the *Préludes*. In a sense we are led to expect an order of disruptions, discontinuities, dissolutions, and indeterminacies. The static *explosante fixe* comes to have a pleasurable fluidity and the impact of the crisis of the *éclat* in 'Pour les Quartes' is numbed. But what 'Petit Air I' and the *Préludes* in particular share is their sense of being suspended, or strangely unmotivated, yet legislated for.

---

[36] *OC*, 17.

The *explosante fixe* and *éclat* are keyholes for picking out the opaquenesses and translucencies created in different ways by patterns of coherence and non-coherence. As Boulez says of the *éclat*, quoted earlier: 'Tous ces mots ont des sens différents qui s'appliquent' (see section 2.4). As concepts, *éclat* and *explosante fixe* are sufficiently mobile to be moulded to these different temporal manifestations, expressing something of them both but differently for each. Neither concept fixes the structures in the poems and pieces rigidly, nor forces them to fit. Neither neutralizes or makes them regular. Each can cope with the differing emotional impacts of the contexts in which it occurs. Like topological shapes, these structures can be stretched and pulled and coiled without their fundamental properties changing. Similarly, Mallarmé's dialectic of listening and reading set out in 'Le Mystère dans les lettres', discussed at the opening of this chapter, is neither a generic musico-poetic term, nor a particular one. Its 'éclat' and 'l'inverse' can be made into models to describe certain specific situations, never imposing certainty on the overlap or allowing its figures to form an order of the unreadable or incoherent, but remaining elusively mobile.

2.9 'ENROULEMENTS'

The discontinuity created by each kind of rupture is filled by a different continuous movement. Mallarmé characterizes this discontinuous continuity in 'Le Mystère dans les lettres' with painstaking attention to detail:

Les déchirures suprêmes instrumentales, conséquence d'enroulements transitoires, éclatent plus véridiques, à même, en argumentation de lumière, qu'aucun raisonnement tenu jamais; on s'interroge, par quels termes du vocabulaire sinon dans l'idée, écoutant, les traduire, à cause de cette vertu incomparable. Une directe adaptation avec je ne sais, dans le contact, le sentiment glissé qu'un mot détonnerait, par intrusion.[37]

Ruptures in instrumental texture are products of transitory coilings or windings. We could be reminded here of the constantly interrupted upwards swing in the line sung by Golaud when he discovers Mélisande by the edge of a well in the opening scene of *Pelléas et Mélisande*. We hear the 'enroulements' and 'déchirures' as configurations of the 'Idée', and as such they can be translated into similar effects notable in language: 'par quels termes du vocabulaire sinon dans l'idée, écoutant, les traduire.' The comparable effect in language ('Une directe adaptation') is in the meeting ('dans le contact') that occurs when two vectors intersect: the rising curve of a glissando is interrupted by the intrusion of another word belonging to a separate mood and of different

---

[37] *OC* (M), 385.

directional force. Typically, this event is more performed than directly explained by the passage. The manner of translation is only faintly outlined in a phrase of hesitating doubt, 'Une directe adaption avec je ne sais', and then interrupted by the interpolation 'dans le contact', an enactment of the 'intrusion' required. Kinetic movements through space, almost abstract mathematical models, recreate the jarring, rebarbative, or exultant complexity of the artistic experience of the 'idea' that breathes through both music and poetry. The 'déchirures suprêmes' combine two movements into one transferable figure.

Winifred Nowottny notes a similar reading experience when she concludes her observations on poetic language in *The Language Poets Use*:

If finally I had to commit myself to a statement of what I understand by the phrase 'poetic form', I should say that it consists in the stasis achieved in the poem between all the interest it activates. I do not know how to think of 'form' except under the image of the 'swift, circular line' described before the mental eye when an impulsion to go in one direction (intellectually, emotionally or pattern-wise) encounters another impulsion that deflects it.[38]

Like Mallarmé, Nowottny conveys her vision of poetic form as a stasis resulting from the magnetic repulsion of sets of read and felt vectors, in an image of circular deflection describing a three-dimensional movement through space: the 'swift, circular line'. Mallarmé is doing something similar with the deflecting vectors or movements of reading in the 'enroulement', which add up to a hovering immobility. The 'fleuron' and 'cul-de-lampe' of 'Le Mystère dans les lettres', together with the arabesque and thyrsus in *La Musique et les Lettres*, are borrowed from the language of ornament, and act as figural representations of these dynamic curves and crossing points. These word images are simple, direct dramatic representations of a particular potential nexus of shapes, patterns, and significations that they unleash from within, around, or behind them. 'Enroulement' is another such term, borrowed from architecture, meaning a volute, scroll, whorl, or coil. This abstract coil or helix traces the pattern made by a set of deflections, the resultant shape from a horizontal pulling against a diagonal, rather like the 'swift, circular line', emanating from a rupture in the texture to create a mobile point of stasis. Here we have a poetic-musical structure that is far more complex than a mere discontinuity. We have a very precise figure that can articulate the particular shape of the activity 'behind', or emanating from, the disjunction.

In 'Petit Air I' overlapping layers and opposing pulls of concurrent antitheses, expressed in differing syntactical, semantic, and rhyming frames of reference, hover between the first and second stanzas. When one reading direction deflects another the poetic surface is pitted and ruptured, as we have seen. But

[38] 221. Nowottny borrows the 'swift, circular line' image from Wallace Stevens's 'Earthy Anecdote'.

ruptures in texture, as they are spatially depicted by Mallarmé in the 'enroulement transitoire', can be articulated precisely as a particular set of forces.
Traditional verse patterns of consecutive progression are disrupted by the
spatialization of the poetic elements in Mallarmé. Sonorous and, by implication, semantic resonances are struck in vertical, circular, horizontal, or diagonal configurations, leading to the simultaneous apprehension of different
parts of the poetic message. The presence (or implied presence) of syntactical
frameworks occurring with these resonant configurations makes for a multiplicity of possible interpretative tools. Instances in the poem, such as the overlapping lines around 'solitude', 'Mire', and 'désuétude', for example, can be
clearly articulated in the terms of the 'enroulement': as projections and interruptions that spiral around one another with an overall effect of mobile stasis.
In 'La terrasse des audiences du clair de lune', the structural equivalent can
be seen in the theme at bar 13. This figure is a static yet circular form that is
at once ornamental embellishment and immobile reflection. The figure is
born out of the ostinato loop of an entirely different goal direction; it assumes
its own life before it disappears but is continued in a varied form (see section
2.4). These lines interrupt and overlap each other in a three-dimensional
space also described by the 'enroulement'. Another 'enroulement' occurs in
the climactic final couplet of the poem, which achieves a resonating stasis
whose texture is composed of the interweaving, in different directions and at
different tempos, of the poetic images and elements.

More striking still are the multifarious narrative chronologies set up, as we
have seen, by the pivotal 'j'abdiquai' in the poem. These share a similar
temporal and spatial structure to key points in the *Préludes*. There is a wider
temporal loop in the poem formed when 'j'abdiquai' throws the tight localized reflections of the first stanza into a more open syntactical arena, adding
a perspective of time and space to the scene. Above all, its presence deflects
the upwards stanza-by-stanza trajectory from earthly reality to sublime heav-
enliness. Instead, the reader is diverted back to the first stanza, through
reversible, mobile syntax, to reread the unfolding events in an entirely new
temporality. 'J'abdiquai' undermines these events in the opening time span, so
that the initial acts of seeing and rejection happen in an atemporal order. This
temporal loop emerging from a pivotal deflection is, once again, embodied in
the time-space continuum delimited by the coil or 'enroulement'.

2.10 TOPOLOGICAL SURFACES

What I have defined through the 'enroulement' is an area of overlap between
music and poetry that can be traced in abstract terms of space and time. A
description of this evolution and interrelation of time and space, unfurled in
unique shapes, figures, and rhythms, can be envisaged in topological terms.

Topology is the branch of mathematics that deals with those relations between points, and those fundamental properties of a figure, that remain invariant when the figure is bent out of shape (for example, when a rubber sheet on which a triangle is traced is bent into conical or spherical form). Topology does not concern itself with specific measures or proportions but with the nature and shape of the movements (turns, twists, and transformations) of objects in space. It sets out to find equations to define how surfaces change from place to place, providing the coordinates for a map of the surface in space. Distances have little meaning in topology. Two geometrical forms are of the same topological type if one shape can be squeezed, stretched, or twisted (without cutting, pasting, or tearing) until it looks just like the other. For example, in topological terms a single-handled mug and a ring doughnut are indistinguishable. A sphere may be stretched to form a bowl, a pretzel, or a soup tureen. The surfaces considered are called minimal surfaces (which can take diverse forms), so called because a surface, like a soap film, for example, will seek the state of lowest energy. If a surface is stretched its potential energy is increased and the surface will seek to minimize itself; hence, minimal surface: a surface's optimal shape for a given contour or boundary. In her book *La Topologie ordinaire de Jacques Lacan*, which examines the topology in Lacanian theory, Jeanne Granon-Lafont highlights the notion of space which these surfaces bring to our attention: 'On voit comment ces relations structurent l'espace, le rendent matérialisable, alors que plus souvent il échappe à notre perception. L'objet spécifique des topologues est cette notion de l'espace et des relations qui le structurent.'[39]

One intriguing minimal surface is the Möbius strip. Granon-Lafont describes the way this object is formed: 'Une bande de papier [est] recollée sur elle-même en lui imprimant un mouvement de torsion.'[40] In effect, the upper face of the strip is twisted to meet the reverse face, to make a continuous band. Only a temporal event (the time it takes to do two circuits of the band) distinguishes the upper and reverse sides of the strip: 'Le doigt qui suit la surface de la bande se trouve après un tour complet, et sans avoir été levé, sans avoir franchi le bord, à l'envers de son point de départ. C'est après un deuxième tour complet qu'il retrouve enfin son point de départ, à l'endroit'.[41] Space in itself has no depth. It is only when an object plunged into space is given a temporal dimension, making a before and after, and by extension an in-front and behind, that there may be a perception of space. (Perception of depth in the movement of revolution defines the space.) In the same way, the Möbius strip has no real depth until given a dimension in time. This makes it a surface of paradoxes, since although we perceive depth at the point where the strip twists, the strip is flat until an event in time occurs. A famous example is of an ant walking along the flat surface of a Möbius strip. As the ant

39 (Paris: Point Hors Ligne, 1985), 18.   40 Ibid. 29.   41 Ibid.

moves towards what is for it the horizon, the point where the strip begins to twist, the time it takes to reach it is a measure of the depth (and therefore a definition of the space). In fact, the ant will never reach the horizon because another one will always present itself. 'Le temps s'impose pour rendre compte de la bande.'[42]

If the figure is represented in a two-dimensional drawing then the twist in the strip or its depth, a figure of eight folded in on itself, is represented 'par un croisement de la ligne sur elle-même'.[43] This crossover point looks like an intersection on the two-dimensional diagram but is in fact a representation of the temporal moment that allows the perception of space. The 'mise à plat' is necessary to dispel the illusion of depth since the strip, in real terms, is flat. In this two-dimensional representation 'une discontinuité de la ligne évoque non pas son interruption, mais le passage sous le ligne, à un moment de son trajet'.[44] Thus the temporal moment in the strip hovers between two and three dimensions. The lines of the strip pass above and below each other in the warp and woof of an interwoven texture. Their superimposition allows the space they represent in a temporal dimension to be imagined and expressed. The topological figure gives a model for the relation of the lines to one another in space and in time. That is, the mobility of the overlapping layers as well as the stasis created between them can be given a shape. The lines of the two-dimensional diagram of the figure weave in and out of each other on paths that progress, are reflected, return, and create diversions and turning points.

Topology studies configurations and perceptions of time and space as observed from nature. The phenomena it observes are far from being isolated ones. What can be observed about spatio-temporal properties visually seems also to be true of our structures of listening and reading. In particular the Möbius strip contains hesitations and paradoxes, *trompes l'œil* and turning points, of a kind very close to those that shape our reading of the Mallarmé text and hearing of the Debussy piece, as well as confirming Mallarmé's 'enroulement' as more than an overtheorized flight of fancy. The kinds of intersection and paradox captured by the 'enroulement' are present in the twist of the strip. The 'enroulement', spiral, or helix is a curve on a developable surface that, like the strip, becomes a straight line when unrolled into a plane. It describes a very real, precise, spatio-temporal curve, punctuated by the temporal paradox of deflection, the twist, which Mallarmé identifies as the linguistic equivalent of the phenomenon of the 'idée'.

The Möbius strip, then, has the properties of the 'enroulement', which can articulate features of the poem by describing the complex patterns of syntactical, metrical, and semantic rhythms, and the stasis and movement between

---

[42] Ibid. 30.   [43] Ibid.   [44] Ibid. 31.

them. The point of intersection is at the rhythmic heart of the exciting tensions of verse, full of the motion of reflections and diverted expectations yet hovering away from them, immobile and removed by the stasis achieved between them. The figure illuminates the separate elements that strain against one another, whilst maintaining a sense of their simultaneous apprehension and the inseparability of their interwoven layers.

Boulez's sense of the spatio-temporal in his work resonates with the twists and curves of the Möbius strip: 'Quand une ligne mélodique dérive par rapport à elle-même dans le temps, on ne peut plus parler d'imitation mélodique, de canon exact . . . nous n'écoutons pas deux lignes . . . Nous écoutons une seule ligne dédoublée par une sorte d'étirement du temps.'[45] The interweaving progression of the figural lines in the *Préludes*, continually reabsorbed into themselves to create diversions and turning points, can also be seen in topological terms. Musical lines grow out of or merge into each other, inspired by their own inner logic like the interlacing, structuring threads of the poem. The helical twist defines in time and space the kind of effect we hear in bars 16–19 of 'La terrasse des audiences du clair de lune' (see section 2.4), when distinct lines form a texture of opposing forces of inertia and movement. These are akin to the complex overlapping layers around 'Mire' in the poem, which are simultaneously held apart and collapsed. The twist expresses the way in which the lines strain apart yet are inseparably interwoven. The misleading and obstructive multiple mirror images of the first stanza are more solid than the objects of which they purport to be reflections. The ripples of rich sonority, rhyme, and fragmented syntax they create around them across the stanza make a texture of collisions, collapses, and diversions. These mirages are full of the deceptive perspectives of the twist, leading and misleading to the fruitful blind alley. The complex overlapping layers of 'Mire' are a prelude to the culminating mirage of the 'oiseau'-*nageuse*.

The dislocated semantic reverberations in 'Petit Air I' are not lost at each word or stanza boundary. Instead each particular line of poetic enquiry (be it semantic or syntactical), arriving at an obstacle, is diverted from its path and submerged beneath the line that takes over in prominence. Rather than disappear the strand is absorbed and contributes to the rhythmic tension of the stanza as a whole. We recall the definition given by Granon-Lafont of the torsion in the Möbius strip: 'Une discontinuité de la ligne évoque non pas son interruption, mais le passage sous le ligne, à un moment de son trajet' (above, this section). As with the strip, which has no real depth until given a dimension in time, reading the spatial separation of the geographical loci backwards and forwards between the first and second stanzas cannot be made sense of until the arrival of the temporal element 'j'abdiquai'. The sky and earth can

---

[45] *Jalons (pour une décennie)*, 418.

only be experienced in terms of their separation once the chronological (or narrative) element is introduced. The illusion of their separation, highlighted by the awkward narratorial move, can easily be collapsed to make them inhabit the same poetic plane. The poetic space is essentially always flat; the reader too becomes a voyeur, able to share with the narrator a simultaneous vision both of the scene and of the decision-making process involved in arriving there. The reader is led to look for a chronological clue to the geographical layout, but in doing so finds herself heading for a horizon that never arrives, or caught up in a loop back to the first stanza and forced to view a simultaneous, timeless, flat picture.

This model, of a line that appears to intersect itself but is actually held apart by time and depth, also describes the tension between bipolar oppositions that are at once held apart and collapsed in the first stanza of 'Petit Air I', just as in the Möbius strip the two faces are at once distinct but inseparable. A perceived horizon in a Möbius strip, the indication of depth which can never be reached, also has an equivalent in the poem, whose overall structure works like an interlace of threads that appear to be leading somewhere. They enter the texture and appear to end but in fact do not. The end cannot be reached because it is continually absorbed by a new telos. Ends that are not ends occur in the chiastic reading process across stanzas too.

In the third stanza, as we have seen, the two movements of 'longe' and 'plonge' combine in a culminating mobile stasis. The glimpse of an ambiguous mobile form is like the horizon that is never reached. The relation of the travelling movement against that of the occasional dipping ('plonge') in and out of the telos is a translation of the structure of the space we witness in the 'enroulement'. In terms of the strip, it is the helical twist of perceived depth measured by time that articulates the effect of the blurred, glimpsed motion of the 'oiseau'-*nageuse* diving and swimming in tandem.

We are readers of and listeners to horizons. In the contained futurity of the final nexus of images Mallarmé creates hope, hope that is almost but not quite fulfilled. Reading the horizon involves the knitting together of two possibilities that are never reached and always remain possibilities. One negative outcome lying on the horizon is the possibility of catastrophe, of there being a *néant* or empty solitude that cannot be overcome. The other possibility is one of joy, a positive futurity that allows a real engagement with the present. The sense could be tipped either way according to interpretation. Similarly, in 'Bruyères' (Example 2.12), from the first book of the *Préludes*, identical, repeated phrases are tipped between two meanings by the harmony changing underneath them from major to minor. Since no clear resolution follows we remain hovering between the senses of each mode.

Example 2.12 Debussy, *Préludes*, book II, 'Bruyères', bars 23–8

When we read Mallarmé or hear Debussy we are held on this horizon in *moto perpetuo*. We are in the 'centre de suspens vibratoire',[46] caught in almost-hope between two states, standing 'dans un équilibre momentané et double à la façon du vol'.[47]

[46] 'Le Mystère dans les lettres', *OC* (M), 386.   [47] 'Solennité', ibid. 333.

3

'L'ADORABLE ARABESQUE'

The two works for alignment in this chapter are extraordinary landmarks in each artist's individual *œuvre*. Written at the pinnacle of Debussy's career, and exploring new reaches of form and fragmentation, *Jeux*, an orchestral ballet composed in 1913, shares the position that is held by *Un coup de Dés* in Mallarmé's poetic output. These two works were radical and disruptive in their own fields. My analysis of them here brings a period of particularly intense musico-poetic cross-fertilization under close scrutiny.

On a first hearing the magical sensuousness of *Jeux* may seem a far cry from the extreme loss of sensuousness in *Un coup de Dés*. Silence in *Un coup de Dés* is a constant reminder of *le néant*, that we are 'captifs d'une formule absolue que, certes, n'est que ce qui est'.[1] The senses both of *hilarité* and of *horreur* in the sea-filled Mallarmé poem pull at different angles across the poem. In *Jeux* silence is more seductively fleeting.

3.1 *UN COUP DE DÉS*

Un coup de Dés is the culmination of Mallarmé's poetic output, written in 1897, and today is still considered one of the works most radically disruptive of established poetic codes. In his earlier poems the main challenges to interpretation and to logic arise at a semantic level, through sensuous, visual imagery and unconventional syntax. The 'Ouverture d'"Hérodiade" ' ['Ouverture ancienne'] is a richly woven web of phonetic resonances and visual images the initial confusion of which can gradually be diminished as the reader becomes attuned to the reflexive thinking.[2] But in *Un coup de Dés* our most fundamental notions of intelligibility are put to the test.

The concept of the symbol and the primacy of the metaphoric and connotational in Mallarmé's aesthetic lent poetry the possibility of much more complex associations with music. We are reminded of this by a passage whose routine citation has made it a *locus classicus* in the Mallarmé literature: 'Je pense qu'il faut, au contraire, qu'il n'y ait qu'allusion. La contemplation des objets, l'image s'envolant des rêveries suscitées par eux, sont le chant: les Parnassiens, eux, prennent la chose entièrement et la montrent: par là ils manquent de mystère. . . . *Nommer* un objet, c'est supprimer les trois quarts de

---

[1] *La Musique et les Lettres, OC* (M), 647.   [2] *OC* (M), 135 (see Chapter 1, section 1.5).

la jouissance du poème qui est faite de deviner peu à peu: le *suggérer*, voilà le rêve.'[3] The aim of the poetic symbol according to Mallarmé is not to reveal objects directly but to allow the reader to witness their revelation. The abstract patterns of symbol to which Mallarmé aspired suggest a yearning for the mystical *au-delà* that comes from the power of music to transport the listener emotionally through and even beyond a wordless realm. Oscar Wilde described the notion of symbol in *The Picture of Dorian Gray* (1870) as 'the mere shapes and patterns of things becoming, as it were, refined and gaining a kind of symbolical value, as though they were themselves patterns of some other more perfect form whose shadow they made real'.[4] Jean-Pierre Richard echoes the emphasis on the Platonic aspect of the symbol, noting: 'C'est Mallarmé qui nous a permis de comprendre Mallarmé. . . . La poésie doit selon Mallarmé exprimer le "sens mystérieux des aspects de l'existence." '[5]

In addition to this impulse to transcend (which Mallarmé describes in his letter to Verlaine as 'l'explication orphique de la Terre, qui est le seul devoir du poète et le jeu littéraire par excellence'),[6] expressed in his letter to Edmund Gosse is the desire to reach the relations behind the words, whose 'rythmes entre les rapports'[7] are the unheard music of poetry ('l'air ou chant sous le texte').[8] The underlying patterns created by the dynamic relations of words or *vers* (for even prose is *vers* without explicit rhyme for Mallarmé) are also part of the poetic mystery. This mystery is inclusive of its own linguistic patterning whilst at the same time pointing beyond experience to the Ideal essence: 'L'existence littéraire, hors une, vraie, qui se passe à réveiller la présence, au-dedans, des accords et significations, a-t-elle lieu, avec le monde.'[9] The dynamics enacted on local levels in literature are shadows of the dazzling moment of unifying vision (the 'vraie existence' that informs them), a pattern for all things whose ultimate enactment constitutes 'le Livre'. The complex rhythms held in precarious simultaneity by *vers* are miniature versions of the Book-to-be: 'Le Livre—expansion totale de la lettre.'[10]

Since Mallarmé sees poetry's task as to free linguistic objects from their contingent relations and transpose them into a network of reciprocal relations reflecting the 'Idée', there can no longer be a clear line of demarcation between language and music. Like that of music, the identity of the linguistic object lies in its own nature rather than in an external signified. *Un coup de Dés* is an enterprise in restructuring language by challenging its familiar boundaries and logic. The result is well observed by Valéry, who sees 'la musique déduite des propriétés des sons; l'architecture déduite de la matière et de ses

---

[3] *Réponse à une enquête*, *OC* (M), 869.

[4] Ed. Peter Faulkner (London: Everyman, 1993), 31.

[5] *L'Univers imaginaire*, 15.   [6] 'Autobiographie', *OC*, 786–90 (788).

[7] 10 Jan. 1893, ibid. 807.   [8] 'Le Mystère dans les lettres', *OC* (M), 387.

[9] 'Solitude', ibid. 405.   [10] 'Le Livre, instrument spirituel', ibid. 380.

forces; la littérature, de la possession des mots'.[11] With the primacy of the suggestive over directly referential language, the materiality of the signifier is foregrounded and the envisaged *rapports* between words can have an architecture more closely shared with the sonorous signifiers of music: signifiers can share similar movements in the signifying field. The underlying rhythmic patterns created by words trace the abstract, non-mimetic patterns that music and poetry have in common, held in precarious simultaneity by a language whose space allows their cohabitation.

The structural traces of the shared architecture at once hide and reveal the configurations of the 'Idée' that is 'scintillante'. The veiled, intermittent 'meaning' of music is the preferred partner of language whose aim is to be 'suggestive' and for whom meaning is also problematic and intermittent. Simultaneously conceding and withdrawing meaning, in the manner of music, entrenches language on a hesitating, shaky, epistemological boundary between the certainty of knowledge and its contingency, between order and chaos. The constant threat of collapse into incoherence is the metaphysical crisis at the heart of Mallarmé's work, and its culmination *Un coup de Dés*. Certainty, coherence, knowledge, and order all come up against and are destabilized by doubt, incoherence, and chance in Mallarmé's world.

3.2 CHROMATIC COMPLEXITIES

The special pulses in and out of sound and the spectral, evanescent textures of *Jeux* make it one of the most enigmatic and intellectually elusive works of twentieth-century music. Analyses of Debussy's musical language, especially in his later works, have not always succeeded fully in capturing its spirit or its acoustic 'letter'. There is something in Debussy's music that escapes when put solely in musicological terms. *Jeux* remains tantalizingly mysterious. It is one of Debussy's most radical departures from familiar musical territory and exhibits the uneasy relationship of much twentieth-century music with traditional form.

At the time of *Jeux*, music was also undergoing some radical reinvention in the hands of Debussy's Austrian and German near-contemporaries. Debussy, however, was on the sidelines of this development and the nature and consequences of his revolution were not to be recognized fully until later. Richard Strauss, Mahler, and the young Schoenberg, unlike Debussy, followed in a more or less direct line from Wagner, who had broadened the scope of permissible harmonies and of harmonic change. Strauss and Schoenberg were pressing towards atonality, Strauss with the chromaticism of *Elektra*

---

[11] *Écrits divers sur Stéphane Mallarmé* (Paris: Gallimard, 1950), 57.

(1909) and Schoenberg with *Erwartung* (1909). Charles Rosen writes: 'By 1908 Schoenberg demanded not only the full chromatic complexity that other composers such as Skryabin and Strauss had already won, but even more: a release from the basic harmonic conception of the cadence, the movement toward release of tension, toward absolute repose, which had been fundamental to centuries of music.'[12] *Erwartung* was thoroughly revolutionary in this respect, doing away with all the traditional means by which music made itself intelligible and that Debussy retained, such as the discursive transformation of clearly recognizable motifs and the repetition of themes. As Debussy premiered *Jeux*, Stravinsky's *Sacre du printemps* (1913) also appeared in Paris, provoking a violent reaction. Stravinsky's ballet score exposed the complacency of the predictable repetition in much traditional music by revolutionizing rhythm, using ironic distancing effects from tonal relations, and making discontinuity a profoundly disturbing musical experience. *Jeux* was also rhythmically diverse and made extremely subtle use of the orchestra. Debussy had already been composing in new forms. The *Préludes* (1910 and 1912–13) for piano, as we have seen, eschewed the continuity and development of the symphonic manner of the Austro-German tradition but retained a structural logic by working against, not relying upon, accepted conventions of tonal language. However in *Jeux* formal and tonal structures disappear even further under the surface, giving way to a freer ongoing associative form in which there is a strange mixture of improvisation with control. *Jeux* embraces continuity and discontinuity, coherence and non-coherence, and pushes them to new limits.

So far, the exploration of the intervening space between music and poetry in this book has looked at mobile models of comparison organized around certain figures taken from the third-party sources of Boulez and topology (*éclat, explosante fixe*, Möbius strip), which shed new light on an element of Mallarméan vocabulary, the 'enroulement' (see Glossary for a definition of these figures). In Chapter 1 I discussed some features of Mallarmé's 'music', namely the 'thyrse' and 'arabesque', in his lecture *La Musique et les Lettres*, arguing that his poetic theory allows the cohabitation of music and language in the text. The arabesque reappears here, now taken from both Mallarmé's and Debussy's writings. In this chapter, the arabesque will be used to harness and articulate the overlap in a specific encounter, that between *Un coup de Dés* and *Jeux*. It will be tested as a site of shared structural rhythm and then used to evaluate the various dynamics of music *in* text and of music *and* text.

---

[12] *Schoenberg* (London: Fontana/Collins, 1975), 41–7.

3.3 TOWARDS THE ARABESQUE: THE LAW AND GRAMMAR OF ORNAMENT

Mallarmé conceived of his writing in terms of directional energies. The general motion he describes as 'la totale arabesque' in *La Musique et les Lettres* traces a shape of generative expansion: 'La totale arabesque, qui les relie, a de vertigineuses sautes en effroi que reconnue; et d'anxieux accords.'[13]

The Mallarmé text figures itself self-reflexively as ornament. Ornament, as commonly understood, is a decorative accessory to the object, artefact, or musical piece, which is designed to be supplementary to the main business of the work. In the Mallarmé text, however, ornament as arabesque has a central function, shape, and place in the text.[14] Obviously an ornament raises questions about which material is essential and which inessential, especially if the inessential seems to have been promoted to the place of the essential. Rather than embellishing the essential structure of the text, the arabesque generates the underlying structure. It is not mere decoration. In the period 1830 to 1900 the ornamental principle was at the heart of the aesthetic imagination for painters, poets, and musicians alike. Rae Beth Gordon writes:

For Félix Braquemond, painter, print-maker, ceramicist, and theorist, art is an abstraction—not a copy—of natural form, and its essence is the 'ornamental principle'. Simply put, the latter is an *agent* of transformation in the metamorphosis of nature into art. It is what Mallarmé will call 'la totale arabesque': the essential movement of the composition that defines the artist's personal vision of the object. It is the manifestation of the artist's power of imagination in the face of nature and as such reunites the palpable and the ineffable. Far from being something added on to structure, it is the core of that structure.[15]

The ornament, then, is an essential movement of metamorphosis, a process of 'becoming' from the natural form to its abstract artistic representation. The very nature of the arabesque, in its perennial structure of alternation and return, is a symbolic representation of this process: from its earliest Islamic origins it has depicted earthly life, in the intricately intertwined foliage, conjoined with the infinity of other-worldly transcendence. As a symbol of the link between the *objet de circonstance* and the 'Absolu' in Mallarmé's thought it is immensely powerful. The ornament holds the earthly and transcendental in an eternal relationship.

---

[13] *OC* (M), 648.

[14] Rae Beth Gordon puts forward in her *Ornament, Fantasy and Desire* that the shape and position of ornament in literary texts from 1830 to 1900 anticipates the way psychiatry, perceptual psychology, and aesthetics converge at the *fin de siècle*. Nerval, Gautier, Mallarmé, and Huysmans, she argues, were at the forefront of a re-evaluation of ornament. Ornament moves from a peripheral position in Nerval and Gautier to become the core of language and composition in Huysmans.

[15] Ibid. 5.

The arabesque is perceived in nature but is also part of the process that transforms it. Gordon quotes another pertinent extract from Félix Braquemond: 'The ornamental conception ... is of even greater importance than the natural structure of the object represented. And this is due to the fact that the former *provides* the structure that gives the work its importance.'[16] The appeal of ornament to Mallarmé is clearly that it embraces the process of transformation without direct recourse to the object. Through its precisely marked structuring function it expresses the 'Notion' or the essence of the object with immediacy but by *suggestion*. Using the ornament is a mark of the imaginative power of the artist, the 'Maître' of *Un coup de Dés* or the 'opérateur' of 'le Livre'.

For the aestheticians of the late nineteenth century a 'grammar of ornament' had to specify the figures that constituted its repertoire. These figures served as immutable frameworks that supported the invention of individual style.[17] Gordon's list of figures of the repertoire includes many of those given structural function in Mallarmé, which have been under discussion here: the *rinceau* (foliage or scrollwork), volute, border, fleuron (finial or tailpiece), and arabesque, among others. The ornamental repertoire falls into distinct configurative patterns, which Ralph Wornum, writing in 1873, set out as three forms of ornamental syntax: 'The whole grammar of ornament consists in contrast, repetition and series.'[18] Governing the grammar of ornamental syntax are two main laws: 'eurythmy' and 'complication'. Gordon writes: 'Eurythmy is thus a law in the interests of harmony, complication is a law that takes into account a quite contrary aesthetic desire.'[19]

The laws of ornament laid down by the aestheticians follow principles of order and chaos that are present in early Islamic visual art. Gordon points out: 'The apparent disorder in Islamic art in fact obeys a rigorous order.'[20] The conflict between disorder and order is dramatized by the arabesque. Initial disorder seems to set off regularly ordered patterns concurrently. Focillon illustrates this well in *La Vie des formes*:

Qu'y a-t-il de plus éloigné de la vie, de ses flexions, de sa souplesse, que les combinaisons géométriques du décor musulman? Elles sont engendrées par un raisonnement mathématique, établies sur des calculs, réductibles à des schémas d'une grande sécheresse. Mais dans ces cadres sévères, une sorte de fièvre presse et multiplie les figures; un étrange génie de complication enchevêtre, replie décompose et recompose leur labyrinthe. Leur immobilité même est chatoyante en métamorphoses, car, lisibles de plus d'une façon, selon les pleins, selon les vides, selon les axes verticaux ou diagonaux, chacune d'elles cache et revèle le secret et la réalité de plusieurs possibles.[21]

---

[16] *Ornament, Fantasy and Desire*, 5. Félix Braquemond, *Du dessin et de la couleur* (Paris: Charpentier, 1885), 216.   [17] A list of figures can be found in *Ornament, Fantasy and Desire*, 12.
[18] Quoted ibid. Ralph Wornum, *Analysis of Ornament: The Characteristics of Style* (London: Chapman & Hall, 1873), 14.   [19] *Ornament, Fantasy and Desire*, 13.
[20] Ibid.   [21] (Paris: Alcan, 1939), 12.

The intense interest in the Orient was of great importance to the evolution of ornament in the realm of the imaginary, and nowhere more so than in music. The notion of arabesque had been brought into the musical arena earlier in Robert Schumann's *Arabesque* for piano, Op. 18 (1839), possibly inspired by the associations of the arabesque with the grotesque in E. T. A. Hoffmann (who also inspired Schumann's *Kreisleriana* (1838, revised 1850)). Edgar Allan Poe referred to his early tales, which he started writing around 1833, although they never appeared in a single volume in Poe's lifetime, as 'Grotesques' and, occasionally, as 'Arabesques'.[22] 'Arabesque' has come to mean something quite specific in musical parlance, namely a florid melodic line free from harmonic constraint, perhaps based on an arpeggio of irregular intervals; but for Debussy the term has quite another significance. He writes in *La Revue blanche* on 1 May 1901:

Ysaÿe joue le concerto en solo pour violon, de J. S. Bach, comme lui seul est peut-être capable de le faire, sans avoir l'air d'un intrus. . . . Pourtant, ce concerto est une chose admirable parmi tant d'autres déjà inscrites dans les cahiers du grand Bach; on y retrouve presque intacte cette arabesque musicale ou plutôt ce principe de l'ornement qui est à la base de tous les modes de l'art. (Le mot *ornement* n'a rien à voir ici avec la signification qu'on lui donne dans les grammaires musicales). Les primitifs, Palestrina, Vittoria, Orlando di Lasso, etc. . . . se servirent de cette divine 'arabesque'. Ils en trouvèrent le principe dans le chant grégorien et en étayèrent les frêles entrelacs par de résistants contrepoints.[23]

Debussy supports his claim for the supremacy of line, for which he uses the term 'arabesque', by appealing to the authority of the fathers of Western music. The armature of polyphonic counterpoint supports the frail interlace above and around it, serving as a structural model for comparison with the 'divine arabesque'. It is a model concordant with Braquemond's idea of the 'armature' of ornament. In *Musica*, October 1902, Debussy writes:

Dans la musique de Bach, ce n'est pas le caractère de la mélodie qui émeut, c'est sa courbe; plus souvent même c'est le mouvement parallèle de plusieurs lignes dont la rencontre, soit fortuite, soit unanime, sollicite l'émotion. . . . Le vieux Bach, qui contient toute la musique, se moquait, croyez-le bien, des formules harmoniques. Il leur préférait le jeu libre des sonorités, dont les courbes, parallèles ou contrariées, préparaient l'épanouissement inespéré qui orne d'impérissable beauté le moindre de ses innombrables cahiers. C'était l'époque où fleurissait 'l'adorable arabesque', et la musique participait ainsi à des lois de beauté inscrites dans le mouvement total de la nature.[24]

The vogue for thinking about music in terms of its line rather than as representation of feeling, reflected in Debussy's admiration for the 'courbes'

[22] *Tales of the Grotesque and Arabesque, With Other Stories* (London: G. Newnes, 1903).
[23] *Monsieur Croche et autres écrits*, 2nd edn. (Paris: Gallimard, 1971), 33–4.
[24] Ibid. 66–7.

in Bach, can be seen in Eduard Hanslick's famous aesthetic treatise 'Vom Musikalisch-Schönen', written in 1854. Hanslick was concerned with the detailed formal properties of music, refusing to concern himself with its emotional impact and regarding it instead as an object of contemplation. He writes:

> The content of music is tonally moving forms. How music is able to produce beauti-ful forms without a specific feeling as its content is already to some extent illustrated for us by a branch of ornamentation in the visual arts, namely arabesque. We follow sweeping lines, here dipping gently, there boldly soaring, approaching and separating, corresponding curves large and small, seemingly incommensurable yet always well connected together, to every part a counterpart, a collection of small details but yet a whole. Now let us think of an arabesque not dead and static, but coming into being in some continuous self-formation before our eyes. How the lines, some robust and some delicate, pursue one another! How they ascend from a small curve to great heights and then sink back again, how they expand and contract and forever astonish the eye with their ingenious alternation of tension and repose! There before our eyes the image becomes even grander and more sublime. Finally, let us think of this lively arabesque as the dynamic emanation of an artistic spirit who unceasingly pours the whole abundance of his inventiveness into the arteries of this dynamism. Does this mental impression not come close to that of music?[25]

Debussy had already written two *Arabesques* for piano (1888) when he wrote *Jeux*. There is a very fertile crossover between the languages of Mallarmé and Debussy as they describe their respective arts. Obviously they are both appeal-ing to the language of ornament, the pool of common aesthetic terms of their time. The fact that Mallarmé and Debussy share an aesthetic vocabulary is, of course, an inevitable result of their mutual immersion, as near-contempo-rary artists and friends who moved in similar circles, in the artistic 'period-style' that filled the Parisian air. By the same token, the shared vocabulary cannot disguise the great differences between their two forms of artistic expression. The internal constraints of diatonicism that govern or are implied in Western music are very far from the internal constraints within French versification. Debussy and Mallarmé are using the term arabesque to describe very different media. Arabesque, then, is a figure that both connotes common ground between music and poetry and differentiates them.

3.4 *UN COUP DE DÉS* AS MUSICAL SCORE

Mallarmé argues in *La Musique et les Lettres* that the rhythms of prose are as good as those of verse if in the hands of an 'écrivain fastueux'.[26] Whereas the

---

[25] Trans. Guy Payzant in Edward Lippman (ed.), *Musical Aesthetics: A Historical Reader*, vol. ii (New York: Pendragon Press, 1988), 265–307 (288–9).   [26] *OC* (M), 644.

Romantic alexandrine fused music and metre, Mallarmé proposes that in the new, internally fluid line of verse 'la fusion se défait vers l'intégrité'.[27] Out of the ruptured line, the affronts to logical and syntactic sense, and the tensions between syntax and metre comes a heady mixture of sound and silence, verse at once fluid and restrained: 'Surtout la métrique française, délicate, serait d'emploi intermittent: maintenant, grâce à des repos balbutiants, voici que de nouveau peut s'élever, d'après une intonation parfaite, le vers de toujours, fluide, restauré, avec des compléments peut-être suprêmes.'[28] The 'compléments peut-être suprêmes' here must include music. Traditional verse will appear intermittently with the 'repos balbutiants' that punctuate and compose the verse.

Just as the line of verse has become less uniform, so in music expressivity has moved from the rigid 'mélodies d'autrefois très dessinées' to the more supple but angular 'mélodies brisées'.[29] If the pulse of the line of verse is fragmented, as in music, the structural rhythms of words on the page, conflicting frameworks of phonetic patterning, interrupted syntax, metre and so on, are closer to Adorno's 'truly musical' than to his 'musicalized'.[30] Whilst Mallarmé pays tribute to the musical versatility of *vers libre* in *La Musique et les Lettres*, describing it as 'modulation', he reaches far beyond its 'musicalized' notion of music as sonority and euphonious phonetic patterning to write the 'truly musical' as poetry. In *Un coup de Dés*, as we will see, the interruption of the 'blancs', which prevent coherent meaning from taking permanent hold, gives the poem a recurring tension in the pull between gaps, ellipses, interruptions and silences, and the promise of coherence. It is this alternance of coherence and non-coherence that is profoundly linked in essence for Mallarmé to musicality.

It may not seem too far-fetched, then, that Mallarmé felt able to claim that the spatially separated groups of words in *Un coup de Dés*, which create an extremely mobile text and a fluctuating, rubato-driven reading tempo, were akin to the musical score: 'Tout se passe, par raccourci, en hypothèse; on évite le récit. Ajouter que de cet emploi à nu de la pensée avec retraits, prolongements, fuites, ou son dessin même, résulte, pour qui veut lire à haute voix, une partition.'[31] To use the word 'partition' of *Un coup de Dés* is highly significant. The poetical drama of *Un coup de Dés* takes place between the instant and the space ('blanc') which reabsorbs it. Mallarmé writes further:

---

[27] Ibid. 644.   [28] Ibid.   [29] *Réponse à une enquête*, ibid. 387.

[30] See Chapter 1, section 1.10. Adorno draws a distinction between two types of representation of music in literature by opposing the 'truly musical' to the 'musicalized': 'Kafka treated meanings of spoken, intentional language as if they *were* music: parables broken off in mid-phrase. Contrast this with the "musical" language of Rilke and Swinburne—their imitation of musical effects and their remoteness from true musicality.'

[31] 'Observation relative au poème *Un coup de Dés jamais n'abolira le Hasard*', *OC*, 391.

Les 'blancs' en effet, assument l'importance, frappent d'abord. . . . Le papier inter-vient chaque fois qu'une image, d'elle-même, cesse ou rentre, acceptant la succession d'autres et, comme il ne s'agit pas, ainsi que toujours, de traits sonores réguliers ou vers—plutôt, de subdivisions prismatiques de l'Idée, l'instant de paraître et que dure leur concours, dans quelque mise en scène spirituelle exacte, c'est à des places vari-ables, près ou loin du fil conducteur latent.[32]

Unusually large spaces interrupt all statements in the poem. This disruption of propositions by the 'blanc' creates an irregular rhythm of sonorous and semantic traits interwoven with silence. The novel layout of the text is a new verse form, the shape assumed by the mixture of 'vers libre' and the prose poem, akin to symphonic structure: 'Leur réunion s'accomplit sous une influ-ence, je sais, étrangère, celle de la Musique entendue au concert. . . . Le genre, que c'en devienne un comme la symphonie, peu à peu, à côté du chant personnel, laisse intact l'antique vers.'[33] Traditional verse has not been aban-doned, simply expanded in time and space ('le tout sans nouveauté qu'un espacement de la lecture'), resulting in 'une vision simultanée de la Page' constructed around a single principal sentence.[34]

There are two main interconnected vocabularies at work in the poem: that of seafaring, shipwreck, and tempest, and that of the perilous pursuit of knowl-edge. Just as the key to sense in this poem is offered, it slips from our grasp. The imagery of sea and shipwreck, and indeed of gambling, is enacted in the very violence, risk, and chance of reading when the poem swirls and surges between points of climax and convergence that can never gain a strong enough foothold not to be the next victim of the disjointed syntax or typographical space around them. The reader has to develop keys to understanding, which are prone to dissolving instantaneously once replaced by a different possibility, over a back-ground or foreground of simultaneous blankness and multiplicity. This rhythm of reading within and across groups of words is illustrated by a set of images in the 'Observation relative au poème', which, it will be remembered, was not intended by Mallarmé for reading with the poem itself:

L'avantage, si j'ai droit à le dire, littéraire, de cette distance copiée qui mentalement sépare des groupes de mots ou les mots entre eux, semble d'accélérer tantôt et de ralentir le mouvement, le scandant, l'intimant même selon une vision simultanée de la Page. . . . La fiction affleurera et se dissipera, vite, d'après la mobilité de l'écrit, autour des arrêts fragmentaires d'une phrase capitale dès le titre introduite et contin-uée.[35]

Polarized groups of images sit uncomfortably alongside each other, their multiple voices requiring rereadings and the shuffling of pages backwards and forwards to give a fluctuating tempo of stops and starts ('d'accélérer tantôt et de ralentir le mouvement').

---

[32] *OC*, 391.   [33] Ibid. 392.   [34] Ibid. 391.   [35] Ibid.

The analysis that follows is not designed as a thorough critical exegesis of *Un coup de Dés*. It is offered within the strict comparative framework I have set up for the exploration, definition, and description of the intermediary; and at no point is it intended to have the function of a full explanatory survey. It seeks to assess the importance and real significance of music in *Un coup de Dés* and in turn to consider the usefulness of the poem as a site for modelling the interface between music and poetry. It will reaffirm the achievement of the poem in its own right but, rather than doing so as an end in itself, will use the poem as a staging post or fresh coordinate in the interconnecting web between music and poetry.

My analysis owes much to the extensive and distinguished body of critical literature devoted to this poem. Gardner Davies offers, through careful analysis of the syntax, 'une explication rationnelle', whose taxonomy, like Claude Roulet's, serves as a tribute to the very plurality of the poem.[36] Robert Greer Cohn's *Mallarmé's 'Un coup de Dés': An Exegesis* traces the poem's expansion, through its syntax, from the initial paradox of the title phrase at the poem's seminal centre, which he calls 'the naked armature', to the periodicity of history and knowledge unfolded page by page.[37] His reading, in its consideration of circular syntactical rhythm, is (perhaps unwittingly) nearer to grasping the musicality of the poem than that of Suzanne Bernard, which sets out with that specific aim.[38] Cohn writes: 'From this beginning the syntax emanates as follows: the oscillation of opposites in paradox shadows forth the phenomenon of rhythm. From inorganic rhythm, that of the ocean, rises the rhythm of life. . . . Each page corresponds, roughly, to a level of the hierarchy of sciences.'[39] By contrast, Malcolm Bowie rejects any allegorizing approach in danger of 'falsely normalising the texture' of the poem.[40] His analysis confronts and theorizes the difficult, broken textures of the poem, encouraging links between these patterns and other systems of thought in ways which more closed, hagiographically minded readings of Mallarmé cannot.[41]

Roger Pearson stresses that his own search for 'le profond calcul' differs from the approach of his predecessors and colleagues, largely characterized, he claims, by an undervaluation of Mallarmé's pursuit of mastery in the

---

[36] *Vers une explication rationnelle du 'Coup de dés'*, rev. edn. (Paris: José Corti, 1992); *Élucidation du poème de Stéphane Mallarmé: 'Un coup de dés jamais n'abolira le hasard'* (Neuchâtel: Aux Ides et Calendes, 1943). Gardner Davies sees the poem as a rewriting of *Igitur*. For Roulet the poem is 'une Ode allégorique, écrite en style lapidaire. Mallarmé y transpose la Fable du Monde, telle qu'elle est définie dans la Bible et par le corps des croyances chrétiennes' (12).

[37] (New Haven: Yale University Press, 1949).

[38] Bernard, *Mallarmé et la musique*; see Prologue.

[39] *Mallarmé's 'Un coup de Dés': An Exegesis*, 10–11.

[40] *Mallarmé and the Art of Being Difficult*, 124.

[41] Roger Pearson is overlooking the significance of the linguistic detail of these analyses when he accuses Bowie's account of minimizing the linguistic nature of thought (*Unfolding Mallarmé: The Development of a Poetic Art* (Oxford: Clarendon Press, 1996), 244).

poem. Derrida and Kristeva, he maintains, 'both champion Mallarmé for
his "revolutionary" displays of linguistic powerlessness and "failure" rather
than for any mastery by which he might be seeking to harness and exploit
the "disseminating" tendencies of language'.[42] Pearson revels most persuasively in what he sets out to prove is a scrupulously planned and tightly
controlled play of language as an alternative to traditional versification, and
concentrates on the spatialized ('cubic') alexandrine whose number (twelve)
governs the text. Pearson is right to argue that 'the "disseminating" tendencies of language' are all the more powerfully explored in the poem through
a highly ordered, determinedly non-traditional system of versification.
However, in spite of Pearson's fresh awareness of Mallarmé's playfulness,
there is a sense in which seeing the 'profond calcul' behind every page of *Un
coup de Dés* can become an endgame. If such a reading were too predominant it might inhibit the element of mobility in the poem that can make it
appear different with every reading, and the new sense of panic the reader
enjoys with every page-turn, which Malcolm Bowie brought to critical
attention.

Critics have, on the whole, tended to ignore the question of the significance
of music, in a poem whose author claimed for it the status of musical score.
Virginia La Charité goes so far as to state: 'Mallarmé did not really know
music and did not understand it technically. Moreover, *Un Coup de dés* has no
resonance, no formal rime or meter; it is not an orchestration, but a fully inte-
grated work, whose circular structure denies identification of direction,
progression, sequence. Music is a metaphor, just as theater, dance, mime and
the church are metaphors.'[43] What follows is intended to reinsert a consideration of specific music back into the discussion of *Un coup de Dés*.

3.5 ANALYSIS OF *UN COUP DE DÉS*

The intermittent rhythm of reading in the poem, which I have discussed with
reference to the 'Observation relative au poème', is produced by the interaction of the 'blancs' with the different poetic procedures that I shall be dealing
with here in turn: structural, syntactical, semantic, phonetic, and associative.[44]

---

[42] *Unfolding Mallarmé*, 1–2. He is referring to Derrida, *La Dissémination* and Julia Kristeva, *La
Révolution du langage poétique: L'Avant-garde à la fin du XIXe siècle: Lautréamont et Mallarmé* (Paris: Seuil, 1974).
Pearson discusses most of the important criticism of *Un coup de Dés* chronologically in *Unfolding
Mallarmé*, 244–5.

[43] *The Dynamics of Space: Mallarmé's 'Un coup de dés jamais n'abolira le hasard'* (Lexington, Ky.: French
Forum, 1987), 128.

[44] For a detailed discussion of the editorial history and controversy surrounding the poem see
Roger Pearson, *Unfolding Mallarmé*, 243–55.

3.5.1 *Telic expectation*

At first glance *Un coup de Dés* has a studiously randomized appearance: words are strewn across the page in the absence of traditional versification. Rather than being given a familiar poetic framework, as she would in a sonnet, the reader is given certain structural clues to reading that can then be applied to other parts of the poem. The tension resides between poetic order and apparent 'hasard' in this thoroughgoing investigation of chance as aesthetic principle, foreshadowing the permutational structures of 'le Livre'.

As is well known, the play of typefaces in *Un coup de Dés* constructs a dramatic presentation of simultaneous events, those in capitals, in smaller capitals, in italics and in lower case. Each distracts attention from the others as they run concurrently at intervals through the multi-layered text. 'UN COUP DE DÉS', a throw of the dice, sets the linguistic ball rolling on the first page.[45] The smaller capitals of 'QUAND BIEN MÊME LANCÉ DANS DES CIRCON-STANCES ÉTERNELLES | DU FOND D'UN NAUFRAGE', coupled with its position on the second page, are visual suggestions that the phrase is parenthetical. However the parenthesis does not close. Rather it lingers over the next two pages, linked by its typeface to 'SOIT' and 'LE MAÎTRE' (on the third and fourth pages respectively). After 'SOIT' the page plunges downwards in an ideographical swoop, the typographical tempest in which 'LE MAÎTRE' ('hors d'anciens calculs') of the fourth page is caught, hesitating between the possibility of 'l'unique Nombre qui ne peut pas être un autre' (fourth page) and the dicethrow ('ancestralement à n'ouvrir pas la main | crispée | par-delà l'inutile tête') on the fifth page. Yet at the same time this impotence is counteracted by the appearance of words having been scattered on the page by the dice-throw. On this page logical inconsistencies are made to seem natural partners. Reluctance to throw will avoid the possibility of being governed by chance; yet the dice has been thrown already: the decision to act or not to act cannot be non-contingent upon chance. Indecision and decision have the same outcomes. The end result is a number, but this too is a product of the chance or probability governing the dice-throw. Mirror-imaging and transformational mirror images around the fold on the 'LE MAÎTRE' page make of this hesitating doubt a local diversion, a moment of immobility, whilst the large space on the fifth page, with the larger capitals and rhyme, draws the eye dramatically back down again. The movement is from a double page centred by the fold, a perpendicular support, to a decentred one, destabilized and skewed in favour of a lower-right gravitational pull. 'N'ABOLIRA' continues the opening phrase of the poem, a simultaneous but unconnected event, underpinned by the extremity of the shift from multiplicity to the solitude of this word, and throwing into question the idea of a traditionally developing

---

45 Henceforth all page references to *Un coup de Dés* refer to the double pages of the text.

poem. What Mallarmé calls elsewhere the 'reflets réciproques', resulting from 'L'œuvre pure' which 'cède l'initiative aux mots', at once undermine and construct the poetic structure in an unfolding that seems endless.[46] At the same time the visual and semantic structural pulls are between rising and falling, a dice being thrown upwards and falling.

'*SI*' on the sixth page becomes central to the poem's drama. The feather-spiralling movement of the text is contained by '*COMME SI*' which causes a fluctuation in the tempo and flow of the poem. There is a sensation of lightness after the weight of 'N'ABOLIRA' (fifth page); the spatial focus is non-linear and indirect. In some sense these differences of heaviness and lightness would contribute to the dynamic markings of the typefaces that Mallarmé envisaged for his musical score.[47]

This '*SI*' is linked to those beyond the space of the page by its typeface and position on the page. The phrase '*rire que SI*' on the eighth page is left hovering, to be picked up by '*C'ÉTAIT | LE NOMBRE | CE SERAIT* | LE HASARD' on the ninth. The hypothetical '*SI*' hovers over each of these pages and over the doubt-filled conditional clauses 'EXISTÂT-IL | COMMENCÂT-IL ET CESSÂT-IL' and so on of the ninth page, which throw the textual weight up into the top right-hand corner to pull against the bottom-heavy 'LE HASARD'. Again the end result is a number, but again it is still a product of chance; probability ('hasard') is involved in the throw of the dice: '*SI C'ÉTAIT*' could be heard 'si sept est' (seven is the number of stars in the 'Septentrion') or 'six sept est'. The final presence, on the eleventh page, of 'UNE CONSTELLATION' forms an immobile cluster in the bottom right of the page that is offset by the downwards assonantal pull of 'veillant | doutant | roulant | brillant et méditant', which throws its status into doubt, and by the vast space of silence on the left-hand side of the double spread. Even as the landing dice seem to offer a fixed certainty of the poem in the final line ('Toute Pensée émet un Coup de Dés'), the niggling doubt that 'RIEN N'AURA EU LIEU QUE LE LIEU', that all the reader has witnessed is an 'inférieur clapotis quelconque comme pour disperser l'acte vide', hovers over it from the preceding page. The descent to the final line is balanced by the potentially liberating, but only glimpsed, constellation (whose ascent mirrors the transition in the whole of the *Poésies* from the blue sky of 'l'Azur' to the night sky). However, the last line is no mere resolution or calm after the storm. Together with the principal proposition of the poem it offers an overarching framework for the poem as a whole, an 'all-at-once' perception rather than a real-time encounter, plunging it back into the hypothetical:

---

[46] 'Crise de vers', *OC* (M), 366.

[47] See 'Observation relative au poème': 'La différence des caractères d'imprimerie entre le motif prépondérant, un secondaire et d'adjacents, dicte son importance à l'émission orale et la portée, moyenne, en haut, en bas de page, notera que monte ou descend l'intonation' (*OC*, 391–2).

A—'UN COUP DE DÉS JAMAIS N'ABOLIRA LE HASARD'
B—'Toute Pensée émet un Coup de Dés'

These are two terms of a syllogism. Although the shadow of the third resultant term of the syllogism is the expected outcome of the poem (to give something approximating to 'toute pensée—jamais n'abolira le hasard'), it is never actually stated. The syllogism promises a linear journey between two points and a result once the poem has travelled somewhere. Instead, the result of the non-statement is that the poem hovers on a dialectical edge. The attempt to control the contingency that permeates all mental acts, to arrive at pure thought, is futile because the act of rejection of contingency (of which the example here is the potential for numerical control in the throw of the dice) actually reaffirms the presence of that which it is trying to escape. Chance must have a role to play in the act of repudiation itself. The question in *Igitur* is whether a controlling structure may be found to order the chaos. Here, the dice-throw epitomizes the fragile possibility of controlling chance with numbers. The possibilities are limited by the action but it itself is still under the ultimate dictate of the uncertainties of probability. Ironically, to throw the dice is at once to acknowledge and to give in to chance. The gambling imagery, that of chance versus strategy, expounds the threat of 'le néant' that underlies the fact that the pursuit of knowledge will be constantly beset by the unknowable. To complicate things further, the Arabic for 'hasard' is /dɛ/('le dé'): so whilst 'le hasard' is presented as diametrically opposed to 'un coup de dés', it is actually etymologically linked.

When the other main group of images in *Un coup de Dés* is added, that of the sea and shipwreck, we are tempted to allow the metaphysical question to become a secure centrality in the poem around which semantic clusters hang as kinds of allegory. Indeed, the sea imagery is a clear reference to violence, risk, and chance. It is also a fitting motivation for the typographical tempest that confronts the reader across every page. However, the terms of the allegory are not given long enough to settle. No one strand is given priority over another. None falls into the positions of figure or ground. The concrete and the abstract are set up as different levels but the distinction is blurred. The poem swings between points of climax and convergence in the argument, whose firm grounding is shaken by the disjointed syntax or typographical space around them, the threat of chance. It contains a single idea, that is, the exploration of the vacillating centre between two opposite pulls, the threat of the void versus the threat of the uniform mental act that hovers behind 'toute pensée'; an idea that is explored and qualified in various ways from start to finish. The binary opposition is presented but destabilized. *Un coup de Dés* is about creating frameworks and violating them, about setting up a telos and throwing it into the uncertainty and violent rupture of the metaphysical crisis; and about moments of hesitancy, of gaping holes or vacant spaces in the texture, across or from which stretches the confusing eddy of superfluous semantic and phonetic resonance.

Having examined the poem broadly on a semantic and structural level, I shall now show how the same features of difficulty and resistance are at work on a syntactic and phonetic level in the text, complicating further the experience of reading.

3.5.2 More hesitations

The reader is faced with a succession of phrases, which appear to organize themselves into recognizable patterns but will, as soon as formed, be challenged immediately by other possibilities. All the possibilities that arise seem viable since there is no overriding norm. It is this tension, caused by the poetic text organizing and disorganizing itself, that lies at the poem's heart. The deflections take place from one group of phrases to another sense group, or within the internal workings of a line that presents itself as a coherent unit. A line or group of phrases invites examination as a coherent whole because of its visual organization on the page. The opening of the poem, for example, introduces three signposts for reading on, each offering a different direction, but suggests that each should be followed simultaneously. In despatialized form this opening reads:

Un coup de dés jamais | quand bien même lancé dans des circonstances éternelles, du fond d'un naufrage | soit que l'Abîme, blanchi, étale, furieux, sous une inclinaison plane désespérément d'aile la sienne par avance retombée.

Reading involves proposing new syntactical scansions for each sequence, which brings different sets of affinities and contrasts to the whole.

Breaks within the phrase group shown in Example 3.1, from the tenth page, are not syntactical markers but instead highlight the easily ignored separations between the words themselves. This line slips down the page, dramatizing the difference and sameness of the separations, drawing attention to the discrete breaks in the phrase, the silences glossed over in speech and taken for granted in reading. The reader is encouraged to think of the interstice and forced to work for sense in this vivid enactment of continuity and discontinuity. The margins are a disruption to the centrality of the word; the voids threaten the apparent solidity of their presence. Ways in which to read are constantly

Example 3.1 Mallarmé, *Un coup de Dés*, from the tenth page

dans ces parages
        du vague
                en quoi toute réalité se dissout

suggested but these cannot be applied in a consistent linear progression through the poem. At times elements of traditional syntax are still necessary to sense-making, and in effect are reinstated as a way of reading by their very distortion. In some clusters syntactical patterns are suggested strongly enough for a particular syntactic telos or expectation to be set up but pulled against simultaneously by alternative and equally compelling possibilities. On the third page, for example, we read the sequence shown in Example 3.2. Here familiar elements of syntax are strongly suggested. The position of 'SOIT' upholds the left-hand margin as a landmark from which the initial chaos of scattered words on the page may be ordered, although the drift of 'blanchi' into a somewhat ambivalent position to the right throws this into doubt. As the apparently random dispersal of words on the page begins to reorganize itself, disorganizing elements disrupt the order once more. 'que' has slipped down from its usual place next to 'SOIT', leaving a word space, thereby changing 'lines' but retaining the reference to its usual grammatical slot. The downwards line beginning 'blanchi' enacts the typographical action of 'plane', whose equivocal status as adjective or verb requires a shift in reading practice, from simply reallocating words to their rightful syntactical slots to calculating their syntactic value:

> blanchi
>   étale
>   furieux
>   sous une inclinaison
>   plane désespérément

At the same time, this same phrase sets up a firm diagonal pull to the right, defining a diagonal pull (depicting 'une inclinaison') against the notional vertical margin set up by 'SOIT'.

Hiatuses, moments of immobility in the forwards momentum, are created by the overspill of possibilities for certain words. Take, for example, the phrase '*rire que SI*' on the eighth page (Example 3.3). The space surrounding '*SI*' is filled with polysemic directions for reading onwards. The eye could travel diagonally left down the page, to give: '*SI* | La lucide et seigneuriale aigrette | de vertige' (and so on). The search for sense in this cluster involves making visual leaps across the fold in the page to find words on the right-hand side which might clarify those on the left, although this can disrupt the separate story they seem to tell alone. At the same time '*SI*' is transformed into a pivotal element and key component in the later phrase (ninth page):

(*SI*)   *C'ÉTAIT*   *LE NOMBRE*

Such hesitations arrest the momentum of the forwards reading while concurrent readings are constructed or evaporate alongside. The possibilities for 'cela', at the bottom of the fourth page, are another example of a moment of

SOIT

que

l'Abîme

blanchi

étale

furieux

sous une inclinaison

plane désespérément

d'aile

la sienne

par

avance retombée d'un mal à dresser le vol

et couvrant les jaillissements

coupant au ras les bonds

très à l'intérieur résume

l'ombre enfouie dans la profondeur par cette voile alternative

jusqu'adapter

à l'envergure

sa béante profondeur en tant que la coque

d'un bâtiment

penché de l'un ou l'autre bord

Example 3:2 Mallarmé, *Un coup de Dés*, third page. (Example reduced by 10%.) In this and the following examples from Mallarmé's poem, the central fold of the double page is represented by the large central gap.

soucieux

expiatoire et pubère

muet

rire

que

SI

de vertige

La lucide et seigneuriale aigrette

au front invisible

scintille

puis ombrage

un stature mignonne ténébreuse

en sa torsion de sirène

debout

de souffleter

bifurquées

par d'impatientes squames ultimes

le temps

un roc

faux manoir

tout de suite

évaporé en brumes

qui imposa

une borne à l'infini

Example 3.3 Mallarmé, *Un coup de Dés*, eighth page

immobilization caused in the text while another direction of reading seems to be forming. 'Cela' seems to point nowhere; 'this' refers to nothing in particular. Its other possible meaning, as the third person singular of the verb 'celer' in the past historic, raises further doubts about its status.

The dissolution of interpretative keys, in a background-foreground of blankness and multiplicity, takes place, as we are told by this phrase from the tenth page, in the 'parages du vague en quoi toute réalité se dissout'. The process is suggested by several other image groups: for example, the siren's rock on the eighth page: 'faux manoir | tout de suite | évaporée en brumes | qui imposa | une borne à l'infini.'

At times the reader's search for syntactic sense is frustrated by having to extend her quest across the page or to other parts of the poem. It is not clear whether the subject of the third person verb 'hésite' is 'LE MAÎTRE' or 'l'unique Nombre' (fourth page). If reading back does not clarify then reading on might point to 'LE MAÎTRE' as subject ('en maniaque chenu'), but in the course of this discovery many other possible unrelated sense groups arise. When it comes to 'la partie | au nom des flots | un', 'un' is so far separated from its syntactic dependents that the eye is drawn by the visual pattern of 'un naufrage cela'. The syntactical criteria of reading left to right and of the indefinite article belonging to a noun are at odds: following the syntactical direction offered would give 'un | envahit le chef | coule en barbe soumise'. Each word, rather than assuming the relative importance it would in its usual syntactic ordering, assumes an autonomy from linguistic labelling as it acts as a free unit in a semiotic system that creates and recreates its own ordering principles.

At some points the multiply reflective surface of sound provided by phonetic patterning appears momentarily to provide a directing signpost, indicating that this or that group of phrases belongs together, or else creates a diversion away from one possible route by pointing to another. Sense cannot always be expected to arise from words in apposition. On the fifth page, for example (shown in Example 3.4), the two distinct rhythms suggest separate momentums and cohesions that will lead to sense. Conflicting horizontal and diagonal paragraphs seem to offer a spatial and typographical enactment of the meeting of 'le vieillard vers cette conjonction suprême avec la probabilité'. Assonance and visual effect build a centrally placed vertical stack at the bottom of the page ('chancellera | s'affalera | folie | N'ABOLIRA') in a rhythm entirely distinct from the preceding one. The horizontals of the first rhythm let it maintain an initial semblance of traditional linearity, whereas the vertical rhythm is formed purely by phonetic effect.

The poem is thus punctuated by resonant eddies of reflective phonetic patterns, and the cancelling effect of points of hesitation that operate in magical otherness of time, in the absence of a fixed temporal-spatial rhythm for comparison. Flickers of coherence are diverted immediately by another shape, as, for example, on the sixth page (Example 3.5). The phrase continued by

N'ABOLIRA

ancestralement à n'ouvrir par la main

          crispée

             par-delà l'inutile tête

legs en la disparition

               à quelqu'un

                    ambigu

            l'ultérieur démon immémorial

ayant

    de contrées nulles

        induit

le vieillard vers cette conjonction suprême avec la probabilité

                celui

                    son ombre puérile

caressée et polie et rendue et lavée

        assouplie pa la vague et soustraite

        aux durs os perdus entre les ais

           né

              d'un ébat

la mer par l'aïeul tentant ou l'aïeul contre la mer

        une chance oiseuse

                    Fiançailles

dont

    le voile d'illusion rejailli leur hantise

    ainsi que le fantôme d'un geste

        chancellera

        s'affalera

            folie

Example 3.4 Mallarmé, *Un coup de Dés*, fifth page. (Example reduced by 15%.)

Une insinuation   simple

au silence   enroulé avec ironie

ou

le mystère

précipité

hurlé

dans quelque proche   tourbillon d'hilarité et d'horreur

voltige   autour du gouffre

sans le joncher

ni fuir

et en berce le vierge indice

Example 3.5 Mallarmé, *Un coup de Dés*, sixth page

'N'ABOLIRA' (fifth page) is suspended and disappears into the texture to make way for this twisting, winding, parenthetical addition. The sentence will appear to be completed syntactically by 'LE HASARD' later in the poem.

Although standard rhyming patterns are missing from *Un coup de Dés* in their overt form, the play between word identities and phonetic clusters is not. Words slip in and out of the ordering frame that they appear to inhabit, sometimes hovering between two frames of reference, fitting either way depending on how they are read. Those frames rub against each other and dissolve into one another: certain words in one syntactical group may be linked by homophony to another with which they have no obvious syntactical link. Sometimes pure assonance connects a phrase or phrases, suggesting a synchronic, vertical stacking of meaning by association, a centre of gravity operating in a rhythm different from that of its surrounding areas. Assonance can be so dominant as to drown the poetic texture in pure sound, giving an impression of unity and a desire for semantic coherence that may be at odds with the discontinuous syntactic ordering underlying it, or pre-empt any sense of unity or arrival in the structural development. For example, sound likenesses can occur within lines and neighbouring phrases, presenting abstract symmetries to groups that otherwise appear disparate. In the example quoted above, the capitals of 'N'ABOLIRA' suggest that it belongs with the rest of the capitalized phrase, although in terms of sound it is very closely tied to the adjacent phrases ('chancellera | s'affalera').

Assonance, alliteration, and internal line rhyme are part of the more general phenomenon of repetition and playing with similarity and difference. The superficial sense of unity they give is in fact a very unstable support of near-identities, blurred polarities, and overlapping margins. Resonance of sound can at one moment be the dominating, ordering principle of or for the words and at the next a subsidiary echo behind them; a moment of immediate unity and disruption in the line or group, or an overarching link across the poem that may concur with or cut across a far-reaching syntactic link already made. Phonetic and syntactical orders weave in and out of the texture, disappearing and reappearing. The undercurrents diverge and reconverge, shift between the margins and the centre of the poem, emerge and are submerged.

Resonances are so powerful in places that they provide multiple reflections and symmetries. This can work on the level of the word (for example, *silence*, 'si lance'; *si c'était*, 'si sept est'; *la voile* (third page); *le voile* (fifth page)). In the exploitation of pun (or, in the last example, homonym) sound identity is undermined by crucial but almost imperceptible differences. Rich phonetic reflection can also take place internally to a phrase group, as on the sixth page, for example:

Une *insin*uation | *simp*le | au *silen*ce | *enroulée* avec *ironie*

Where semantic development or an accumulation of layers of meaning might be expected as a motivation for the sound patterning, phonetic reverberations in this instance create a cluster, a moment of stasis or immobility. But the repetition of sound patterns points here to an internal emptiness. The predominance of the /s/ phoneme in particular is a dramatization of a winding 'insinuation', an enactment of a spiralling (or 'enroulement') that embraces presence and absence in a typographically scattered phrase that seems to rise clear of the text.

3.6 THE ACOUSTIC DRAMA OF *UN COUP DE DÉS*

In the 'Observation relative au poème' Mallarmé writes of the 'blancs': 'La versification en exigea, comme silence alentour, ordinairement, au point qu'un morceau, lyrique ou de peu de pieds, occupe, au milieu, le tiers environ du feuillet: je ne transgresse cette mesure, seulement la disperse.'[48] The *pli* (fold of the page) both divides and joins each double page, and forms a V shape belonging to both halves. If the page takes over the function of the traditional line of verse, the *pli* acts like a caesura in the middle of the 'line'. Each 'line' has been dissected and expanded to occupy several horizontal, vertical, and diagonal planes with different emphases. On the third page the diagonal of 'une inclinaison | plane désespérément' operates against the rigidity of the notional left-hand margin; and on the fifth page the 'inclinaison' works around horizontal paragraph-like statements. These *inclinaisons* seem to act like moments of musical simultaneity expressed in typographical terms. At a glance the eye appreciates the vertical and diagonal co-presences of a text in space and time, as the ear would hear a rhythmical passage played over a held chord or an ostinato rhythm.

The chance to test the poem's use as a musical score, that is to say, of reconstructing the typographical layout of the text from an audition or performance of the text, remains an inviting one. It is made even more so by Valéry, who has left a mystery surrounding Mallarmé's intentions for the text. He describes a certain visit to the poet at Valvins, during which he heard 'ce grand homme discuter (au sens presque de l'algèbre) les moindres détails de position du système verbal et visuel qu'il avait construit ... vérifiant minutieusement le montage de cette figure en qui devaient se composer le simultané de la vision avec le successif de la parole, comme si un équilibre très délicat eût dépendu de ces précisions.' He also recounts how on one occasion in Paris the poet read the poem aloud to him.[49] It may well be that performance was part of Mallarmé's plan for the poem as 'score'.

---

[48] *OC*, 391.

[49] *Œuvres*, ed. Jean Hytier, Bibliothèque de la Pléiade, 2 vols. (Paris: Gallimard, 1957–60), i. 625, 623.

Gide's reaction to the poem in a card to Mallarmé dated 9 May 1897 may have pleased him. He writes: 'La dernière page m'a glacé d'une émotion très semblable à celle que donne telle symphonie de Beethoven.' Indeed the visually and semantically dramatic ascent towards the shimmering 'CONSTELLATION' of the last page, from the 'gouffre' of the ninth and the hopeless statement of the tenth ('RIEN N'AURA EU LIEU QUE LE LIEU'), does have the grandeur and finality of such a symphonic conclusion.

This poem, then, is about reading as movement, in a combination of weight, space, time, and flow. Time flows onwards, interrupted in its path of gradual ascent by destabilizations, diverted by the distraction of local events (themselves composed of tensions between the multiple and the single, between meaning-forming clusters and solitary words with no meaningful status), leaving in its wake a sensation of 'everywhereness' that finally escapes categorization.

3.7 FIGURING THE ARABESQUE

Mallarmé's use of the arabesque figure in *La Musique et les Lettres* is an articulation of the way the text weaves in and out of itself, disappears into itself to re-emerge later, an enactment of the tension between control and chance, of the uncertainty over the ability of language to fill the void. The manifestation of the arabesque is the pull between the desire to read on and forward and the interruptions created by offbeat centres of gravity in the poem ('le simultané de la vision avec le successif de la parole', as Valéry put it (see section 3.6)).

The operation of the curling in on itself and the forking outwards again of the arabesque in *Un coup de Dés* takes place in the play between words and space in the spiralling ascent of its acoustic drama. 'Le montage de cette figure', as described by Valéry, is a structure that delimits the dynamic and mobile text. The curlicues and forkings of the arabesque articulate the textual play of horizontal, vertical, and diagonal planes in the organized complexity of the poem. It is the figure of the 'chiffration mélodique tue',[50] knitting together incompatible movements, impossible collisions, and instantaneous contradictions. It sets up limits and violates them, plays mobility against immobility, and diverges from a cantabile, forwards-moving telos with offbeat pulls. Binary oppositions are stretched and loosened. The harmony of assonance is shot through with dissonance. Hesitations caused by phonetic and semantic spillage resonate across gaps and spaces and silences in the text.

The sum of the parts of the poem forms a structure comparable in many ways to the acoustic drama of *Jeux*, to which I will turn my attention over the

[50] *La Musique et les Lettres*, *OC* (M), 648.

next few pages. My analysis will first take *Jeux* on its own terms, before exploring the arabesque as a site for expressing the mutual transformability of the poem and piece.

3.8 JEUX

The music of *Jeux* is cinematic in its shifts in and out of focus. Images of waltzes and of marches fade in and out of each other in a strange, dreamlike logic. The piece is always in motion, in one long transition of undulating weight and lightness, surging and receding on a journey that must never consent to arrive. It is the first time that Debussy keeps for such a long stretch (about seventeen minutes) to one continuous form. Melody is constructed out of colours; the shapes and the shadows are as important as the fact of the notes themselves.

There is nowhere near as much written about *Jeux* as there is about *Un coup de Dés*. Jann Pasler writes that *Jeux* was 'ignored for many years because of its banal scenario'.[51] More recently it has prompted more interest amongst composers and musicologists, which has resulted in work that provides several useful frames of reference for grappling with the piece. Herbert Eimert discusses the concept of form, which is challenged by *Jeux*, in relation to analysis. He writes: 'One can see what Debussy's form "no longer" is; much harder to say what it is. One makes least progress if one tries to apply to Debussy the standard concepts of musical theory. . . . The same applies to formal schemes. To describe Debussy's music, a fluctuating middle layer of concepts would have to be specially discovered.'[52] Arguing against other criticism anxious to describe the work in traditional formal terms as a rondo, Eimert searches for language to convey what he evokes as the vexing experience of listening to *Jeux*, finding terms such as 'rhythmicised time' and 'endless melody'.[53] The conclusion at which he arrives ('the inconspicuous novelty of *Jeux* lies not in its construction, but in time')[54] leaves the way open for Pasler. In her article she repositions the importance of the plot of *Jeux*, suggesting a connection between the ballet's scenario and the temporal organization of the piece. This connection is given as evidence of one type of continuity in the piece, along with four motivic and temporal types. Other important analyses of *Jeux* include Laurence Berman's, who characterizes *Jeux* in the light of *Prélude à l'Après-midi d'un faune* and of Mallarmé's 'Eclogue'.[55] Boulez's language for describing *Jeux* is

---

[51] 'Debussy, *Jeux*: Playing with Time and Form', *Nineteenth-Century Music*, 6/1 (1982), 60–75 (60).

[52] 'Debussy's *Jeux*', *Die Reihe*, 5 (1959), 3–20 (3).   [53] Ibid. 6, 10.

[54] Ibid. 20.

[55] '*Prelude to the Afternoon of a Faun* and *Jeux*: Debussy's Summer Rites', *Nineteenth-Century Music*, 3/3 (1980), 225–38.

mimetic of its contained, mobile plurality and closer, perhaps, to Eimert's 'fluctuating middle layer':

Or, loin d'être chétivement morcelée, la structure, riche d'inventions, d'une complex-ité ondoyante, instaure une forme de pensée extrêmement ductile, fondée sur la notion d'un temps irréversible; pour *l'entendre*, on n'a que le recours de se soumettre à son développement, car une évolution constante des idées thématiques écarte toute symétrie dans l'architecture. . . *Jeux* marque l'avènement d'une forme musicale qui, se renouvelant *instantanément*, implique un mode d'audition non moins *instantanée*.[56]

Although these analyses have succeeded in demonstrating a certain unity between the complex layers of interaction in the texture, not enough has been said, following Eimert, about the elusive difficulty of grasping the whole expe-rience of *Jeux*, nor about the aspects of its acoustic drama that are not cohe-sive or unified and do not fit comfortably into overarching schemes. The tension in *Jeux* lies in hearing the music both as a fragmented series of instants, that is, hearing the ruptures and intersections in the foreground, and as an organic whole, bound by temporal unity.

There are elements in the texture of *Jeux* that, even after several hearings, prevent the piece from becoming a totalizable listening experience. Essentially *Jeux* abolishes the musically predictable. It conjures up an alluring mixture of magic, hedonistic joy, furtive desire, and mystery, partly through the choreo-graphed scene of desire, which involves two girls having a game of tennis with one boy and, when they lose the ball, a frenzied kiss-chase.[57] The music seems to awaken flirtatious desire and then teeter on the brink between coy resis-tance and total abandon. It escapes the listener's grasp because it never sounds like the same piece twice.

In his essay 'Sonate, que me veux-tu?' Boulez writes: 'Mettre les pouvoirs formels de la musique en parité avec la morphologie et la syntaxe; la fluidité de la forme doit intégrer la fluidité du vocabulaire.'[58] Language that is adequately descriptive of *Jeux* needs to capture the sound in process, under-going constant evolution. This demands a rethinking of the musical notion of form. Concepts such as periodicity and symmetry will be of diminished importance in the descriptive vocabulary for music in which the melodic, harmonic, rhythmic, and timbral ideas are blended so as to become aspects of a single, simultaneous conception and realization.

It is hard to squeeze the complex interplay of elements in *Jeux* into all-encompassing frameworks, since, as André Souris has said of Debussy's music: 'Tout se passe chez Debussy comme si la substance sonore trouvait sa continuité en elle-même, comme si elle était à la fois l'agent et le produit de

---

[56] *Relevés d'apprenti* (Paris: Seuil, 1966), 344.

[57] The analyses of the piece here will not be filtered wholly through the action. The importance of the plot for the music will be discussed later.

[58] In *Points de repère* (Paris: Christian Bourgois, 1995), 152.

sa propre liaison, comme si rien d'extérieur à elle-même n'intervenait dans son mode d'être.'[59] My analysis will attempt to pull the elements in *Jeux* together in a way that illustrates their simultaneous bid for, and affront to, coherence. My aim is to discuss some of the aesthetic effects of their interaction. *Jeux* is characterized by rhythmic and timbral contrast between sections. Each section has its own unique quality, a characteristic motif and palette of instrumental colour. The form of the piece is based on a rhythm of sections whose organization is broadly complementary to the action. Continuity between the sections is less of a concern than the creation of surprise effects of sudden metamorphosis, that is to say, changes in texture and mood without preparation or transition.

3.9 AN INITIAL ANALYSIS OF *JEUX*

For the purposes of this analysis, I shall treat the three most important aspects of the various episodes of *Jeux* separately: motivic, timbral, and temporal.

Whereas in Debussy's piece for flute, *Syrinx*, sheer melody seems to predominate over rhythm and harmony, in *Jeux* rhythm and harmony are explored to a much greater extent. The use of small fragments, or motifs, usually two bars in length, built out of one-bar elements, shifts attention away from the level of sustained melody, which is now fleeting and elliptical.

Example 3.6 Debussy, *Jeux*: (i) Figure 1; (ii) Figure 4 and preceding 4 bars; (iii) Figure 6

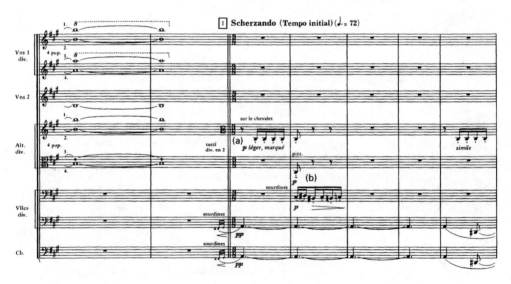

[59] 'Debussy et Stravinsky', *Revue belge de la musicologie*, 1–4 (1962), 45–56 (47).

Example 3.6 (ii)

Example 3.6 (ii) (cont.)

Example 3.6 (iii)

Distinct sections are built up by the reiteration and slight variation of the rhythmic groups. The motifs are tiny melodic fragments whose outlines return throughout the piece but exhibit many variants and metamorphose into new motifs. The quantifiable aspects of a motif, its metric, melodic, and harmonic shape, are fixed for an unpredictable duration. The repetition and reworking of the motif do not construct a melody or formal scheme but draw attention to the different harmonic, instrumental, and temporal contexts in which the motif appears. Each motivic instant is juxtaposed with the next, rather than evolving smoothly from one to the next, allowing the fault lines between them to be fully displayed. Each motif is rewritten back into the texture, caught up in and an agent of its own process. A motif is passed between different voices, transformed slightly each time, woven in and out of the texture and then recombined to form new variations, referring to its own limits and overstepping its own boundaries. For example, before the curtain rises on the scene two sections of musical material are introduced. There is a very slow, pianissimo 'Prélude' in four time and a Scherzando waltz (piano and pianissimo) that crescendos into a brief return to the 'Prélude' (Example 3.7).[60] The Scherzando is composed of various combinations of the foreboding and furtive staccato motivic shapes (a) and (b) (Example 3.6 (i)). A crescendo builds from 6 bars before figure 4, as (b) is extended into a snatch of the waltz theme (heard in violas and cor anglais) that will only be heard fully at the climax of the piece (Example 3.6 (ii)). But the crescendo recedes abruptly to pianissimo once more, heralding the return of the 'Prélude' for four bars. At the curtain rise (figure 6), a new motif (Example 3.6 (iii), (c) and (d)), a variation of (a) and inversion of (b) is heard in the clarinet, followed by different combinations and variations of (b) and (d) (Example 3.6 (iii)).

Elements (a), (b), (c), and (d) recur throughout *Jeux* in a variety of such arrangements and metric positions. Only motif (c)–(d), with its self-renewing, rising and falling contour, retains its identity. Its initial hearing with the rising curtain sets up the expectation that it will be the main motif. However, it constantly hovers between figure and ground. At figure 14 it is stated clearly in the clarinet, doubled by the oboe over a menacing form of (a) in 'cellos' and basses. From figures 21 to 22 it moves in and out of the foreground as a countermotif to the flighty dotted rhythms of the flute, but from then on it is alluded to only by fleeting fragments. It continues to weave in and out of the texture at figure 51, giving way to the waltz theme after figure 64 (Example 3.13) and later to the build-up of frenzied sound into figure 75. Eventually it disappears.

On the timbral level, oblique references to and echoes of timbres heard elsewhere in the work offer illusory *points de repère*. The brief section of the

---

[60] The rehearsal figures given in Example 3.6 and following correspond to those in *Images, Jeux and The Martyrdom of St. Sebastian* (New York: Dover, 1992), 206–323. While the extracts here are adequate, this analysis is most easily read with the complete score to hand.

Example 3.7 Debussy, *Jeux*, Figure 5

'Prélude' heard again before the curtain rises (Example 3.7) would point up a moment of calm repose in a quite expected development were it not for, amongst other things, its timbral differences from the opening bars (the shadowy suggestion of Scherzando elements in the string writing, for example). The original 'Prélude' pedal on an octave B remains in the second violins, but is now tremolo; the other string parts, including the cellos, prominent for their former silence, are now instructed to play *sur la touche*; their parts, a ghostly, slow-motion recalling of motivic material from the Scherzando, are now accompanied by timpani rolls. When at figure 29 the strings have hushed descending parallel chords, deliberately reminiscent of the opening 'Prélude', the listener has to rethink the opening as a beginning. For a few bars the reference back to the origin of the piece offers it as the home base, a point of reference from which the material will grow and to which it will return (see Example 3.8 (i)). For a moment the piece seems to promise organic coherence; yet the character of the reference is changed by the evocative cymbal note that shimmers before a mysterious, coquettish rising glissando in the harp (Example 3.8 (ii)). The celeste retains the mysterious timbre in the sudden switch back into the whispering fragility of string tremolo in 3/8 time, with nervous, melismatic chromatic flurries in the solo violin (Example 3.8 (iii)). Elements are brought together to create changes of mood and produce a fine and subtle synthesis.

Similar tensions between different frames of reference can be seen at the temporal level. Boulez writes: 'l'organisation générale de l'œuvre est aussi changeante dans l'instant qu'homogène dans le développement; l'œuvre a besoin d'un seul tempo de base pour régler l'évolution des idées thématiques, ce qui rend l'interprétation fort difficile, puisqu'on doit conserver cette unité fondamentale, tout en mettant en relief les incidents qui ne cessent d'intervenir.'[61] Driving the piece is the manic pulse of the Scherzando waltz first heard after the 'Prélude'. The fast 3/8 pulse (dotted crochet=72) is the constant temporal reference point of the piece, referred to as 'Mouvement initial' when it is required. Within the central pulse there are constant, sometimes very swift, relaxations and reintensifications in the tempo, marked 'Retenu', 'Sans rigueur', 'Cédez', 'Rubato', followed by 'au Mouvement'. Example 3.9 shows how swift these local temporal hesitations can be. The approach to figure 24 is in the 'Mouvement initial', the rapid 3/8. For two bars at figure 24 the tempo pulls up, aided by the lines over the staccato quavers indicating the heavy articulation required and the sudden forte dynamic. But the tempo is picked up again almost immediately and the dynamic drops dramatically down to pianissimo. Local rubato is dramatically expressive and never threatens the unity of the fast 3/8, if anything it confirms the precedence of this tempo.

[61] *Relevés d'apprenti*, 344–5.

Example 3.8 Debussy, *Jeux*, Figure 29

At some points then, sections that pull apart in every other way are held within the larger limits set by the constant quaver pulse. On a grand scale, metric changes seem to shape the ballet into a broad rhythm of sections. But events from different temporal worlds intervene at unexpected moments to upset the familiarity of the 3/8 pulse. Set against the three time, in the 'Prélude' initially are sections in two or four, more reminiscent of marches than waltzes. The 'Prélude' opens in 4/4 (crotchet=52) and only briefly interrupts the 3/8 Scherzando again until it is heard again at the very end of the piece. The fundamental tension between two and three time, however, persists.

At figure 29 (Example 3.8) an echo of the 'Prélude' is heard, although it seems all the briefer since it takes place in three time, at exactly half the speed of the 3/8. The contraction of time has quite a disarming effect on the listener,

Example 3.9 Debussy, *Jeux*, Figure 24 and preceding 5 bars

Example 3.9 *(cont.)*

Example 3.9 (cont.)

Example 3.10 Debussy, *Jeux*, Figures 32–3

Example 3.10 (*cont.*)

who is placed in the uncanny position of fully recognizing the motif yet finding it new and strange; there is a sense of *déjà entendu*. Yet when the 3/8 returns two bars later, the listener has to ask herself whether the surreal intervention was just a passing *trompe l'oreille* or whether it has actually changed the musical order. There is no comforting return of the old, familiar tempo. Instead the 3/8 has slowed to a more lethargic, dreamlike speed of dotted crochet=52.

From figures 32 to 33 (Example 3.10), three time and two time are more closely juxtaposed; in fact, they cut directly across one another in abrupt, unpredictable alternations (an example, perhaps, of one of Boulez's 'incidents qui ne cessent d'intervenir'). The slower waltz (mentioned above) builds into an expansive quasi-Viennese figure in the strings, marked 'Passionnément (sans presser)', which is then echoed by the cor anglais in a sustained six-bar ritenuto and diminuendo. Suddenly the tempo switches to 2/4 time, the value of the new crotchet equalling the length of the quaver in the slower 3/8 tempo. After six bars the 'Passionnément' waltz motif bursts out of the 2/4 march as quickly as it disappeared, for a brief four-bar interjection. No sooner than a waltz or march audaciously claims the musical foreground, it is cut short and challenged by a rhythmically dissonant passage.

Similar effects are achieved by mixing harmonic stylistic features. For example, after sixty-nine bars of chromaticism, a sforzando chord in trumpets, flutes, and piccolos (four bars after figure 8) suddenly opens up a field of triads (Example 3.11). The music literally jumps from what seems like the freedom of endless harmonic variation to a logic of fixed, organic formations for a few bars. It is as though this music is charged with a current that pulses with elastic brilliance.

3.9.1 Misleading plots

The scene takes place in a park, the action a chance encounter between two girls and a young man who woos them after he is first seen chasing a strayed tennis ball. After coy prevarication and displays of jealousy by each of the girls, the three eventually dance together to the climax of the piece, when they join in a triple kiss. The return of the stray tennis ball interrupts them and they disperse into the depths of the night.

Commentators who have read the musical events in *Jeux* as purely allegorical of events on stage overlook the importance and autonomy of the musical texture itself. Although they should not be ignored, much critical time is spent on puzzling over the choreographical instructions marked onto the score, and on proposing the plot as the simple motivation for the temporal changes in the music. Eimert, for example, claims that Debussy 'composed "along the text" with divine eloquence'.[62] Jann Pasler reinstates the scenario as an explanation

---

[62] 'Debussy's *Jeux*', 8.

of the effects of time and form in the music, assuming an unproblematic relation of the choreographical markings to the action 'narrated' by the music: 'The scenario of a tennis game provided Debussy with an ideal context for experimenting with time and form as functions of invention rather than as formulae.'[63] She also suggests that the way one motif links to the next is driven by the action: 'The motif in the oboe with the indication "marqué" just before 24 not only accompanies the young man's appearance on stage, but also comes to be identified with his invitation to dance between 25 and 26.'[64] Roger Nichols goes as far as to use the vocabulary of tennis as a rather overdetermined metaphor for the musical gestures: 'The vulgar forehand drive from the string section is deftly returned by a mysterious lob from the solo flute.'[65]

Example 3.11 Debussy, *Jeux*, Figure 8

[63] 'Debussy, *Jeux*: Playing with Time and Form', 61.
[64] Ibid. 69.
[65] *Debussy* (Oxford: Oxford University Press, 1973), 36.

Example 3.11 (cont.)

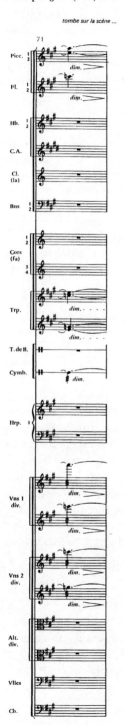

There is a sense in which the motivation for the music is so flimsy and superficial as to be ironic; there is a danger of its being taken too seriously. In fact the autonomy of the music's self-perpetuating progression vastly outstretches the relevance of its relation to particular actions. (Obviously there is a difference between what the listener to the orchestral ballet will perceive, what an audience might register, and what a reader of the score might note.)

A unique sound and time is created for each section of the ballet in the form of a new motif, a rhythmic variation, often following the same pitch outline, inverting the melodic outlines or juxtaposing two fragments of the motifs heard in the introductory section. The organization of the sections is broadly complementary to the plot of the ballet, although the sections are not by any means self-contained. The actions of the three characters on stage do seem to motivate the sectional organization of the work superficially.

However, the instructions can be misleading if treated as keys to the music. The absence of really precise directions means the central drama is in the music. For example, continuity between the sections is often challenged by sudden metamorphoses in the music quite unprepared by the plot, accompanied by constant relaxations and intensifications in the tempo and density of texture within the overall drive of the dance. The release from the triple kiss is so harmonically ambiguous in its irresolution that it just merges into a new musical flow, which we assume is leading us in a new direction. The music constantly bursts out of its fragile frame. The lack of musical closure at the end of the piece, for instance, makes the end of the action seem less a closure than just a dissipating from view. So, it could be said that, in fact, it is the music's 'action' that determines the character of the stage action.

Since ternary patterns can be found at all levels of the work, from the choice of metre to the suggestions of a ternary structure ('Prélude', 'Scherzando', 'Prélude') the drama of the three characters on stage begins to seem superfluous. These ternary suggestions are founded on a binarism: the 'Prélude' and 'Scherzando' are essentially the two conversant threads of the piece. This may in some broad, indirectly mimetic way reflect the boy–girls dynamic on the stage. On the other hand, it seems more that the inherently unbalanced pattern of two against three informs or generates both the plot and the music. There is no denying, of course, that Debussy composed to a given scenario. But the listener–viewer does not experience the theatrical patterns as more basic than the musical patterns.

There are other ways in which *Jeux* works against bits of frameworks implicit in its structure. Form is created by orchestral colour more than by traditional developmental and variational principles of tonality and functional harmony, yet the 'Prélude' provides a skeleton of conventional patterns of organization. The return to the 'Prélude' material at the end of the ballet serves as a kind of recapitulation, although it does not simply conclude what has gone before it but is also a proliferating echo. A snatched chromatic frag-ment leading back to the home key escapes beyond the recognized ending, raising a distinctly mischievous question mark to hover over it, now poised to tip back into the heady momentum of the piece.

On a melodic level, the listener's nostalgia for a full-bodied, Romantic orchestral sound is fed by snatches of phrases that seem to belong to a complete yet unheard lyrical phrase. Fleeting references to silence make the fragmentary moment become one of fulfilment, all the more ecstatic for its brevity. Barraqué notes: 'Le compositeur tient parfois compte de "développe-ments absents" comme si la musique s'était déroulée ailleurs, suivant un parcours logiquement déductif, mais se trouvant sapée, par interruption, en des tranches d'oubli.'[66] The snatches of waltz tunes that fade in and out of *Jeux*'s fugitive texture are the glimpses and prefigurations of the principal 'Viennese' waltz theme (Examples 3.6 (ii) and 3.10, for example). They suggest the presence of an external melody that is never allowed to intrude into the limits of the piece and be indulged to completion.

When all three characters finally dance together in the build-up to the triple kiss, the heady, merry-go-round waltz is allowed to surface for longer (three bars before figure 65 (Example 3.12)). This time, rather than following straight on from the regular four-bar passage, which slows up and crescendos in anticipation, the new theme is delayed by the hiatus of a fifth bar of breath-takingly sudden pianissimo (Example 3.12, four bars before figure 65, 'a Tempo') before shifting into the irregular five-bar melody in cor anglais, horns, and cellos (three before figure 65).

After thirteen bars—an odd number of bars prevents symmetry in the melody—and a diatonic cadential preparation in D♭, there is a dizzying modulation to B major, which sounds as an enharmonic change (a modula-tion via a whole tone from D♭ to C♭; Example 3.13). The theme then disap-pears slowly into the texture in truncated rhythmic shadows of its former self, against the dry staccato and pizzicato of the strings. This is the most marked occurrence of the constantly recurring pattern that forms the piece; no musi-cal signposts are set out to indicate its approach.

So far I have been suggesting that *Jeux* is working in various ways to create friction with the different types of telic expectation it sets up. Ruwet makes a very detailed study of the minute degrees of variation that exist between repeated fragments in Debussy's writing: 'Cette identité est souvent—si pas toujours—illusoire. . . . Sur les plans de la mélodie, du rythme, des timbres, des intensités, des modes d'attaque, la duplication introduit souvent des vari-ations subtiles, qui ressortent d'autant plus qu'elles se présentent sur un fond identique.'[67] The shadow of the unheard 'model' fragment, which gives rise to the motivic variations, serves as a telos, a lurking expectation. There is an

[66] *Debussy* (Paris: Seuil, 1962), 169.　　　[67] *Langage, musique et poésie*, 72.

Example 3.12 Debussy, *Jeux*, Figures 64–5

Example 3.12 (cont.)

Example 3.13 Debussy, *Jeux*, Figure 66 and preceding 6 bars

Example 3.13 (cont.)

implied original from which all the variations are derived, 'un fond identique', yet it is never stated.

3.9.2 Return of the arabesque

In *Jeux* 'courbes' or themes curlicue in and out of each other. Arabesque is the force of contrasting shapes and directions, the 'jeux' of *Jeux*.[68] There are several instances of arabesque in *Jeux*. For example, at figure 8 (Example 3.8) the insistently descending line is followed by a brief, sharply rising one that suggests the tennis ball. Three bars later (six before figure 9), the line tumbles down again. At figure 9, the direction of the motion is ambiguous, a turning on the spot (this can be seen in the flute line in Example 3.14). This motion evolves at figure 10 into a more defined melodic movement in the harps and violins.

A frequently occurring dynamic outline that has been discussed in this analysis is one that surges out of the texture and disappears into it again. This is a microscale version of what happened to the waltz theme (in the way it emerged from and re-entered the general mêlée at odd intervals). The undulating rise and fall in pitch in two-bar elements within the four-bar phrase is accompanied by a sudden crescendo to forte and decrescendo, often emerging from a texture of light staccato, marked 'piano' (in a wave-like contour also characteristic of *La Mer*, see Chapter 2). Four bars before figure 15 in the first violins, for example, a sudden rise in pitch and dynamic for a bar is followed by an eddying descent and diminuendo. This powerful surge of vertical movement creates a texture of varying crests and troughs, leaving linear time in suspension (Example 3.15).

Between figures 14 and 15, there are elements pulling in many different directions at once. The lower strings give four bars of the pulse rhythm, in almost as foreboding a fashion as the famous string passage from the opening of *Sacre du printemps*. The bouncing upbeat from the first scherzando, heard on the viola, is now simultaneously heard rhythmically augmented in the cellos. The violas give a mechanical, insistent beat, marking each of the three quavers of the bar. There is a wild tension, contained in a piano dynamic, waiting to be unleashed. Motifs from the Scherzando are added to each other without warning, in an effect of vertical stacking. The (c)–(d) motif is now in unison between clarinet and oboe. Irregular, fragmented time, as the listener has grown accustomed to it, appears to be squashed in a concertina motion. The texture is occasionally thinned when two lines coincide for a moment in unison. Any sense that the piece was progressing through rhythmic and melodic variation is upset as the motifs of the opening appear to have self-replicated exactly, yet

---

[68] As well as suggesting the tennis game, *Jeux* could also signify the 'play' of the text-score. *Jeu* is also a musical term for 'style' or 'technique'.

Example 3.14 Debussy, *Jeux*, Figures 9–10

Example 3.14 (*cont.*)

Example 3.15 Debussy, *Jeux*, Figures 14–15

Example 3.15 (*cont.*)

now in different places again. This could be a moment of startling clarity where patterns fall into place. But it is not accompanied by a sense of arrival in this case. Instead, we hear the void in the texture left by the point of union; it is passed over as an insignificant event. The result is the juxtaposition and combination of vertical-stacking and thinning effects in the density of the orchestral texture, which could be quite precisely expressed through the all-encompassing multiplicity and unity of the arabesque figure.

There is no question in *Jeux* of passages simply tumbling haphazardly into one another; rather, they are poised in arabesque-like grace. Jonathan Kramer writes: '*Jeux* is highly sectionalized to be sure, but the sections are as often in motion towards other sections as they are static.'[69] The excitement in this piece comes from brushing close to a collapse into chaos, from following a journey through critical complexity and from the grace and poise of the Viennese waltz being maintained throughout the succession of impulses, destabilizations, and recreations of new balances. The waltz would again become the subject of an orchestral work in Ravel's *La Valse* (1920). Feeding on elements of Johann Strauss's Viennese waltz, as well as tapping sources from Liszt, Chabrier, Debussy, Stravinsky, and Schoenberg, Ravel expands the dance in a mixture of grotesque, irony, and nostalgia with modernity. There is a new intensity to the vertiginous rhythms of the waltz, underpinned by fragmented and heady asymmetrical counter-currents and a pulsing, hypnotic stillness. The result is a grim and exhilarating parody that tries to see how far it can distort the familiar and conventional. It traces a direct lineage from *Jeux* in order to do so.

3.10 'LA TOTALE ARABESQUE': THE ORNAMENTAL PRINCIPLE

The arabesque is the moment of balanced tension in space and time when a fragment emerges from the texture and then returns to silence, at once emptying and filling the space in the text. In *Jeux* the arabesque manifests itself as a rupture in the texture caused by atemporal slippage, creating a gap in the texture in which the absence of the expected transition is felt, which it fills with a different rhythm, tempo, texture, or harmonic structure. The figure can provide a paradigm for those phrases or points in the music and poem that do several things at once, that change or tip semantically as you look at them or hear them. Both *Jeux* and *Un coup de Dés* are made up of these slippages, surprise shifts, and promises of reintegration.

The play between mobility and immobility that characterizes *Jeux* is also a fundamental part of reading *Un coup de Dés*. The desire for a forward impetus of reading in the poem is encouraged by the natural downward typographical

---

[69] 'Moment Form in Twentieth-Century Music', 177–94 (189).

contours on the page, but constantly deflected by the pulls of changing centres of gravity. The interruptions by the 'blancs' emit conflicting signals, causing moments of hiatus and hesitation.

In both works we are dealing with limits that are set and then need to be redrawn, units with strange autonomy, hovering between frames of reference and resisting categorization, and textures that set up a telos, a destination, and the rules of their own game in order to violate them or overstep their boundaries. The grammar of this ornament can describe these mobile, spatial events precisely.

3.11 DIFFERENCES

The terrifying threat of complete silence in *Un coup de Dés* is perhaps stronger than in *Jeux*. The sensuousness of the texture of *Jeux* is made more tantalizing by its permanent deferral, by endings that are left open and mysteriously unresolved; but moments of very sparse writing are not dwelt upon in the forward course of the piece. The limits of the temporal structure might vary but the chance retrospectively to construct is severely limited in comparison with *Un coup de Dés*. References back in *Jeux* are like subliminal appeals to the subconscious; hesitations take place within the distant world of musical events. Doubt and hesitation in *Un coup de Dés* is a more gnawing metaphysical doubt whose temporal power is not so controlling of the reader. He or she is free to be thrown into the 'tourbillon' with fewer guiding constraints than in *Jeux*. The promise of sonority and unity is sucked dry of its sensuousness and attractiveness by being drawn into the fear of the inescapable impossibility of the chance-abolishing act.

To summarize, the arabesques in each work are through-composed to differing degrees. Mallarmé makes the arabesque a site for the self-reflexive rhythms of expansion in the text, and of the shared structural performativity of music. The enactment of order and chaos in the arabesque finds form in the rhythm of grasping and releasing clusters of meaning. Debussy's 'critical' exposition of the figure is a lot less precise than Mallarmé's, although his 'frêles entrelacs' offer a point of structural similarity between Mallarmé's composition and his. In his music too Debussy seems to keep on the side of ornamental 'eurythmy' in his perception of the beautiful 'courbes', whereas Mallarmé favours 'complication'.

Silence, for example, although saturated in the semantic resonances that fill the 'blancs', is a more marked feature of the poem. The fragments of *Jeux* are linked in a more seamless *découpage*. The changes in temporal mode in the twists and turns of the arabesque are those that prevent the listener from hearing *Jeux* in the same way twice. These are recognizable in the experience of the reader who cannot find a fixed, external position from which to view the poem, but he or she never feels marooned in the same way by *Jeux*. Ultimately, the reading experience is a very different one.

3.11.1 Similarities

In the ascent, turning, spiralling, and bifurcating of the arabesque—recalling the impassioned description of the figure by Eduard Hanslick, quoted earlier—there is a shared, precise rhythmic articulation of the rising and falling, ordered and disordered space in both poem and piece. It is also the symbol of structure, as against the 'frêles entrelacs' of Debussy's Palestrina and the overarching coherence in conflict with local digression of Valéry's phrase 'le simultané de la vision avec le successif de la parole'. Since it has moved from being the non-essential figure in the margins of the work to being the structuring element, it shares at once the properties of the digressional, peripheral, and central, capturing the delicately fragile balance in the two works.

Derrida illustrates the phenomenon of mobility within a fixed structural framework in *L'Écriture et la différence*:

On perçoit la structure dans l'instance de la menace, au moment où l'imminence du péril concentre nos regards sur la clef du voûte d'une institution, sur la pierre où se résument sa possibilité et sa fragilité. On peut alors menacer *méthodiquement* la structure pour mieux percevoir, non seulement en ses nervures mais en ce lieu secret où elle n'est ni érection ni ruine mais liabilité. Cette opération s'appelle (en latin) *soucier* ou *solliciter*. Autrement dit ébranler d'un ébranlement qui a rapport au *tout* (de *sollus*, en latin archaïque: le tout, et de *citare*: pousser).[70]

Derrida's metaphor is of the cornerstone that gives both solidity and fragility. Moments that threaten chaos within the possibility of a coherent structure focus our attention on the structure's relative solidity at others.

Mallarmé's statement in *La Musique et les Lettres* harnesses both musical and poetic discourse: 'Je réclame la restitution, au silence impartial, pour que l'esprit essaie à se rapatrier, de tout—chocs, glissements, les trajectoires illim-itées et sûres, tel état opulent aussitôt évasif, une inaptitude délicieuse à finir, ce raccourci, ce trait—l'appareil; moins le tumulte des sonorités, trans-fusibles, encore, en du songe.'[71] Music and the poem in this instance can, in the manner proposed by Mallarmé, share the behaviour of 'text', by going beyond their own rules and transgressing their own limits. In 'Qu'est-ce qu'un auteur?' Foucault uses the term 'jeu', when discussing the self-reflex-ivity of the modern text, to describe the weaving of lines in and out of the textual or textural (in the musical case) framework that appears to circum-scribe them:

---

[70] (Paris: Seuil, 1979), 94.   [71] *OC* (M), 649.

On peut dire d'abord que l'écriture d'aujourd'hui s'est affranchi du thème de l'expression: elle n'est référée qu'à elle-même, et pourtant, elle n'est pas prise dans la forme de l'intériorité; elle s'identifie à sa propre extériorité déployée. Ce qui veut dire qu'elle est un jeu de signes ordonné moins à son contenu signifié qu'à la nature même du signifiant; mais aussi que cette régularité de l'écriture est toujours expérimentée du côté de ses limites; elle est toujours en train de transgresser et d'inverser cette régularité qu'elle accepte et dont elle joue; l'écriture se déploie comme un jeu qui va infailliblement au-delà de ses règles, et passe ainsi au dehors. Dans l'écriture, il n'y va pas de la manifestation ou de l'exaltation du geste d'écrire; il ne s'agit pas de l'épinglage d'un sujet dans un langage; il est question de l'ouverture d'un espace où le sujet écrivant ne cesse de disparaître.[72]

Such a notion of text seems to summarize the behaviour of the shared aesthetic features of *Jeux* and *Un coup de Dés*. It resonates with Mallarmé's vision of how 'vers' lends a crucial semantic dimension to music, which makes clear the extent to which his concept of the two arts is intertwined:

Par contre, à ce tracé, il y a une minute, des sinueuses et mobiles variations de l'Idée . . . (une réminiscence de l'orchestre); où succède à des rentrées en l'ombre, après un remous soucieux, tout à coup l'éruptif multiple sursautement de la clarté, comme les proches irradiations d'un lever du jour: vain, si le langage, par la retrempe et l'essor purifiants du chant, n'y confère un sens.[73]

3.12 CONCLUDING REMARKS

In *Jeux* and *Un coup de Dés* models of conventional musical and linguistic syntax have been radically reorganized in similar ways. It is clear how the resonance and recall set up in the poem by phonetic patterning and wordplay, the contingent display of language performing according to its own polysemic possibilities, which involves moments of mobilization and immobilization by withdrawal into and emergence from its own texture, can be applied equally to the behaviour of *Jeux*. In 'Sonate, que me veux-tu?' Boulez writes: 'Il nous appartient désormais—nous inspirant des exemples de Joyce et de Mallarmé—de ne plus concevoir l'œuvre comme une trajectoire simple, parcourue entre un départ et une arrivée.'[74] *Un coup de Dés* and *Jeux* are not works that follow a single course. They do not offer themselves as single objects of contemplation in relation to which a reader or listener assumes a fixed position. Boulez finds in this aesthetic the concept of a maze: 'La notion moderne de labyrinthe dans l'œuvre d'art est certainement un des sauts les plus considérables, sans retour, qu'ait accompli la pensée occidentale.'[75]

The opening and the ending mirror one another in *Jeux* although there

---

[72] Printed as 'Compte rendu de la séance', *Bulletin de la Société Française de Philosophie*, 63 (1969), 75–95 (77–8). [73] 'La Musique et les Lettres', *OC* (M), 648.
[74] *Points de repère*, 152. [75] Ibid. 153.

appears to have been random digression in between: a similar technique is exploited by Joyce in *Finnegans Wake* (1939), which ends so that the next word could be the first word of the book, giving a finite frame to what seems a realm of infinite possibility. Schoenberg's *Verklärte Nacht* (1899) begins in D minor and ends in D major, having undergone a radical transfiguration that is suggested in the title. The tortuous complexity of the harmony means that it cannot be described as a journey moving from a beginning towards the end. The ending of *Un coup de Dés* seems to promise a conclusion that brings the loose ends together ('Toute Pensée émet un Coup de Dés'), but in fact reopens the questions and points the reader back into the 'tourbillon' of the text.

But Boulez's maze is not a specific enough metaphor for the many directional energies of *Un coup de Dés* and *Jeux*. From my analyses, the figural motif or structure that best fits, and is shared by, the works is the arabesque. The arabesque is mobile, has dynamic space and works in three-dimensional non-linear space alongside the linear. It is adopted by literary and musical languages from the language of ornament in search of greater mobility in the text. Its status as ornament can be exploited by music and literature since it may be both inherent in the texture and additional to it. It can carry meaning from a suppressed central field and occupy the position of figure or ground, centre or margin, thereby embodying the structural process of boundary creation and transgression. Henri Focillon writes: 'Avant même d'être rythmé et combinaison, le plus simple thème d'ornement, la flexion d'une courbe, un rinceau, qui implique tout un avenir de symétries, d'alternances, de dédoublements, de replis, chiffre déjà le vide où il paraît et lui confère une existence inédite. Non seulement il existe en soi, mais il configure son milieu, auquel cette forme donne une forme.'[76]

Clearly, there is a parallel vocabulary in use in the syntax of ornament which is readily transferable to both works examined here. These twisting, expanding forms are dynamic features of each and can be used by both as a structuring device. In the architectural spaces Focillon describes, form is created by the breaking up of volumes, the play of empty space against shapes, the sudden gaps, and the collision of multiple planes. Mallarmé's poetic architecture is structured by a play between voids and complex reflections and by spatial planes and perspectives that generate various levels of meaning. Debussy's musical architecture is composed of the recessions and advances of motifs, colliding rhythms, expansions and contractions, and pulses in and out of sound. Focillon's ornament models space and confers on it a new and original existence. This is the function of arabesque on this intermediate ground. Arabesque is the directing force of intermediacy, describing the interplay in each piece and the inter-art interplay in the tight interlace of ornamental overburdening and nothingness.

[76] *La Vie des formes*, 36.

This arabesque does more than the figure taken by Nerval in *Aurélia* and *Voyage en Orient* to be the *mise en abyme* both of the writer's style and the writing process, and to be the form or mode of romantic expression through which to find aesthetic freedom and fantasy. This arabesque is transformed to pulsate with the flexions and curves of the sinuous, intricate, and complexly ordered paths cut by these two extraordinary works. Arabesque inhabits both the spiralling pull of the diagonals against the verticals in the poem and the carved-up flow of linear time in the snatches of waltz grasped quasi-simultaneously by the eye and the ear. Rhythmically and spatially the arabesque strongly inhabits time as it billows forwards and tips back again, bifurcates and conjoins in three-dimensional space. On the one hand, light, dancing trills, motifs, 'insinuations', 'écume', spirals, flurries, and curlicues take place in the arabesque's foliage. On the other, there is also a robust, linear, and planted telos of pulse, forward flow, recapitulation, recall, and return running through the arabesque. The intermediary embraces both sides of this opposition in the arabesque, which holds them in the exquisite poise of a delicately traced filigree.

4

SONG AND THE *ÉVENTAIL*

In song is to be found perhaps the most intense and immediate instance of the intermediary. It is the form in which the relationship between words and music becomes unmistakably the subject in the foreground. Poem and music are forced into very close, and sometimes uncomfortably close, contact. Some of the great composers of lieder in the nineteenth century turned to some equally great poets (although as often, of course, they were inspired by mediocre ones). Schubert set Schiller, Petrarch, Dante, and Walter Scott, among others; and both Schubert and Schumann set Heine, Goethe, and Shakespeare. Fauré composed poems by Hugo, Gautier, Villiers de l'Isle-Adam, Sully Prudhomme, Baudelaire, and Verlaine as song.

Vocal music is frequently interpreted along naive mimetic lines. A common model for song is to let the 'theme' of the text dictate what the listener 'looks for' in the music. It is this tendency Edward Cone tries to avoid with the methodology he proposes in *The Composer's Voice*.[1] If the distinction between author and narrator in literature, he asks, can be multiple and ambiguous, why should music not have such narrative voices? He writes: 'If an analogous element could be established as functioning in musical composition, it would save us from the kind of oversimplification that detects obvious suicidal intentions in Tchaikovsky Symphony number 6.'[2] Cone goes on, in his analysis of the narrative voices in Schubert's 'Erlkönig', to show that of all the potential combinations of voices offered by the poem, Schubert opts for the simplest narrative option in his version, that of a single narrator quoting dialogue. The problem with Cone's argument is that there is not necessarily reason to suppose, even if Schubert were this kind of reader, that the other narrative voices of the poem are subdued when the poem inhabits his music. Cone's example does illustrate well the complex criss-crossing of voices in the forum where text meets music, however: 'The art of song thus exploits a dual form of utterance, related to but not to be confused with the dual medium of voice and instrument. It combines the explicit language of words with a medium that depends on the movements implied by non-verbal sounds and therefore might best be described as a continuum of symbolic gesture.'[3] But Cone's

---

[1] (New York: Columbia University Press, 1957), 1–5.   [2] Ibid. 3.
[3] Ibid. 17.

theory of song is limited by his conception of text. 'A composer cannot "set" a poem directly', he writes, 'for in this sense there is no such thing as the "poem": what he uses is one reading of the poem—that is to say, a specific performance.'[4] Cone seems to be appealing in this to a Stanley Fishesque notion that there is no text *per se* until it is instantiated in an interpretation, reading, or, to use Cone's musical term, 'performance'. There is, therefore, no object for the composer to set other than his own reading of a poem. A musical instantiation, he implies, is a single reading, a particular performance or version of the poem that fixes it; contained in music, it is no longer able to disseminate along other semantic wavelengths. Cone's theory does not allow for the possibility that music might diverge altogether from any story told in the poem, or that music might not fix the poem, but instead open it to various kinds of interpretation. In addition, we cannot claim to know what kind of readers various composers were. Such approaches to song should not, of course, be discounted altogether, but neither are they satisfactory as the sole source of enquiry.

Susanne Langer's work on song in *Feeling and Form* went a long way towards shifting two oft-rehearsed commonplaces persistent in writing about song, that the music of song is an imitative footnote to the poem and that the musical setting of words acts as a supplement to insufficiently expressive poetic meanings. She writes, mindful of Wagner: 'Eminent aestheticians have repeatedly declared that the highest form of song composition is a fusion of perfect poetry with perfect music. But actually a very powerful poem is apt to militate against all music.'[5] Langer is motivated by a deep consciousness of the inadequacy of musical critical discourse for articulating the interlocked performance at the interface by music and poetry in song. She quotes, as an example, Schumann's youthful essay in praise of the union of music and poetry in song: 'Still greater is the effect of their union: greater and fairer, when the simple tone is enhanced by the winged syllable, or the hovering word is lifted on the melodious billows of sound.' Although her indignant response is rather undeserved in this case, her point is still important to make: 'This is typical literary musical criticism, that treats music as a soft romantic accompaniment duplicating the sound effects of poetry.'[6]

Langer argues, although 'the very powerful poem is apt to militate against all music', that song is an appropriation of the text rather than an imitation of it. A poem, once enveloped by music, loses its individual identity:

When words enter into music they are no longer prose or poetry, they are elements of the music. Their office is to help create and develop the primary illusion of music, virtual time, and not that of literature, which is something else. . . . When words and

---

[4] (New York: Columbia University Press, 1957), 19.   [5] *Feeling and Form*, 153.
[6] Ibid. 153–4. Schumann's essay can be read in *Gesammelte Schriften über Musik und Musiker*, 2 vols. (Leipzig: Breitkopf & Härtel, 1914), ii. 171–5 (173).

music come together in song, music swallows words: not only mere words and literal sentences, but even literary word-structures, poetry. Song is not a compromise between poetry and music, though the text taken by itself be a great poem, song is music.[7]

But the degree to which the text is swallowed varies according to the kind of poem it is. Some composers, like Beethoven, are excited by great literature, she argues, while others see a potential musical score 'in quite insignificant verses as often as in real poetry'.[8] Her point is, really, that composers choose poems for a whole host of reasons. In a sense, whether or not the words are emotionally trite need bear little on the musical outcome, as is the case with Schumann's sublime settings of Adelbert von Chamisso's poems in the cycle *Frauenliebe und Leben*. But, at the same time, Langer points out that certain types of poetry are more likely to be swallowed than others: 'A poem that has perfect form, in which everything is said and nothing merely adumbrated, a work completely developed and closed, does not readily lend itself to composition. It will not give up its literary form.'[9] Some fine poetry, however, is easy to set because 'the form is frail, no matter how artful, the ideas it conveys are not fully exploited'.[10] Certain poems will dissolve at the touch of an alien imaginative force; others, more dramatically built up, such as those of Goethe, will not. Perhaps Langer has Verlaine's ideal of musical verse in mind, that it should be 'Plus vague et plus soluble dans l'air', when she suggests that verse with an incomplete, fragile quality lends itself more readily to setting.

But how can the critic decide in each case whether or not the poem is solid enough to resist the will of the composer, or whether its frailty allows it to be overwhelmed and 'swallowed' up by the music? These do not seem adequate criteria upon which to analyse song, or to judge whether or not verse is annihilated in song. Clearly Langer's valuable work does not present a sufficient model for the music–text interface in song and could benefit from the help of a literary criticism that could not be accused of engagement in the subjective judgements of 'literary musical criticism'. While it may well be true that more 'robust' poetry is less easily overcome by music, from the listener's perspective, than other kinds, and that song is primarily about music not poetry, at a certain level of self-consciousness this does not tell the whole story about song. Perhaps when any poetry, even 'frail', enters the musical arena it does not lie down as easily as Langer and Cone would have it.

For Lawrence Kramer, the music of song becomes a kind of deconstruction of the poem. A composer may set a poem only by reinscribing it, so that 'a poem is never really assimilated into a composition; it is *incorporated*, it retains its own life, its own "body" within the music'.[11] Music enters into a

---

[7] *Feeling and Form*, 150, 153.   [8] Ibid. 153.
[9] Ibid. 154.   [10] Ibid.
[11] *Music and Poetry*, 127.

contest with the poem in the forum of song. The fusion of words and music is a simultaneous act of dissociation and violence upon the text, since the music overrides speechlike patterns of repetition and alternation. The singing of words alienates them from their spoken form. Above all Kramer emphasizes climactic moments in music, interpretative gestures expressive beyond the scope of the poem, which all but erase the words of the poetry.[12]

In a similar vein, Katherine Bergeron writes, in her essay 'The Echo, the Cry, the Death of Lovers':

Such a disintegration of the material word ... effects a release from language and certainly accounts for the pleasure—as well as alienation—one might feel on hearing a familiar text set to music. In other words, pleasure is produced by translating the relations that order the surface of the poem into a set of purely *musical* relations. Singing 'opens' the poem, allowing the boundaries of the word to be blissfully transcended, allowing speech to slip into new, unaccountable realms.[13]

Both Kramer and Bergeron equate moments of disarticulation with pure music. Such accounts still rest tacitly upon the assumption that the composer was foe not friend to the text. They do not give a sufficient picture of what lies under the mysterious and very different surfaces of songs and poems or an incisive analytical tool or model with which to do so. Approaches that favour the process of musicalization over the text as 'music' do little to enhance our understanding of the true complexity of the conflict and resistance between the two arts at this site of overlap. They fail to account, for example, for songs in which the impression is given that the voice is just one tone colour among many, as in Mahler's 'Der Abschied' from *Das Lied von der Erde*, for example. Mahler, like Debussy, paid scrupulous attention to verbal and poetic patterning in his songwriting, encouraging first and foremost structural assonance between poem and piece. There is much value in the work of Cone, Kramer, Langer, et al., but my own approach to song comes at the interface from a different angle, one which puts poem and music on a more equal footing, by looking at Debussy's settings of Mallarmé in *Trois poèmes de Stéphane Mallarmé* with the aim of opening up the musico-poetic tensions in song to critical view.

In song the specific syntactical, metrical, and phonetic frameworks superimposed in the poems are brought into conflict with a different set of musical frameworks. In each song the listener apprehends these layers simultaneously, each working at different levels, each complementing, transforming, disrupting, subverting, echoing, or challenging the other. Whereas a work like *Jeux* can be heard with no knowledge of the story from which it was born, the intrusion of the Mallarmé poem in each of the *Trois poèmes de Stéphane Mallarmé*

---

[12] *Music and Poetry*, 125 ff. Kramer uses the vocal quartet in the 'Ode to Joy' from the last movement of Beethoven's Ninth Symphony as an example of musical misreading of Schiller's allegorical symbol of Joy, and gives other examples from Schubert and Brahms.

[13] *Nineteenth-Century Music*, 18/2 (1994), 136–51 (144).

is unavoidable: each song is an epicentre of aesthetic overlap. Song is a place where music and text are brought openly together, creating patterns of similarity and difference. I shall examine what happens when the independent frameworks of the poem as poem and the poem as song are brought together in two of the *Trois poèmes*, *Soupir* and *Éventail*. The aim is to allow the complex interaction of the surfaces and insides of the poem and of the piece to give a detailed picture of the overlap as it takes place in song. Rather than reading song as a form in which the poem is engulfed by the music, or choosing to interpret the poem in song along simple mimetic lines, it is by looking at the level of their shared structural rhythms that we can have greater insight into the particular nature of this contact between music and poetry.[14]

4.2 *TROIS POÈMES*

Debussy had already achieved an extraordinary blend of music with speech rhythms in *Pelléas et Mélisande*, writing varied and flexible melodic contours in the vocal parts. He had emancipated discords and used their sonorous qualities as expressive in their own right. Treated as plain speech, the words of the libretto have an extraordinary theatricality and could not be further from the grand-opera style of a Gounod or a Meyerbeer.[15] When the lines are performed there often seems to be little 'singing' implied, an effect given by the relative lack of motivic or thematic shape, which makes moments of actual melody all the more striking.

It would be difficult to argue, therefore, that setting Mallarmé had a particular role to play in the development of Debussy's style, although Mallarmé must have offered the ultimate challenge to any composer who was as aware of the patterns and shapes of words as of music. Debussy's last encounter with Mallarmé had been between 1892 and 1894, when Debussy was working on *L'Après-midi d'un faune*. After this Debussy did not return directly to Mallarmé again until, in 1913, he wrote *Trois poèmes de Stéphane Mallarmé*, 'settings' of 'Soupir', 'Placet futile', and 'Autre Éventail de Mademoiselle Mallarmé', and it is unclear what exactly made him do so.[16] These songs offer

---

[14] What the audience actually hears of the poem in the song when performed may differ from the ways in which the overlap can be represented in criticism. One hearing might be coloured by the prior knowledge that these Mallarmé poems each yearn for an inaccessible woman. Another might interpret the poem's content in terms of the overall shape of the music. Rereading the Mallarmé might become a more directly musical experience if accompanied by echoes of the Debussy song. Questions there is no space to address here still need to be asked and have not been touched in the undeservingly small amount of writing there is on these songs. Why were these poems chosen in particular? What is the effect of placing three poems side by side in a form that the poet probably never envisaged?

[15] Robin Holloway notes the influence of Mussorgsky in the naturalness of the vocal part and the spontaneous orchestral gestures, in *Debussy and Wagner* (London: Eulenberg Books, 1979), 17.

[16] Ravel set 'Soupir', 'Placet futile', and 'Surgi de la croupe au bond' for voice and chamber ensemble in the same year.

a fascinating opportunity to unravel a moment when music and poetry are staged together.[17] It is clear that the powerful tonalities and sonorities born out of the radical reinventions of syntax and textual space in poetry were an important influence on Debussy's compositional palette. And nowhere other than in Mallarmé were these reinventions so radical.

In this chapter as in the last, I shall be using figures drawn from Mallarmé's critical prose and poetry, namely the thyrsus, *pli*, and *éventail*, to discuss the tensions, as well as the shared ground, between poem and music as they are brought to life by their intensified confrontation in song. As shown by arabesque, *enroulement*, *explosante fixe*, *éclat*, and Möbius strip, certain Mallarméan, and other, figures, if viewed as three-dimensional, dynamic, and abstract patterns, can be used as a way not only of reading his poetry but also of articulating the space shared by the poem and the piece. In turn this suggests a way of understanding the unseen text, or structural literary frames, in Debussy's music, to which very little detailed critical attention that indicates a clear understanding of Mallarmé has been paid. In particular it is the way in which Mallarmé challenged poetic language and ways of reading, through an increasingly fragmented textual medium, as well as his special awareness of the dual nature of music and letters, that are of special significance when considering the *Trois poèmes*.

4.3 FIGURE AND FRAGMENTATION IN THE LANGUAGES OF DEBUSSY AND MALLARMÉ

Figures that recur time and again in Mallarmé, enacted by specific textual manoeuvres, describe the abstract relational patterns shaped by *vers*, which, as Jean-Pierre Richard notes, 'il [Mallarmé] s'efforce d'apercevoir, en filigrane, derrière tout évènement sensible'.[18] The dynamic presence of the figures choreographs ways of reading Mallarmé, as we saw in Chapter 1, and allows us to reflect on the text's own status as literature. Mallarmé's vision of the twin intellectual process ('Ce procédé, jumeau, intellectuel') holds music and poetry in a joint architectural structure. Using this vision as a guide, it is a question here of identifying the 'rapports' set up by the proposed relation of simultaneity that shapes the music–poetry interface. My search is for the deeper underlying 'accords et significations' which, Mallarmé suggests, both conjoin music and poetry and constitute them individually.

---

[17] Mallarmé's poem 'Soupir' appeared in *Parnasse Contemporain* in 1866. 'Placet' was written in 1862 (marked 1762) and submitted to Verlaine for publication in *Poètes Maudits* in 1883. It actually appeared in an article by Verlaine before this in *Lutèce* in 1883. The final version 'Placet futile' appeared in *La Décadence* in 1886, revised in *La Revue indépendante*, with the Louis XV date suppressed. 'Éventail' appeared in *La Revue critique* in 1884 and *Le Décadent* in 1886 before being published in *Poésies* in 1887. I shall be considering 'Soupir' and 'Éventail' here.   [18] *L'Univers imaginaire*, 15.

For Mallarmé the new flexibility of the alexandrine, within its old para-meters, which he puts forward as his poetic aesthetic in 'Crise de vers', gives it a powerful claim to musical status. The fragmentation of verse is key to its shared status with music. The ear, 'affranchie d'un compteur factice, connaît une jouissance à discerner, seule, toutes les combinaisons possibles, entre eux, de douze timbres'.[19] He hears a corresponding dissemination of possible sounds within contemporary musical melody: 'D'ailleurs, en musique, la même transformation s'est produite: aux mélodies d'autrefois très dessinées *succède une infinité de mélodies brisées* qui enrichissent le tissu sans qu'on sente la cadence aussi fortement marquée.'[20] In the vaguely defined 'mélodies d'autre-fois', Mallarmé may have been referring to his perception of a pre-Romantic clearly orientated system of harmony in music, giving it a stability which Charles Rosen characterizes thus: 'What gives the motif its significance and its solidity in a work written between 1700 and 1900 is its movement within a symmetrical and stable structure defined by modulation away from and back to a perfect triad.'[21] In the emergent, new 'mélodies', as Mallarmé identifies them, motifs no longer have this solidity and stability. They enrich the fabric of the music while blurring and covering, in the stricter sense of 'cadence', regular and overtly recognizable rhythmical, metrical, and harmonic struc-tures.

This self-conscious and audacious claim of Mallarmé's for the outward alignment of music and poetry actually contains its own hidden counter-claim. On the face of it, the desire of Mallarmé's contemporary music to conceal and ambiguate its own rhythmical and harmonic frames of reference is shared by a literature that can engulf its own structuring skeleton, incorpo-rating and enveloping it as it unfolds:

Éviter quelque réalité d'échafaudage demeuré autour de cette architecture spontanée et magique, n'y implique pas le manque de puissants calculs et subtils, mais on les ignore, eux-mêmes se font, mystérieux exprès. . . . L'armature intellectuelle du poème se dissimule et tient—a lieu—dans l'espace qui isole les strophes et parmi le blanc et du papier: significatif silence qu'il n'est pas moins beau de composer, que les vers.[22]

Part of the art of poetry, or so we are led to believe, is for technical wizardry to slip seamlessly into the background, rather in the manner of the Flaubertian 'livre sur rien'. The use of the phrase 'armature intellectuelle' is far from arbitrary, since armature can be taken to signify a musical key signa-ture as well as, in this case, a poetic framework.[23] Nor is the armature always

---

[19] 'Crise de vers', *OC* (M), 362.
[20] 'Réponse à une enquête', ibid. 867 (my italics).   [21] *Schoenberg*, 50.
[22] 'Sur Poe', *OC* (M), 872.
[23] Mallarmé also uses the term 'armature' in 'Crayonné au théâtre' to capture the concurrent temporalities in dance, but it describes equally the textual blend of controlling framework and elements trying to escape it (see Chapter 2, section 2.1).

on the surface. It can indeed mean an external framing device, as in 'une charpente', but has an alternative sense, 'l'armature (du béton)', a trellis or gridwork of steel that is put into making a 'coffrage' (the support walls of a man-made channel or canal in the earth). In the second case the armature is an interior supporting device, the support of a support. Armature is a term that signifies an external and internal structure in one simultaneous apprehension. Alternatively expressed, the armature contains its own 'negative' version: it may be perceived in both its states (support or support of support) according to interpretation, like the black and white gestalt images that represent both a vase and two faces:

Écrire –

L'encrier, cristal comme une conscience, avec sa goutte, au fond, de ténèbres relative à ce que quelque chose soit: puis, écarte la lampe.

Tu remarquas, on n'écrit pas, lumineusement, sur champ obscur, l'alphabet des astres, seul ainsi indique, ébauché ou interrompu; l'homme poursuit noir sur blanc.[24]

Black and white, word and blank, language and silence, order and nothingness: these are the recurring oppositions in Mallarmé's metaphysical universe.

As a comparative term the musico-poetic armature works in so far as the silent architecture of the poem in the blank spaces (which, as we saw in the case of *Un coup de Dés*, can resonate with polysemic possibilities) has its equivalent in musical rests. Rests or silences in music are equally articulating and 'heard' as sounds. They can have rhythm or hold poignant tensions in play. Alternatively, they can be vehicles of obstruction that carry potential energy or echo with certain recalled sonorities. In both Mallarmé and Debussy the hidden armature seems to come hand in hand with, or as a by-product of, increased fragmentation.

This armature, then, is the site of unseen text in music and unheard music in poetry. In verse unheard music is created between or beneath new combinations of words and rhymes in overlapping and conflicting frameworks, which are developed to their extreme limits by Mallarmé at the end of his career. At once framing device and interior support, the armature presents a model of form that can be turned inside out and seen one way or the other according to interpretation. Simultaneous inside and outside surfaces are revealed in the manner of, for example, an early Cubist sculpture of a guitar by Picasso. Self-revealing and spontaneously evolving, the armature is a mobile structure, changing in appearance before the gaze and never locked into one position, opening out in a series of metamorphoses that can almost be viewed like sculpture. Delimiting surfaces are porous and shifting, giving the word and sound structures a sensed plasticity of form. Interlacing frameworks of sense, syntactical, metrical, phonetic, and semantic, engage the

---

[24] 'L'Action restreinte', *OC* (M), 370.

poem in this process of formal metamorphosis. To the ear, the mobile repetition of figures in Debussy and indeed Mahler means they reappear in ever-changing contexts. Themes appear and dissolve in an instant with the utmost flexibility, shifting from foreground to background, and changing their roles in the hierarchy of sound. In Debussy themes intrude upon and then retire from the patchwork of the texture in an almost perfunctory manner.

Here, guided by Mallarmé's shared architecture (armature) as musico-poetic model for song, I shall open out the differently interlocking and conflicting sets of structures (syntactic, metrical, phonetic, and semantic) at play within the poems and shaping them. Aligning these structures with an analysis of the composition of mobility in the music will enable us to look more closely at the particular force and nature of the meeting of music and poetry in these songs.

4.4 DEBUSSY'S *SOUPIR*

The first of the songs, *Soupir*, unfolds along an overarching line of accumulation and release of musical tension, according to the following broad dramatic plan.[25] The exposition is calm until 'Mon-te' in bar 13, when a slow building of uneasy tension starts. Bar 18 ('Vers l'Azur'), marked *en animant un peu*, is the broadest point in the song as well as the pivotal, central point in the poem, an energetic bursting out after the tightly contained and sparse pitch groups of the previous few bars, only for the mood to relax again shortly afterwards (bar 22). But the relaxation does not signal a final closure. Instead the pianissimo passage from bar 13 on a tightly rhythmic, repeated D♭, which was stopped short at bar 18, now resurfaces a semitone higher in a similar figure in the vocal line. Now back in the original tempo, the phrase reaches a bittersweet climax of a quite new quality on 'creuse' (bar 25). The final phrase is marked 'plus lent' for the dying 'long rayon de soleil', the parallel motion of voice with piano making for a stilted effect, disappearing to a triple piano dynamic at the end.

Fluid and asymmetrical in structure, the song is given phrases of irregular length by its changes of time signature. Features such as changes of tempo, and of dynamic, melodic, and rhythmic shape, mark out other sections of varying length in keeping with the line breaks and enjambements of the poem. After the introduction the piano is heard only against the voice, or else disappears entirely, until a moment near the end of the song (bars 26–7) where it is left alone in a link passage to the last section. Only in bar 30 is the piano's

---

[25] I shall refer to the Debussy song as *Soupir* and to the Mallarmé poem as 'Soupir'. The song is reproduced in full in Examples 4.1–4.3. This score should be consulted for the general references to the song that follow in this section.

opening figure (bars 1–2) recalled in the piano, in the same rhythmic configuration as the beginning (although the voice echoes the pitch outline of this figure at its first entry in bars 6–9). This time it is a more distant echo, taking up only two beats before its sonorous cluster dies away with the voice. This reappearance is enough to suggest in the mind of the listener that the closing passage has somehow resolved the tensions accumulated through the earlier harmonic indirections of the piece. But recalling the opening rising figure of the piece here does not actually resolve any ambiguity or provide the conclusion it should, because it is too short-lived. Instead the recurrence heightens the tensions by implying but not supplying a closure that the listener has not been led to expect or to need. It is a closing gesture that, by association with its former position, simultaneously reopens. The figure rises and hovers, held between these two gestures.[26]

4.5 MALLARMÉ'S 'SOUPIR'

Mon âme vers ton front où rêve, ô calme sœur,
Un automne jonché de taches de rousseur,
Et vers le ciel errant de ton œil angélique
Monte, comme dans un jardin mélancolique,
Fidèle, un blanc jet d'eau soupire vers l'Azur!   5
—Vers l'Azur attendri d'Octobre pâle et pur
Qui mire aux grands bassins sa langueur infinie:
Et laisse, sur l'eau morte où la fauve agonie
Des feuilles erre au vent et creuse un froid sillon,
Se traîner le soleil jaune d'un long rayon.[27]   10

At the heart of 'Soupir' lurk echoes of the Romantic topos in which the poet desires to reach the inaccessible/dead woman and needs to organize the poetic self, as a function of this desire, around the sexual deferral caused by the absence/death of the beloved. Eric Gans's discussion of the development of this topos in the post-Romantic lyric, poetic voice, starting from the celebrated model in Lamartine's 'Le Lac', is pertinent to 'Soupir'.[28] Gans outlines the development in the post-Romantic poetic self of 'its dependence on the Other's expulsion for its very existence'. The sign, he argues, is given origin

---

[26] The second song, *Placet futile*, which I do not have space to discuss here, has a quite different character. Debussy plays on the antiquated, precious rhythms of the minuet by interrupting their unperturbed regularity with more disturbing, dislocated phrases ('Nommez-nous', for example, bars 19 and 24). The elaborate surface of appoggiaturas, snatched motifs, and fleeting trills is constantly threatened by the silences around it, which build up a structural drama of their own.

[27] *OC*, 15–16.

[28] 'The Poem as Hypothesis of Origin: Lamartine's "Le Lac" ', in Christopher Prendergast (ed.), *Nineteenth-Century French Poetry: Introductions to Close Reading* (Cambridge: Cambridge University Press, 1990), 29–47.

by death, created from a locus of absence (as the Greek suggests, *sema* meaning 'sign' and 'tomb'), and holds a unique position in relation to the personal and the universal. In Mallarmé the 'Tombeaux' and the prominence of images of oceanic drowning suggest the reconstruction of the Other's death as the sole constitutive experience of the self. In 'Soupir' the Romantic aesthetic that locates the desire to expel the Other within the experience of a differentiated individual is stretched to its limit. The very category of the individual is problematic. Through the search for the woman the forces of desire are dislocated and generalized, as the traditional I–you rhetorical voice of lyric poetry is fragmented.

In line 1 the eyes, agent of the gaze, are suppressed in favour of a metaphysical entity, 'mon âme'. The contrast created by the physical presence of the 'calme sœur' is immediately dissipated through metaphorization. Her forehead is a dreaming autumn scattered with freckles or spots of russet light.

The unreliability of the relationship posited between 'mon âme' and 'ô calme sœur' is felt as it becomes subject to the power of the symbolic language as the poem progresses. As the trustworthy categories of the physical and real break down, so do the conventional poetic categories of voice and nature. These categories are allegorical poetic constructs, whose elements become forces in a mystical and symbolic network, the explicit material of which is shaped and coloured by the different nuances and moods of the suppressed fragments.

The whole sighlike breath of 'Soupir' unfolds in two sentences, the second of which is a reflection and expansion of the first. The syntactical patterns in which the sentence unit is laid out in the poem create different rhythms of reading. The traditional hierarchy of grammatical, syntactical, metrical, and semantic sense-making elements is upset to the extent that the reader of the last line, 'Se traîner le soleil jaune d'un long rayon', has had to construct a reading premiss entirely different from that promised by the opening lines. The metaphysical subject ('subject' indicates the poem's voice in this instance) is juxtaposed closely with the physical body of the 'calme sœur' by leaving the verb, which in conventional syntax would follow the subject, until the beginning of line 4. The desire for a verb following 'Mon âme' is instilled from the beginning of line 1 ('vers ton front'). However, this vector is suppressed in favour of a verb and adjectives that create an undercurrent of tension with the desired movement, such as 'rêve', 'calme', and 'jonché'. The two former are languid and still, whilst the latter scatters and fragments the colour of the metaphor.

The adjective 'errant' deflects the direction suggested by the rising arc of 'vers ton front'. The deflection is mirrored syntactically and semantically by the search for the subject of 'errant' necessary at this point. 'Le ciel', a conventional Romantic image for a transcendental abstract truth, seems unlikely to be 'errant'. If the 'œil angélique' is the subject, then the verb has been displaced and invested directly in the metaphor for the eye, 'le ciel'. A third possibility is that the 'âme' is 'errant': not clearly placed in the *moi/toi* dialectic of the lyrical voice, it searches for another Other to construct. The prepositional phrase that follows quickly excludes this option, but the mere suggestion of so many choices for 'errant' shocks, excites, and causes doubt.

Locating the voice of the *je* in 'âme' sets the poet's quest for the woman on a spiritual plane that descends immediately to the level of the woman's body, introducing a clear sexual tension. The woman's body can be perceived only in two fetishized fragments, 'front' and 'œil'. The relation of the poet to the 'sœur' is ambiguated by the Platonic and sexual potential held in tension by this name. Coupled with this, the overloaded Romantic connotations of 'automne' suggest the lassitude of the latter stages of life in direct contrast to the taut fetishization.

The adjective 'calme' suggests a still pose, perhaps sleep. But in spite of the visual suggestiveness of the adjective, the aperture of the poetic 'âme' allows an intensely focused view only of the 'front' and the 'œil'. Whereas in traditional lyric rhetoric the woman is often absent from the scene, leaving an empty centre filled by the poet watching from the periphery, here the boundaries of centre and periphery are not clearly delineated. The reader can be aware only of a distant, ambiguously related woman as a locus of fragmentation—a fragile springboard for the leap upwards of the sigh, if this is to be ecstatic. From the beginning the mood of loss, deferral, and dissatisfaction is engendered by this subtle play of suggestion and contradiction.

The traditional Romantic topos of nature is introduced and treated in quite disarming ways here. In 'Le Lac', the lake and its surroundings are in structural harmony with the inviolable forces of desire of the poem. In 'Soupir' nature undergoes a metonymical transformation into the woman. The woman's body parts are immediately metaphorized, shifting with no warning into the 'natural' frame of reference: 'vers ton front où rêve, ô calme sœur, | Un automne jonché.' The poet's soul moves upwards to an isolated part of his subject's anatomy. It wanders, although its own movements and location become bound up as part of her metaphorical space ('le ciel errant de ton œil angélique'). There is no fixed scene in which this mixing occurs: the detached, generalized forces of desire strain against the apparently tight control of the chiasmus. The absolute desire to transcend, expressed in the opening by 'Mon âme', is mediated or deviated by the feminine presence.

All these elements are forerunning strands of the tendency, which will become much more highly developed later in Mallarmé's career, to make every element of the text take part in its own process of enactment through an absence of fixable external referents, and through the use of insubstantial metaphorical frames. The contrast between the ease of transition into metaphor and the marked leverage into the simile draws attention to the fragility of the comparison and of poetic language. This is underlined by the shifting positions of syntactic and metrical patterns into and away from the foreground. Semantic deferral finds a local enactment in such metrical and syntactic cross-rhythms.

In syntactic terms, delaying the verb and the simile in the poem places expectation on the simile for clarification, especially as 'comme' receives special emphasis, following 'Monte' after a comma. The blurring of abstract and concrete in the early lines of the poem is a continued tension as the expected concretizing power of the simile is undermined by the juxtaposition of 'jardin' with 'mélancolique'. The image is of the soul as fountain reaching faithfully and diligently for the sky but being pulled back to earth again in a slower, repetitive motion: a sigh that is long and yearning but never satisfied. The adjective 'Fidèle', standing alone in the line like 'Monte', has to be reinserted into the poem, since it has been detached from its logical syntactic slot following 'Mon âme' or 'Monte'. Thus displaced, it invades the domain of the simile, upsetting its potential for explanation and concretization.

Metrically, the lie of the syllables in each line of verse creates certain accentual patterns that can be at odds with those created by the syntactical framework, sometimes falling with them but sometimes providing an alternative rhythmic sense. For example, the first alexandrine has syllable measures of 2+4+2+4, suggested by the underlying syntactical grouping, which are accented as follows: 'Mon **â**:/me vers ton **fro**nt//où **rê**/ve,ô calme **sœur**'. But the elision between 'rêve' and 'ô', which maximizes the voluptuous potential of the /v/ phoneme to contribute to the dreamlike flow of the two hemistichs, is disrupted by the syntactical break, which almost forces the *e atone* into an autonomous third syllable, making a *coupe lyrique* ('où rêve,/ô calme sœur'). By the end of the line the hemistich seems to vacillate between the six syllables suggested by the metre (2+4) and the lengthened seven suggested by the syntax (3'+4). Since 'où rêve' is in the complementary position in the second hemistich to 'mon âme' in the first, the reader is taken back to the beginning of the line. There is similar doubt about the length and accentuation of the *e atone* of 'âme', which could, equally, be read as needing the fullness of articulation of the *coupe lyrique*. The '-me' syllable seems to detach itself on a path towards 'ton front'.

In the second line, the breadth of the 'calme' instilled by the languor of the first line pervades (3+3+2+4) in the unbroken noun phrase of the first and second hemistichs: 'Un autom/ne jon**ché**//de ta:/ches de rou**sseur**'. The regular syllabic punctuation suggests an aesthetically pleasing regularity to the scattering ('jonché') of the 'taches de rousseur'.

The metrical accent at the end of line 3 (4+2+3+3) does not coincide with a syntactic break and completion, since the enjambement leads the syntactic group into line 4: 'Et vers le ci**el**/er**rant**//de ton **œil**/angé**li**que | **Mon**te,/comme dans un(//)jardin /mélanco**li**que'. For expressive and syntactic reasons, the *e atone* of 'Monte' makes a *coupe lyrique* to give a rhythmic pattern of 2'+6+4 in line 4. Only the ghost of a caesura is present since the syntactical group runs across the hemistichs.

In line 5, 'Fidè/le, un blanc jet **d'eau**//sou**pir**/e vers l'**Azu**r!', the metrical pattern appears to be 2+4+2+4 but the syntactical break after 'fidèle'
suggests the *coupe lyrique* grouping of 3'+4, creating a vacillation between six
and seven syllables similar to that in line 1 with 'rêve, ô'. Thus the reaching
'vers' feels constantly checked, in keeping with the fountain image; the 'whole'
is not reconstructable.

The simile arriving in the middle of the poem offers itself initially as a key
to solidifying the sense of the earlier lines and uniting the abstract soul with
the physical body of the 'calme sœur'. Its climax , 'vers l'Azur', arrives in the
middle of the ten lines, a pivotal moment from which reading the poem now
takes place, backwards and forwards from the middle, to form a whole semantic picture. It is also the point at which the long rising arc of the opening lines
begins to take a turn into a long, drawn-out fall. Lines 5 and 6 mirror the
symmetry of the poem's overall structure. They offer the model of a poem
that can be read in two halves, a structural manifestation of the binary struggle the poet feels between the Absolute and the physically real. However,
rather than act as a clear point of separation, the central boundary becomes
a line across which the reader is constantly having to move back and forth, to
re-evaluate one half in terms of the other. This happens on a more localized
level in the blurring of clear absolute and real categories in the opening lines
and the integration of the poetic self into the metaphorized body.

Reflection becomes an important part of the second half of the poem. The
verb 'mire' has 'l'Azur' as its agent, although 'bassins' are the passive recipients of reflections, especially as 'l'Azur' is softened by 'attendri'. The expanding simile that frames the poem structurally from within (an internal
armature) creates a downward movement since the Idealistic, Romantic
connotations of the spiritual paradise, the blue heavens of 'L'Azur', are
starved when the sky assumes the neutral colourlessness of the 'jet d'eau'. The
dislocated 'âme' of the subject, in its search for the Absolute via the 'calme
sœur', is not satisfied with a vantage position from which it can fully appreciate and reach into one and the other; rather it enjoys the sensation of being
straddled impossibly between the two and the frustrating impossibility of
reaching or constructing the woman through poetic mimesis.

In the second section of the poem there is almost a mirror image of the
syntactical pattern of the first. Now the verbs fall in more expected syntactical positions and the suppressed relative pronoun 'Qui' appears. Disjunction
is caused by the chiastic reversal of 'aux grands bassins' and 'sa langueur
infinie'. The subclausal interruption following 'Et laisse', however, leaves the
qualifying infinitive until the beginning of the last line, embodying the lazi-
ness implied in 'Se traîner le soleil jaune'. Delaying the verb that comple-
ments 'la fauve agonie' until line 9 ('erre'), means that it is placed in
disarming juxtaposition with 'Des feuilles', leaving the reader to search
around for a singular agent for the verb.

Just as 'ciel' is invested with the mobile property ('errant') of 'œil', in lines 8–9 the autumnal 'feuilles' are made capable of intense 'fauve agonie'. It is the 'fauve agonie', not the 'feuilles', that is the subject of line 9; the attributes of the autumnal 'Azur' are displaced by pure feeling, whose agent is no longer locatable. 'Agonie' is a detached, floating force in the poem, which has the deepest impact ('creuse un froid sillon') whilst the other verbs in lines 6–10 (for example, 'mire', 'laisse', 'erre', 'se traîner') are static and passive. The simile reaches the crux of its deathlike despair in the 'sillon'. The 'sillon' is furrowed into thin air, marking the real hollowness of the simile, which the breath of the 'soupir' fills and empties in the poem.

The metre creates cross-rhythms across this continued, intensified, exquisite sensation of dislocation through semantic and syntactic deferral. Lines 6 and 7 can be scanned in this way: 3+3+4+2 | 2+4+3+3, making the enjambement between the two lines their point of mirror reflection (as well as the action of the verb 'qui mire') '—Vers l'**Azur**/atten**dri**//d'Octobre p**â**/le et **pur** | Qui **mi**/re aux grands ba**ssin**s//sa lan**gueur**/infi**nie**'. The second hemistich of line 7 has the seamless rhythmic continuity appropriate to 'langueur infinie', set up by the long four-syllable measure of 'd'Octobre pâle' (whose length is highlighted by the short following 'et pur'). In line 8 'morte' receives a strong accent at the caesura and is elided into the next hemistich: 'Et la**i**sse,/sur l'eau **mort**//e où la fau/ve ago**nie**' (3'+3+3+3). This elision, in addition to supplementary lingering produced by a *coupe lyrique*, stretches the tempo, allowing the line fully to express the deadness of the water. The regular rhythm of the measures infuses this and the following line with a deepening sense of cold futility. In the last line, the syntactical group is stretched over the expected break of the caesura, creating a rhythmic pull between syntax and metre: 'Se traî**ner**/le soleil(//)**jau**/ne d'un long ra**yon**' (3+4+5). The ghost of the caesura means that on a first reading 'jaune' appears dislocated from 'soleil' until a rereading helps the line settle into the syncopated rhythm of an *alexandrin trimètre*.

The drama underlying the poem is excitingly clear. It is about whether or not the woman can be reached, and, if so, whether that outcome is desirable. The excursion into metaphor is at once a path 'vers l'Azur' and an obstacle. Touching or seeing the body is substituted in the poem by the intellectualization of its parts. It may quite simply be more pleasurable to allow oneself to be led into poetic activity than to seek the whole woman.

4.6 WHEN 'SOUPIR' BECOMES SONG: CONFLICTS OF SIMILARITY
AND DIFFERENCE

Debussy's music in the song seems to treat the poem in ways that, far from dissolving language, preserve it by representing it. For example, some words that receive metrical emphasis in the poem are highlighted by one musical device or another. This can happen on the simple level of word-painting. 'Jonché' is dramatized by the staccato, rhythmic pulling of the quaver triplet in the piano. As set up by Debussy, 'creuse' penetrates the musical texture by lingering on a minim and rising a third in pitch. In the poem, 'l'eau morte' is given apparent length by being stretched over the caesura. Musically the effect of 'morte' is achieved by the triplet rhythm and repeated D♭ on 'morte où la'. The melodic shape can adhere closely to the poetic accent. The instances of enjambement of the second half of the poem, for example, are mirrored precisely in the articulation of the song's phrasing.

William Austin observes in his analysis of Debussy's *Syrinx* that 'a leap down to a pitch from the next nearest note' and a 'wide leap up to all that follows it in the phrase' causes the pitch to linger in the memory.[29] The final pitch rise of the melodic phrase leading to 'sœur' in bar 9 accentuates the rhyme word, and is as distinctive as the poetic break away from the repeated phonemes of the rest of the line. Words stressed in the original text are often placed at the beginning of a bar in the song to receive musical stress. This accounts to a degree for the fluctuating time signatures: the metrical time needs to be elongated or squeezed to fit the demands of the poetic metrical stress. The melodic line almost always religiously follows a 'note per word' principle, which means that moments in which pure music dominates over the words do not occur. Yet there are moments when the melody overdetermines certain words, as in bar 11, where the music allows the poetically insignificant and monosyllabic 'le' two quavers.

The enjambements of the poem are also respected by the song's corresponding musical effects. For example, 'Mon-te' is hooked in two crotchets onto the end of a bar, which incorporates them by switching to five crotchets in a bar. This metrical elongation marks the fact that the syntactical group at this point in the poem spills over the edge of the metrical line. The technique works well here because of the dislocation of the verb. The difference between the musical and poetical enjambements is more evident in bar 22, where 'et laisse' is a continuation of a bar which begins with the rhyming syllable 'nie'. It loses the force it has in the poem by being at once an opening and closing gesture, finishing the last line syntactically but starting a new one metrically.

4.6.1 Directions of listening

The upwards flurry of rising fifths in the opening piano figure ((*a*), Example 4.1) stretches away from the originating E♭, hovers at its peak (F, an interval of a ninth), and is then mirrored by a descent to its starting point (bar 2), from

---

[29] *Music in the Twentieth Century: From Debussy through Stravinsky* (New York: Dent, 1966), 10–11.

Example 4.1 Debussy, *Soupir*, bars 1–11

which it stretches a ninth again and descends a second time at half speed. Bars 4 and 5 are diminished echoes of the rising figure played up an octave, only this time no mirroring resolution is heard. The piano opening, then, sets up a very bare melodic line, based on a repeated rise–fall shape and pattern of fifth intervals. The rising echoes (bars 4 and 5) are supported by little local decrescendos and a gradual overall decrescendo and float over a grounding dominant to tonic left-hand figure, which gives an impression of A♭ major (*b*). This figure, usually heard in a cadence signalling closure or semi-closure, seems pre-emptive here, and creates a feeling of destabilization from the outset. Such patterns of unresolved hesitation, combined with the fact that the series of fifths does not fix itself harmonically, evacuate from the introduction any sense of leading to a pre-defined place.

The vocal line moves almost entirely by step or in thirds, from which exceptions stand out clearly. It oscillates within the octave ranges of E♭–E♭′ and F–F′.[30] From bars 6 to 10 the line moves within the E♭ octave, falling towards 'jon-ché' only to be pushed up a tone higher this time as it rises, to F′ (mirroring the pitch range of a ninth of figure (*a*)). In these bars the vocal line also follows the rise and fall shape of the opening figure (*a*), rhythmically and melodically imitating the rising triplet figures (bar 7 (*c*), for example, inverted in bars 9 and 11). The rising minor third (*d*) in bars 8 and 9 recurs inverted later in the piece, with the result that, over this section of the song, lyrical, sweeping gestures seem to anticipate their own dissolution.

The accompaniment reinforces the stasis of the restricted vocal line with long, held, repeated chords. The repetition of bar 9 in bar 10 keeps a rein on the ascending melody. Dissonances, such as the diminished chords in these bars, contain a range of possible resolutions, hovering with ambiguous promises and possibilities, but fulfilling none of them.

Extended over a longer bar of five crotchets, the line seems to linger over a falling third, a stark opposition to the sense of the word it sets, 'Mon-te' (bar 12), which signals the change of mood to come and holds in a simultaneous conflicting pull the upwards and downwards musical directions (Example 4.2). From the beginning of bar 13, tension builds in a three-against-two rhythm between voice and piano, whose disjunction will become more and more uncomfortable as the piece progresses. The E♮ from 'Mon-te' is transferred into the accompaniment in sustained dissonance with the rest of the harmony. The chordal movement in the left hand is awkwardly stilted and anchored. The right-hand E♮ octave staccato triplet leaps (*e*) work against the low repeated D♭ in the voice that rises to a dissonant E♭ at the end of bar 13 ('comme dans un jardin mélancolique'), and are sustained unrelentingly over the following five bars. The flatness of the vocal line at bar 13 (*f*) makes a stark contrast with the rise–fall movement of bars 1–12. The broad sweeps of the opening figure have dissolved into an agitated rhythmic ostinato, neither stable nor dynamic, a small-scale movement that prevents large-scale harmonic movement.

There is an impending sense of urgency in all this contained movement, which suddenly breaks loose in the miniature melodic rise, hesitation, and fall on 'Fi-dè-le!' (bar 15). More patterns of surge and subsidence follow, at 'un

---

[30] F′ indicates the F an octave higher than the F above middle C.

Example 4.2 Debussy, *Soupir*, bars 12–20

blanc jet d'eau soupire vers l'azur' (*g*), for example, but in this case the accompaniment remains stable, not following where the voice leads. 'Azur' (bar 17)
is left in midair as an unanswered question as the mood is changed by the
insistent octave repetition falling downwards, finally releasing its grip. The
left-hand dominant-to-tonic figure (*b*), which has been submerged in the
texture from bars 13 to 18, is now restated in more comfortable tonal
surroundings (bar 18). At last the accompaniment is freer from bars 18 to 22,
now moving in quavers with the melody. The expansive warmth comes as a
relief after the austerity of the last passage. The three-against-two rhythm
subsides into the more fluent dotted-crotchet figure on 'Octobre' (bar 19),
which is a melodic high point in the piece (*h*). At the climax of this passage
the three-against-two rhythm reaches the height of its syncopation and
disunion, when stretched over the crotchet triplet (*c*), colouring the 'in-fi-nie'
(bar 21, Example 4.3) with emptiness.

In bar 23 a permutation of (*f*), the haunting, flat quaver and triplet rhythm
on a repeated pitch, returns a semitone higher ('sur l'eau morte où la fauve
agonie'). The tempo is gradually released by a 'cédez' to 'plus lent' from bar
26. The three-against-two rhythm between voice and piano from bar 27 to the
end feels lazy in this new tempo ('se trainer le soleil jaune'); finally an inversion of (*b*) is heard in the vocal line, now clearly cadential but still echoing the
rise–fall pattern, and the opening figure (*a*) returns in the piano to close the
piece.

4.7 READING 'SOUPIR': TOWARDS DEFINING THE INTERFACE

Externally, 'Soupir' the poem has two clear directions of reading suggested by
its semantic content. One is a compact structure of neat antitheses and mirror
reflections that support the 'âme'–'sœur' relationship, initially set up as a
binary opposition. The poem's second semantic direction is in tension with
the first. As the reaching 'vers l'Azur' is further sustained in a continually
checked movement, the hyperbolic vision of the impossibility of reaching
'l'Azur' becomes increasingly stratospheric in its demandingness, matched by
the strength of the pull between vision and reality.

In order to perform the docking manoeuvre required to bring poem and
piece side by side I shall revisit some of the earlier analysis here. Synthesizing
the main lines of argument and placing them together here will allow the
layout of the intermediary to start taking shape.

4.7.1 *Linear improvisation*

In 'Soupir', it will be remembered, two strains of poetic development run
concurrently. Running against and simultaneously with the horizontal

Example 4.3 Debussy, *Soupir*, bars 21–31

inside–outside conflict between poetic subject and the object of desire (the woman or 'l'Azur') is a vertical pull running through the poem. On the one hand there is a longing for escape from the constantly frustrated desire for 'l'Azur'. On the other hand, formally the simile ('comme dans un jardin mélancolique') provides a linguistic frame in which the *moi* and *toi* can be held in equal relation. But even this balance is offset by diverging forces. The initial suppression of 'sœur' in favour of 'rêve' is continued until dream dominates over the physical in the poem. The mid-point (lines 5–6) marks a transition of focus from an exploration of the 'âme' to the ideal but impersonal and inaccessible 'Azur'. Thus there are two paths offered for a reading of 'l'Azur': one to read an extended metaphor for the woman and the other to replace the woman with an abstract ideal. Each involves following the constant disruption of apparently fixed dualities in an increasingly deep maze of semantic suggestion. Syntactical devices such as inversion and suspension, for example, operating on a figural and grammatical level, disrupt and confuse the clear distinction of the inside–outside binary model of the 'âme'–'sœur'.

The vertical pull running through the poem is exemplified by the action of the 'âme', which is characterized by the upwardly reaching words 'rêve', 'angélique', and 'ciel errant'. This tendency for 'rêve' suffers a sharp pull down when it meets the 'calme sœur', physically rooted in the 'front' and the 'œil'. The syntactic suspension of 'Monte' and 'Fidèle', the adjuncts of the 'âme', leaves the action of the 'âme' similarly in suspension, unresolved, and detached in its pursuit of the higher reality. In its suspended hyperbolic flight, the soul brushes over the 'sœur', who is reduced to two specks on the autumnal landscape (the 'front' and the 'œil') and almost disappears.

At the same time, the metaphorical treatment of the poetic 'âme' and 'sœur', which links their substance inextricably, means the place of both is central. (They are also centrally placed in lines 5 and 6.) The two terms of the simile 'un blanc jet d'eau soupire vers l'Azur' (where 'l'Azur' could be replaced by 'sœur', 'front', or 'ciel de ton œil') frame the central fold of the poem vertically from lines 5 to 6 in the repetition of '—Vers l'Azur', and horizontally within line 5 itself.

4.7.2 *Linear improvisation in song*

The important distinction between Mallarmé's 'Soupir' and Debussy's treatment of it lies in their fundamentally different frameworks of organization. Mallarmé's poem is essentially a fixed form with more mobile structures occurring within and against it. Debussy's version of the poem is more improvisatory and less contained than Mallarmé's, although never straying far from the closely linked motifs and pitch ranges running through it.

The song is dependent upon the narrative of the poetic text as a way of organizing itself, although the temporal framework of the song is not symmetrical and fixed like that of the poem: rather it is made fluid by following the accented and rhyming words of the poem. Whereas in the poem the strong symmetrical frameworks, such as metre and rhyme, contain looser, more mobile ones such as hesitation, dislocation, and suspension, in the piece there is no fight against a retaining frame, but rather a search to find a guiding framework outside itself in words.

The fundamental experiences of reading Mallarmé and reading Mallarmé as stage-managed by Debussy differ widely. Silences in the *découpage* of motifs in Debussy, an undulating flow of interpolated fragments, are fleeting and even violent, as we saw in Chapter 2 in the case of the *Préludes*. But they never have quite the same impact as the angular, blank silences the reader encounters in Mallarmé and that stop him or her in her tracks. The changes of time signature and the rubato, as well as the undulating phrase shapes, make the music seem infinitely supple. The first line, for example, takes time over 'âme vers ton' written as a minim and crotchet triplets, and skips over 'front où rêve', with an expressive freedom that the alexandrine cannot quite achieve. The musical line is not held within a regular constraining metre (the metre moves freely between two, three, four, and five crotchets in a bar). Where the poem takes a natural breath at the comma ending the first line, the musical line avoids such emphasis. 'Sœur' arrives at the top of the musical phrase that falls naturally on to 'un automne' as though it were part of the same poetic line. A performer can take a breath after 'rousseur', since the line of the music aims towards the closure of that semantic group, within the forward-moving pulse of the piece, before starting the tentative descent of the next line, 'le ciel errant'. A recitation of the poem might well do the same thing, given a natural pulse by the metre. But without the expressive rises and falls of musical phrases, the voice has a more monotonous pitch and is more heavily reliant on the phonetic effects of the words to produce the atmosphere and drama, where the singer can work with pitch and the piano accompaniment.

In spite of these fundamental differences, the pushes and pulls that are concealed and revealed in a reading of the poem are also manifest in the song. Separate sections of the piece have their own isolated motifs, such as 'Fidèle!' and 'un blanc jet d'eau soupire vers l'Azur', for example, whose undulating rise–fall phrase shapes give great temporal freedom to the line. The melodic contours are articulated by rests that have no particular musical logic of their own, to the point where each seems a disembodied breath. The sense of distance from the voice and suppressed sensuality is brought about in part by the hushed dynamics, mostly pianissimo and never more than piano. Passages of near-monotone chanting, on 'comme dans un jardin mélancolique' and 'sur l'eau morte où la fauve agonie', for example, increase the sense of coldness. Their linearity offers a stark contrast to the temporal freedom of the other vocal phrases. At the same time the similarity of all the vocal musical material, in terms of the restricted pitch range and repeated rhythms in the

vocal line, gives a sense of through-composition, a sustained line of dissonance. In fact, even the contours mentioned earlier, for all their apparent freedom, contain within their static, circular patterns suggestions of the linear.

Debussy's melodies are not centred on the traditional dominant-tonic
outline, yet there are always suggestions of goal-orientated progressions
sounding through in the piano part (figure (*b*), for example). Often a motif is
a flurry or diversion around a certain final pitch that confirms the tonal orien-
tation of the melody (for example, bars 16–17, 'un blanc jet d'eau soupire vers
l'Azur'). The rise–fall motif implies tonal oscillation, the move from agitation
to stability. A feeling of cadence, created by the linear shapes, results in pent-
up tension because the expressive force has no outlet. Seen in this way, the
rise–fall motif, in tension with these suggested harmonic goals, creates a sense
of oscillation between mobility and solidity. The frameworks do not create in
the music as clear a set of simultaneous vectors as in the poem. There is
greater porosity and fluidity between the musical frameworks, and they are
less tightly confined than in the compact metrical space of the poem.

4.7.3 *Reflections and hesitations*

So far we have seen how for every pull up in the poem there is a pull down
and for every attraction there is repulsion, but that these do not occur neatly
and sequentially. There is a great deal of poetic symmetry but also an element
trying to escape it. Incompletion goes hand in hand with metric continuity
and completion.

The set of compass-point coordinates mapping the semantic texture of the
poem has been demonstrated in the analysis. Both the structural mirrors—
those of sense and syntax—reflect within individual lines and across the
poem. For example, the positions of *moi* and *toi*, horizontally reflected in line
1, are mirrored in line 5 in the simile. Visually, the last five lines of the poem
are symmetrical with the first five. In addition, the syntactic parallels of position in lines 4, 5, and 8 encourage a reading both ways from the middle of the
poem. Lines 3 and 8 are also syntactically parallel but are mirror reflections
(inversions) of each other. In line 3 the inanimate is married to the human ('le
ciel errant de ton œil angélique') whereas in lines 8–9, 'la fauve agonie | Des
feuilles' attributes a human feeling to an inanimate object. The soul's agony is
displaced into its term of comparison. The inversion is a powerfully concise
means of expression in the poem, whose tour de force is reached in line 10, 'le
soleil jaune'. Usually the sum of the parts, here 'le soleil' becomes part of the
sum of the 'long rayon'.

Yet all of the reflections hold at their centre an unresolvable conundrum
which constantly throws the status of 'l'Azur' into doubt. The movement
'vers' of line 1 never attains its goal. 'Monte' is stopped in its tracks by a
comma. The rich phonetic echoes of 'Mon âme' and the union of 'mon' (*moi*)

with 'te' (*toi*) in 'Monte' suggest a completion of sense that is prematurely finalizing, preventing the verb from performing its action. There are other moments of dramatic hesitation creating significant breaks in the smooth, continuous flow of the alexandrine-regulated texture. The awkward apposition of 'calme sœur' and 'automne', for example, makes the reader hesitate over the subject of 'rêve' in line 1. Lines 6–10 of the poem give a greater sense of continuity. The syntax is far less disrupted, except for one pre-emptive parenthesis in lines 8–9, until the dramatic syntactic disjuncture of line 10. The main tensions of the poem are points that do not meet or are not reached, centres that appear to be the source of unfolding but actually write stories of stopping short.

4.7.4 *Reflections in the song*

In the song, patterns of overarching coherence are formed by the shape, pitch, and repetition of figures in the vocal melody. Bare octaves and fifths are given great prominence in the texture (at places such as bars 13–17), adding to the remote coldness of the piece. Other particular melodic shapes recur, such as the rise–fall motif, as I have been calling it. These lend a faint familiarity to each phrase, although the act of recognition is undermined by the refusal of any motif or melodic line to settle into repeated or regular patterns. The strange lack of familiarity that accompanies familiarity is enhanced by the changes of bar lengths. The distancing of tonality in favour of ambiguous dissonance in places contributes further to the unfamiliar familiarity. Reflection in the song leads to aporia, rather as in the poem, although by very different means.

In the poem, on the smallest scale, successions of particular groups of sounds are synthesized into clusters. On a larger scale, the constantly over-lapping frameworks, each suggesting its own linear reading, lessen the burden on the line unit, the result of which is a hovering stasis between simultaneous frameworks in the poem. Whereas the overall structure of the piece is ordered along an axis of accumulation and release of tension, the simultaneity of the poem means that a gap can never open because it will be filled with something else. The music seems to ignore such structures in the poem, gliding over the hesitations between its frameworks.[31]

4.7.5 *Closure and opening*

In syntactical and metrical terms there is a controlling framework in place in the poem which sometimes coincides with the semantic directions and at other

---

[31] In his article 'Mallarmé: Debussy, Boulez' Dominique Jameux notices that Debussy's musical expression in *Soupir* ignores the poetic parentheses: 'la succession sémantique "laisse se traîner", qui est interrompue par une proposition participiale puis relative, pourrait s'énoncer musicalement sans la "parenthèse" qui constitue cette interruption' (*Silences*, 4 (1987), 191–201 (195)).

times creates cross-rhythms against them. Sense groups have as their immediate goal a two-line phrase. Individual lines are suspended to await virtual sense completion from their rhyming pairs. The overall sense direction reaches completion at the end of line 5, although this line, being the complement of the simile, forms a sense group with line 4 ('comme dans un jardin mélancolique'). 'Un blanc jet d'eau' is thus displaced into line 5, breaking the two-lines-per-group pattern. From this point onwards in the poem the sense group falls across the rhyming pairs, leaving line 10 to stand alone also, in parallel with line 5.

The richness of the line-final rhymes in 'Soupir' highlights and emphasizes the direction of these smaller sense groups. They often contain a richly overdetermined semantic resonance incorporated phonetically into the rhyme: the metaphorized woman, 'rousse sœur', incorporating the union of masculine adjective with feminine noun, in 'rousseur', or the 'en gel' in the phonetically approximate 'angélique', which prefigures the 'froid sillon', a cold knife through the poetic 'âme'. The 'rayon' has all the more power because of the preceding 'sillon', both of which are given rich flavour in turn by their predecessors in the rhyme position, 'infinie' and 'agonie', a deep, concise expression of disappointment, pain, and lack of fulfilment whose flavour permeates the mood of the rest of the poem.

All the while the unity of harmonic resonance is disrupted by the excessive richness of the rhymes. Such is the independent power of the *rime suffisante*, for example in 'agonie'/'infinie', that what appear to be moments of closure contain within them a will to life of their own. The rhymes offer at once a close to the line or sense group, but also a diversion, distracting the attention away from the route that was momentarily settled upon. They offer too a compellingly cacophonous shattering of harmonic unity, pulling away from the unified frame of sound. An equivalent phenomenon can be heard in certain repeated dissonant chords of the song (for example, those in bars 9–10 and 13). These imply forthcoming resolutions but do not supply them, disappointing the need for closure. They create individualized, ambiguous moments that hold the latent possibility of harmonic function and tonality, which is not laid to rest but is, rather, diverted and submerged, remaining a possibility and colouring the consecutive notes with its undercurrents.

4.8 FIGURING THE INTERMEDIARY

Some of the intermediary ground between poem and piece, then, has been unravelled. The complex forms of association and dissociation between music and text have been arrived at and characterized in the following terms: types of linear improvisation; reflections and hesitations; patterns of closure and opening; cross-rhythms of pushes and pulls; and conflicting voices. Some figures are required by which these shared and contrasting dynamics may be represented, shorthand pressure points expandable into three-dimensional re-enactments of the middle ground.

In the passage from *La Musique et les Lettres* already discussed in Chapter 1, the figure of the thyrsus is used as an illustration of the textual phenomenon to which it refers: 'Toute prose d'écrivain fastueux . . . vaut en tant qu'un vers rompu, jouant avec ses timbres et encore les rimes dissimulées: selon un *thyrse* plus complexe.'[32] The thyrsus figure is a three-dimensional motif that, in the Mallarmé text, enacts and configures the poetic activity, by following the movement upwards through space of the foliage entwined around the Bacchic staff: it is an elegant, performative vision of the fragile balance between containment and frenzy. The figure holds within it vectors which express the structural interweave of music and verse. In Mallarmé's thyrsus, music and poetry are held in precarious simultaneity.

In Baudelaire's prose poem entitled 'Le Thyrse', this figure is explored as a symbol of duality, the Bacchic paradox of strong will combined with fantasy: 'Un bâton, un pur bâton, perche à houblon, tuteur de vigne, sec, dur et droit. Autour de ce bâton, dans des méandres capricieux, se jouent et folâtrent des tiges et des fleurs, celles-ci sinueuses et fuyardes, celles-là penchées comme des cloches ou des coupes renversées.'[33] It is the symbolic power of the tension between the two composite parts of the figure, withheld in suspended anima-tion from each other, that fascinates Baudelaire: 'Ne dirait-on pas que la ligne courbe et la spirale font leur cour à la ligne droite et danse autour, dans une muette adoration?'[34]

The thyrsus is a symbol of the different impulses held within the text: 'Ligne droite et ligne arabesque, intention et expression, roideur de la volonté, sinuosité de la verbe, unité du but, variété des moyens.'[35] It embodies a coun-terpoint of the contradictory but interdependent modes of rigour and expres-siveness. The rod or baton of the mythical figure is essential to poetic construction, the winding foliage. It is the support or base from which poetic rhythms can depart and are thrown into relief; a strand of unity running through the work; a telos of completion and constancy against which discor-dance and elements of open invention can play.

The tensions, similarities, and differences patterning the intermediary between poem and piece in **Soupir**, can begin to take meaningful shape when seen in terms of this figure.[36] Symbolizing the overlap means it keeps the poem and piece rigidly held apart while intertwining them at the same time. The thyrsus is a keyhole through which the configurations of linear improvisation, reflection and hesitation, and open closure may be articulated and explored.

---

[32] *OC* (M), 644.   [33] *Petits Poèmes en prose*, 162–3.
[34] Ibid. 163.   [35] Ibid. 165.
[36] The form **Soupir** will be used to refer to both the poem and the song.

4.9 THE THYRSUS IN **SOUPIR**: POEM AND SONG

In 'Soupir' the fixed controlling frameworks have working against and within them many more mobile frameworks, 'jouant avec ses timbres et encore les rimes dissimulées' (see section 4.8). The thyrsus dynamic works along several of the poem's axes. For example, the metrical closure suggested by the regular pattern of the alexandrine, as well as the telic closure of the rhyme, coincides with moments of syntactic suspension, such as at 'œil angélique | Monte', creating a counterpoint of independent yet interdependent rhythms. At 'se traîner le soleil jaune' the syntactical group is stretched over the expected caesura, causing a similar phenomenon of rhythmic pull between the syntax and metre. This play of fixed and mobile (of the expected telos and improvisatory pull away from it) is an aspect of the poem that fits the dynamic figure of the thyrsus well. The same is true, of course, of other Mallarmé poems, and indeed of poetry more generally, in which the pattern of expectation of arrival and deferral is enacted in the tension between the syntactical and metrical frames. The straight line of the thyrsus is always implied even if there appears to be nothing but the 'foliage' of poetic elaboration. If the syntactical elements of the poem arrive dislocated and suspended then the absence of the expected syntactical telos is all the more strongly felt.

Part of the bipolar tension is located in the directional ambivalence or conflict between horizontal and vertical structures. The poem rests upon a horizontal framework laid out in the regularity of the alexandrines and the strong, rich rhyme endings. Equally, there is a vertical framework in the semantic content (the pull between the poet and 'L'Azur'), in the patterns of syntactic suspension underpinning this, and in the layout of the ten lines of the poem itself. The constant tension between horizontal and vertical, as well as the internal blurring of these clearly delineated directions (such as the binary boundaries of 'sœur' and 'âme'), also creates a thyrsus effect.[37]

The play of horizontal and vertical is a more distant tension in Debussy's music, but present nonetheless. The melody follows both a linear logic (in passages such as the repeated quaver and triplet motif, 'sur l'eau morte', for example), punctuated by dominant-tonic effects, and an oscillating dramatic shape governed by the patterns of verse (the rise–fall motif in its various manifestations). The thyrsus also describes the relation in the song between the opening material (bars 1–6) and its constantly varied forms as they unfold in the rest of the piece.

---

[37] Both strands of the thyrsus are progressing in time. I am treating the horizontal elements as the 'bâton', and the vertical pulls in tension with them as the foliage.

4.10 CHARGED RHYTHMIC SPACE: 'AUTRE ÉVENTAIL DE MADEMOISELLE MALLARMÉ'

Ô rêveuse, pour que je plonge
Au pur délice sans chemin,
Sache, par un subtil mensonge,
Garder mon aile dans ta main.

Une fraîcheur de crepuscule   5
Te vient à chaque battement
Dont le coup prisonnier recule
L'horizon délicatement.

Vertige! voici que frissonne
L'espace comme un grand baiser   10
Qui, fou de naître pour personne,
Ne peut jaillir ni s'apaiser.

Sens-tu le paradis farouche
Ainsi qu'un rire enseveli
Se couler du coin de ta bouche   15
Au fond de l'unanime pli!

Le sceptre des rivages roses
Stagnants sur les soirs d'or, ce l'est,
Ce blanc vol fermé que tu poses
Contre le feu d'un bracelet.[38]   20

As is generally acknowledged, the fan is one of Mallarmé's most fascinating and elusive symbols. He comes back to it time and again, in 'Autre Éventail de Mademoiselle Mallarmé' (1887), twice in sonnet form ('Éventail' (dedicated to Méry Laurent, 1890) and 'Éventail de Madame Mallarmé' (1891)), and later in the *vers de circonstance* entitled *Éventails*, eighteen gems of rhyme around proper nouns. The fan has an extraordinary power to generate symbols from within and by association with itself. 'Autre Éventail de Mademoiselle Mallarmé' reads as its own *art poétique*.[39]

In the original 'Autre Éventail' the poem's subject and material are literally one, since the poem is written onto a lavishly decorated fan. Each stanza of the poem is one complete sentence, as though it were written on the fan's paper panel. Frivolous and decorative *objet de circonstance*, the fan is pushed into the foreground. Usually an accessory, the ornamental is now the main poetic subject, no longer apostrophized as in the lyric convention but given voice. The poetic object is also the poem's own voice; it becomes the *je*.[40] In

---

[38] *OC*, 31.

[39] Mallarmé's poem will be referred to hereafter as 'Autre Éventail'. *Éventail* refers to the Debussy song.

[40] The poet's desire to become the fan in order to get as close as possible to the 'rêveuse' is, in one sense, parallel to his desire in 'Placet futile' to be depicted on the fan that is the love-god's wings, as the shepherd of the princess's smiles.

Debussy's *Éventail*, the vocal line is declamatory and charged with ambiguous tension. Intermittent, fleeting silences punctuate the music with unsettling presence and irregularity. Interruptions on the piano make the textual material sound breathless, appearing in scherzando semiquavers but constrained within only the tiniest of chromatic pitch movements. The other main piano material to punctuate the silence that so frequently leaves the stark vocal line hanging, unsupported by any complementary line, takes the form of grace notes that replace the sense of progression a tonal accompaniment would provide. By contrast with the sense of repressed desire in Mallarmé's poem, Debussy's song is bare and altogether spikier. The atonality gives a strange sense of the music being unmotivated yet at the same time highly driven, disorientated but too restless to luxuriate or lose its way altogether.

In 'Billet', discussed in Chapter 2, the 'danseuse' is metonymically transformed into a 'tourbillon' by syntactical juxtaposition. Placed over the stanza break, the transit of identity from the 'danseuse' to the 'tourbillon' is marked by the hesitation caused by stanzaic change that, along with the dramatic change of tempo, contributes to the dizzying 'tourbillon' effect. The fan of 'Autre Éventail' does not undergo such a sliding transit: the effect is immediate. The object is not placed within an accumulation of poetic images as the central focus of the poem, but rather, by its content and form, it fills and delimits one poetic frame and plays with the boundaries that dictate and define the fan's status as object. As such it fulfils Mallarmé's ideal of the object becoming its own 'Notion pure'.[41] The object as object flickers in and out of our perception in exchange for the object as 'Notion'. It appears and disappears through its self-reflexivity, a fan filling the present erotic moment and a fan-form pre-dating and outliving the scope of the poem—a beating fan whose movement can appear timeless and static, like the smoke rings in 'Toute l'âme résumée' (see Chapter 1), which reappear as they disappear. The fan at once contains its own armature (the framework of the material object and of the poem) and is the armature of the space around it.[42] Claudel perceived these dissolvable boundaries in terms of a kind of gestalt figure, as he writes in a letter to Mallarmé: 'Votre phrase où, dans l'aérien contrepoids des ablatifs absolus, la proposition principale n'existe plus que du fait de son absence, se maintient dans une sorte d'équilibre instable et me rappelle ces dessins japonais où la figure n'est dessinée que par son blanc et n'est que le geste résumé qu'elle trace.'[43] It is this ethereal counterbalance between poetic

---

[41] See Chapter 1, section 1.6.

[42] Writing onto the object and the poetic personification of the object is also the subject of 'Placet futile', the second of the songs, in which the lover's lips on the Sèvres china cup awaken Hebe, who is depicted thereon. See also 'Las de l'amer repos': 'Imiter le Chinois au cœur limpide et fin | De qui l'extase pure est de peindre la fin | Sur ses tasses de neige à la lune ravie' (*OC*, 12, ll. 15–17).

[43] 23 Nov. 1896, quoted in Henri Mondor (ed.), 'Stéphane Mallarmé et Paul Claudel: *Correspondance*', *Cahiers Paul Claudel*, 14 vols. (Paris: Gallimard, 1959–95), i. 40–55 (49–50).

frameworks that can be so precisely expressed through the representative nodal points and joints, edges and articulations, and mechanical action of the fan.

In the first stanza of the poem, the *je* desires release into 'pur délice', an unmapped freedom 'sans chemin'. *Je* is open to multiple allegorical readings and can be identified either as the fan-object (as suggested by the title and form of the poem) or as the symbol of the flight of poetic inspiration. The fan and the wing are inseparably linked in 'évent-ail', held in the same image. The 'aile' is the wing of a bird-fan resting in the hand of the 'rêveuse'. Rather than existing inside a certain world or context, the fan's internal and external aspects are kept on the same plane from the outset. The reader views the fan-object but simultaneously apprehends its every surface laid open to view like a Cubist sculpture.

Etymologically 'subtil' (line 3, 'subtil mensonge') means 'under the tissue or weave of the text'.[44] A sleight of hand or textual trickery will give the illusion that the fan-*je* is being controlled by his dreamer's hand. This fantasy, that the instrument of flight is being controlled, is what will plunge him into the unlimited space of 'pur délice'. The simultaneous complex of vertical and horizontal movements that we saw in 'Soupir' re-emerges in this poem.

In the second stanza the hand and fan are suppressed. The fan is now delineated in space by the air surrounding it, which it compresses and releases. The textual object in the first stanza, a generator of symbols of production and reflexivity, is dissolved in this stanza, overwhelmed by the space it defines. The content of the poem-object dissociates itself from its formal outline. The textual metaphor itself is prey to the erosion of the object boundaries within the poem's unchanging formal boundaries. The rhythmic, repetitive 'battement' of the repressed fan-object, invaded by the external and held prisoner in the snare of verse, calibrates or scans the space, reverberating as far as the horizon.

The erodible and reconstructable properties of the space occupied by objects, the perception of which can be altered for the observer by poetic 'subtil mensonge', are discussed under the heading 'Aller-retour' by Jean-Pierre Richard, who differentiates Mallarmé's flower imagery from the dynamic properties of the fan: 'Au lieu de se présenter comme un "lucide contour", *comme une clôture bornée par une libre transparence*, la corolle peut nous apparaître alors comme un simple arrêt du jaillissement. Mallarmé s'efforcera donc de rêver une forme qui résolve son problème de façon plus visiblement dynamique: ce sera l'*éventail*.'[45] Richard captures the transmutable nature of the fan, whose edges are porous and translucent.

---

44 I am indebted to Graham Robb for this point (*Unlocking Mallarmé*, 151).

45 *L'Univers imaginaire*, 309. (The quotation from Mallarmé can be found in 'Prose', *OC*, 56, l. 27 (my italics).)

In the third quatrain the contained chaos of the expanding and shrinking space defines the relative positions of the fan; the dreamer becomes charged with the expectancy of an imminent kiss. 'Vertige' is the thrill of the desire for separation from the rhythmic imprisonment of the fan-beat or of verse.[46]

A point of critical complexity, or 'équilibre instable' as Claudel put it, is now reached. The fan-beating is suspended in the timeless, ecstatic inertia of a kiss that is formed but which can neither explode into fulfilment nor subside ('Ne peut jaillir ni s'apaiser'). In the fourth quatrain the exquisiteness of contained ecstasy, 'le paradis farouche', is compared to the dreamer's smile, buried in the folds and concealed behind the fan. The 'farouche' elements of potential fissure and dispersal in the smile are contained at the base of the fan ('l'unanime pli'). The fan-verse, with its unanime fold formed of other, potentially individual, folds ('plis'), symbolizes and is symbolized by the hovering stasis of concealed desire. 'Éventer' has the sense of moving air and can also mean 'to conceal'. The paradoxical image of the fan includes ambiguously revealing and concealing gestures performed by sleights of hand.

4.11 THE *PLI* OF THE FAN

The kind of fan on which Mallarmé wrote his poems was composed of a semicircle of paper partitioned into segments by a series of folds and supported, when fully open, by a spread of wooden spokes placed at equal intervals along the radius of the semicircle. The spokes join at one pivotal point at the base of the fan. Each panel is held in relation to the next by a dividing fold (or 'pli') when the fan is open. 'Plis' articulate the fan structure in three dimensions. Identical individual elements are joined by a common stem to form a whole, held in fragile relation to one another by separate spokes. The fold is the nodal point which articulates the similarity between each panel yet divides it by marking it as different. The 'plis', at first nestled in parallel, are disclosed when the fan is opened into its webbed structure. 'Plis' are figural representations of the cross-rhythms created by the desire for closure being pulled apart by opening gestures.

The 'pli' itself holds opposing pushes and pulls in their simultaneous relation. It represents both the 'gouffre' of the 'néant', which hovers, paralysed, caught between contingency and the futile desire for order; and the stasis resulting when the desire to 'plonge' is checked. The figure of the *pli* contains

---

[46] A flower image hidden within the 'vertige' ('vers-tige') recalls Baudelaire's 'Harmonie du soir': 'Voici venir les temps où vibrant sur sa tige' (*Les Fleurs du mal*, ed. Enid Starkie (Oxford: Blackwell, 1980), 46, l. 1). The poem is the wavering stalk on which the flower of *vers* (or the idea-flowers as 'Prose pour des Esseintes' would have it) is promised to bloom. See also Mallarmé's comments on Dujardin's literary efforts in 'Planches et feuillets': 'Voici les rimes dardées sur de brèves tiges, accourir, se répondre, tourbillonner, coup sur coup' (*OC* (M), 327).

the nexus of movements that occur in the weave of ('subtil') the charged, hesitating surface. It also opens a gap in the surface in which objects can be
hidden (like the smile buried in the text-texture of the fan) and displayed in a
self-reflexive motion. It is the rhythmic figure of the presence that reveals
inner absence (or conceals presence), yielding under external surface pressure
(like the fan defined by the shape of its own course in the air). In the *pli* presence and absence can cohabit. They do not exclude each other; nor are they
reconciled. The *pli* is a vulnerable and rebuildable boundary, the mechanical
articulation point of the fan's wing, representative of Claudel's 'l'aérien
contrepoids', the exquisite tension held between and within syntactical and
metrical frames in *vers*.

The *pli* describes the moments in poetry that are both acts of closure and
also acts of opening in some way. The figure contains opening and closure in
its actual shape (V), the opening in which creates a gap in the surface texture
from which a fragment from a completely different time frame can emerge. It
is also the figure of textual dissimulation, and of the hesitating stasis of being
caught by it (between opening and closure, horizontal and vertical).[47]

Mimesis of the fan pattern is offered by the stanzas and rhyme axis themselves in 'Autre Éventail'. If the *pli* is the horizontal fold between each
quatrain (the blank) and the central stanza is the mainstay ('vers-tige') then
when the 'rire' runs down the back of the fan the 'unanime pli' points to the
other 'tige', the *rimes riches* of the fan-poem. These are the vertical bases from
which the folds emanate as the unanimous *pli*.

As a figure, the *pli* can be a useful heuristic device in exploring other texts
by Mallarmé.[48] The figure occurs in the poem 'Soupir', to take an earlier
example, in line 4, where a syntactic break creates an opening that occurs
immediately after 'Monte'. The break suggests a premature completion of
sense since the verb ('Monte') is prevented from performing its action. In
another pattern of occurrence, the myriad reflective surfaces in the poem
create a tension wherein apparent sites of productivity actually point to
absence at their centre (like the two surfaces of the *pli*), for example, by throwing the status of the clear binary pair 'âme'/'Azur' into doubt. The most striking use of the *pli* is to describe the closure of sound groups and effecting of
sense completion by the rich rhymes, whose overdetermined semantic resonance can be seen as diversions that seem to open the rhyme at the moment
of its closure into multiple new directions. Indeed, there are also elements in
Soupir as song that share the open closure of the *pli*. For example, the dissonant chords in bars 9–10 and 13 are ambiguous moments in the musical

---

47 See Richard when he turns his discussion to the 'pli' of the fan itself: 'L'éventail . . . nous fournira
l'exemple d'un pli heureux, réussi parce que mobile et souple, soumis avec grâce à la loi qui alterne
toujours chez Mallarmé l'ouverture et la fermeture' (*L'Univers imaginaire*, 179).

48 As has been demonstrated resoundingly, of course, by Derrida, one of the great masters of the
pli in Mallarmé.

texture which, whilst suggesting a resolution, or closure within a tonal frame, actually contain elements that keep them prised open, readily suggesting many other possible escape routes for their continuation on a more winding tonal path.

The closed fan or 'sceptre' is also the 'unanime pli' from which the other folds may emerge. In its closed state the poem is a 'vol fermé'. Its potential for flight is checked. The line of the sceptre is as easily dissolvable as the fan, itself the hazy, multiple, indeterminate point at which the shores of the 'rivages roses' meet the golden, evening skies, 'les soirs d'or'. The point where one begins and the other finishes is obscured; which defines which is unclear. The 'vol' is an unfulfilled and futile *blanc* resting against the rich, golden artifice of the dreamer's bracelet. The futility, compounded by the rich surface echoes in the *rime complexe* of 'bracelet', is in the impossibility of making the presence real, in being permanently imprisoned by the reflexive, repeating *pli*. In addition to the rhythms of open closure, then, a further set of rhythmical *rapports* are represented in the fan. The vacillating action of the fan, its 'battement', trapped in a movement back and forth, calibrates the air in a fluctuating rhythm of pushing onwards and pulling back.

In his discussion of the dynamic symbolism of 'l'oiseau' in Mallarmé, Richard touches on some essential properties of the fan. For Richard, the bird, trapped between 'l'écume inconnue et les cieux',[49] represents Mallarméan thought, which 'se trouve ici sollicitée par un double, et contradictoire, dynamisme, à la fois attirée et repoussée par le dehors'. External forces, exerted simultaneously, shape the space by attracting and repelling it. Plunging into the 'gouffre' is counterbalanced by a desire to fly back out of it. 'Ce cri, qui continue à s'élever, pour rien, dans l'altitude, semble vouloir y propager la vibration de notre vide.'[50] The force 'double' and 'contradictoire', then, is the attraction and repulsion for the 'gouffre' and the in-between state of hovering between the two (which is the resultant, non-binary by-product). These are the combined forces that inhabit the fan.

4.12 'AUTRE ÉVENTAIL' AS SONG

Hearing the song *Éventail* is a very different experience from reading Mallarmé's poem. The question I shall ask here is how the particular Mallarméan figures of the *éventail* and *pli* can be used as conceptual figures for the music–poetry interface in song. Do we 'hear' the poetic basis for the song in non-mimetic structural ways in the music? How can the dynamic structure

---

[49] 'Brise marine', *OC*, 15.
[50] *L'Univers imaginaire*, 306. See Chapter 1, section 1.10, for further examples of the use of 'plis' in Mallarmé and Derrida.

of the fan, its clear tensions and points of articulation, its pivots and porous boundaries, its oscillating motion and pinioning of antithetical states, configure the complex overlap between poem and song?

The song opens (bars 1–3; Example 4.4) with a rising sequence, which, when it reaches its peak, drops straight down a third. This burst of activity lacks the support of a sustained bass line in the piano. Briefly snatched chordal interjections on the piano, off the beat, underline the bareness of the tied A♭, an evasion of the point of arrival. Rhythmically, sounds never arrive in any predictable pattern; each one is a shock, a reference to something we have missed or to an event that never took place. Each interjection seems to be lingering at the edge of silence, the messenger of something that is not happening.

A recurring melodic pattern in the voice is one of chromatic stepwise movement above and below a pivot note. These chromatic figures, oscillating above and below a note, shape the insistent pitch repetition in the vocal line of the first verse, which only opens out in bars 11 and 12. In bars 5–10, such figures work against the snatched, staccato grace notes in the piano right hand that start in bar 4. Rhythmic and pitch repetition in bar 7, for example, contributes to a sense of stasis; the figure returns to its starting note, having progressed nowhere. The vocal line creeps up a semitone in bar 8 and the figure in bar 7 is rhythmically augmented in bars 9–10. The very slight chromatic changes hint at progression but in fact keep a very tight lid on the nervous rhythmic twitches, which are constantly contained, doing little more than repeating themselves. A different chromatic progression of three rising notes (F♯–G–G♯) accompanies in the piano left hand the rising chromatic shift in the voice between bars 7 and 8. This sounds in the piano as a sleight of hand ('subtil mensonge'), a momentary harmonic blossoming, rather than a genuine modulation.

As we have seen, in Mallarmé those moments where vacancy or silence seem to threaten are very closely linked to moments where a dizzying blur of potential meanings, sounds, or directions seem crowded simultaneously into one space. Such a blur of meanings also occurs where frames of reference cannot be fixed but shift in and out of focus to fit different agents and recipients of the action. The music of the song seems poised in similar flux between silence and sound. The rhythmic irregularity and brevity of sound is threatened with silence. Musical events are such only by being, equally, simultaneous non-events, thus closely resembling the fan. The fan at once delimits the boundaries of its surroundings and forms the extent of its own universe; it is defined by the space encroaching upon it and the space it fills.

In bars 12–13 a link passage in the piano repeating the opening bars leads into the second verse. This time, however, the tied A♭ falls by step into the oscillating vocal line of bars 14–16 (Example 4.5). The return of the piano's first entry as an interlude underlines the sameness on which the variety is resting.

Example 4.4 Debussy, *Éventail*, bars 1–13

Example 4.5 Debussy, *Éventail*, bars 14–27

The precarious lightness of the music in the second verse gives it the impression of teetering on the brink of two states, pulled apart by the contrary motion between the piano and voice (bars 15–16). Bar-length crescendos from pianissimo emphasize the oscillation of the left-hand octave chords. The stark contrary motion between piano and voice at this point has the effect of opening and closing the texture. The two lines are in direct conflict. Motion is fixed around one spot, progressing by standing still. The nodes of simultaneous convergence and opening fill the music with the simultaneous impulses of the *pli*, a cohabitation of pushes and pulls and distinct textures. The crescendos push each bar on internally until the beginning of the next bar, whose subito return to pianissimo halts the momentum. The rhythmic pace varies from the forwards-moving, energetic semiquavers of 'à chaque battement' to the lazier crotchet triplets stretching over 'un coup prisonnier'. These contrast with the rhythmical simplicity and regularity of the oscillating crotchets in bars 14–16.

Again the upper pitch registers of bars 14–16 are deprived of bass support. Isolated staccato quavers in the left hand hint at dominant-to-tonic closures (E♭ and A♭ in bars 17–18), which pierce the texture in *pli*-like revelatory glimpses, disappearing as quickly as they appear. At bars 19–21 the piano texture opens out, and the repeated rising fifth becomes increasingly insistent in bars 22–5 in the right-hand octaves, where the middle of each bar is emphasized by a dynamic swell. After a brief 'serrez', the tempo accelerates at bar 24 into a sudden explosion of chromatically descending octave triplet semiquavers, which prepares a precipitous F♯ leap down an octave on 'Vertige' in the voice.

The charged, demi-semiquaver ostinato ripples beneath in the piano in a hushed pianissimo *frissonnement*: 'voici que frissonne | l'espace comme un grand baiser' (bars 28–31; Example 4.6). The stepwise chromatic shifting of the left-hand line (bars 28–33) contains the frenzy of the muted ostinatos, 'fou de naître pour personne', sinuous but trapped in the low register. Rubato, the blossoming of an augmented fifth in the voice, and a momentary standstill in the right hand, reveals the moving texture, interrupted and hovering for an instant on the same pitches in bar 30 before continuing its relentless descent in the next bar. This hesitation creates an atemporal moment, in contrast to the relative stillness of the slow octave in the vocal line (bar 31). The piano's agitated, restless, and buzzing line has something of the contained ecstasy of Mallarmé's fan-poem, which, as we have seen, is constricted but potentially exploding ('ne peut jaillir ni s'apaiser').

The thrilling, vertiginous leap of a minor seventh on 'Sens-tu' subsides into a smooth, blossoming melody in the fourth verse (Example 4.7). A simple third is the basis for the enveloping open closure of the melodic phrase for 'au fond de l'unanime pli' (bar 44). A lingering calm arrives at this point (the 'cédez très peu') but is broken again abruptly in bar 46 by the return of the jerkily

Example 4.6 Debussy, *Éventail*, bars 28–36

Example 4.6 *(cont.)*

snatched ornaments and staccato chords. A hovering transition follows (bar 47), which takes off into the opening figure once more.

The final link passage makes one last cyclical gesture when the tied A♮ this time moves back up a minor third to the C from which it came. The tempo of the fifth verse is indicated as 'en retenant peu à peu jusqu'à la fin'. In the last bars of the song the vocal line, which sounds almost effortless and weightless, stays low while a sense of floating higher and higher is achieved by moving the anchoring bass notes in bar 61 up the octave, to be in unison with the voice. A hint of the syncopated left-hand staccato is added in some final ornaments. Each separately articulated note in the rising piano line adds another fold *(pli)* on the same shimmering spot, in a space charged with reverberation, both constructing anew and dissolving (Example 4.8).

4.13 MOBILE FIGURES AND THE *TROIS POÈMES*: A SUMMARY

As a song cycle the *Trois poèmes* represent a special musical engagement with poetry. Although I have treated two of the songs separately for the purposes of these analyses, each song is meant to be heard as a part of a musical cycle for which the poems were not originally destined by Mallarmé. In a sense, the poems have been lifted out of their ordinary milieu and transported onto an entirely new stage or placed in a new set of parameters. The dislocation incurred by such a transportation is accompanied by the meeting and non-meeting, on many different levels—acoustic, structural, and those of performance, amongst others—of two sets of cultural baggage belonging to readers and listeners: song creates an unstable, asymmetrical, and undecidable intervening space between music and poetry. By being considered in conjunction in this chapter, a fresh light has been cast on the poems and songs, their relation

Example 4.7 Debussy, *Éventail*, bars 37–49

Example 4.8 Debussy, *Éventail*, bars 60–5

now intensified and complicated by their interpenetration. From the basis of the analyses, Mallarmé's figures push the cogent strands of resistance and affinity of these instances of musico-poetic interplay through exacting, integral, and intermediary hoops.

The fan, its *pli*, and the thyrsus as conceptual, structural motifs house some crucial points of common ground and difference between poem and song. The oscillating patterns, rhythms, and surges of momentum in *Éventail* and the rhythmical 'battement' or 'équilibre instable' of 'Autre Éventail' can be mapped in the dynamic pulses embodied in the *pli*. As a heuristic device the *pli* can represent the knitting together of antithetical states across the *Trois poèmes* and the Mallarmé texts. As we have seen, the simultaneous gestures of opening and closure in *plis* are also featured in the rich rhymes of the poems, for example, as well as in the dissonant chords of the songs. Nestled in the controlling structure of the *éventail* the *plis* form an internally and externally apprehended armature that configures patterns of silence and sound.

The thyrsus is a further tool for mapping the different dynamic forces in the interface between poem and song, this time the fundamental tension, found both in the poems and in the *Trois poèmes*, that exists between the linear and the non-linear. The thyrsus is a keyhole through which the manifestations of hesitation, reflection, and linear improvisation, either in the poem and poem as music individually or between them, may be viewed. Through the figures, the *pli*, and the thyrsus, the intermediary has moved from its marginal silence in the wings, to resonate on the shared mainstage.

4.14 THE FAN

The representative power of the fan symbol goes beyond that of the *pli* and the thyrsus. The fan is a symbol of the poetics of mobility and hesitation which requires special emphasis in its capacity as generative metaphor for the inter-art dynamic. What the fan in its non-binary complexity allows, beyond its primary intermediary function as vehicle for the *plis* in the *Trois poèmes* and 'Autre Éventail', is a more general articulation of the nature of the inter-change between music and poetry.

Poetry and music as manipulated by Mallarmé and Debussy have a common root yet a fully differentiated outcome, as in the parts and the sum of the fan. The parallels between their arts escape one another, the gaze obstructed, yet they may be brought back into alignment. Instead of a vague mêlée of stock, mimetic truisms informing our understanding of the relationship, incompatible features and movements of each are knitted together in a tensile, malleable construction that may be controlled, whose movement or *épanouissement* may be directed, but that becomes more itself (more fully into being or into its function as fan) as the bonds uniting its individual parts move towards disarticulation, until only a single nodal point pinions them. The fan is a webbed structure in which disclosure of the *plis*, at first nestled in parallel, is what generates its productivity as an agent of air movement. The *rapports* between the sections are vital. The air of the intervening space pulsates in rhythms of mobile stasis, resistant affinity, and open closure.

A full exploration of the fan, in the light of a proper understanding of the implications of music for Mallarmé's verse, not only revitalizes the full complexity lying within his work, but also maps the three-dimensional geography of the space that both poem and music inhabit.

EPILOGUE

Including music as a structuring element in the composition of the text allows Mallarmé to overreach himself as creator and to push the text dangerously towards overreaching itself. In *La Musique et les Lettres* textual and musical textures are made to coexist in figural and rhetorical form (see Chapter 1). Music and letters shadow one another exactly, as if two sides of a coin, but only first by becoming silent structural frameworks. Music is almost emptied of its sonorous content, and letters are detached, in the signifying vessels of words, from a conventional syntax, so that structurally they can meet in the middle. Mallarmé was acutely aware of the possibilities for the text of this site of plurality, and patterns of listening are an essential part of his playful, mobile, overdetermined texts. Recognizing the extent and validity of the musical in the Mallarmé text is a way to appreciate and to articulate more fully the exciting and pleasurable overspill afforded by his writing.

But illustrating this aspect of reading Mallarmé has only been a secondary aim of this book. What is strikingly original and successful about Mallarmé's aesthetics of the overlap, and what can be taken from it for the purposes of exploring the interdiscipline, is the precise modelling of the relation that is performed through musico-textual structures. I have gone beyond the discovery of the musical in Mallarmé, by bringing a comparative method derived from him to bear more generally on instances of crossover between music and verse by him and Debussy, either those instances that already exist, or those specially manufactured for the purpose. In *La Musique et les Lettres* the intermittence of meaning and non-meaning becomes the joint (musico-poetic), motivating, structural rhythm of the prose. My argument and analysis have been designed to offer a conceptual apparatus through which to explore the intervening space between letters and music, a necessary supplement to the individual criticisms of each art, which illuminates both the coherence and the affront to coherence that are fundamental to our inter-art experience.

In the writing of this book, as I have focused on just how close a *rapprochement* Mallarmé achieves in his lecture, I have been mindful of the overwhelming asymmetry between the levels and types of semantic referential power belonging to each art. In fact, Mallarmé deals with the asymmetry by levelling out the two arts more than my figures have done. The *décalage* between frames of reference in the works discussed here is engaged with through their analysis and expressed in a series of figures or, as they could also be termed, neutral conceptual motifs ('neutral' in the sense that they are independent, taken from outside or from the writings of both artists, yet belonging to each art: they dwell both in neutral and partisan territory at once). In the intervening space between the Debussy *Préludes* ('La terrasse des audiences du clair de lune'; ' "Les fées sont d'exquises danseuses" '; 'Brouillards') and 'Petit Air I', for example, the pitted intermediary texture of conflicting temporalities, and atemporalities, is drawn together and expressed in various ways and at various levels through language borrowed from Boulez (*éclat* and *explosante fixe*), Mallarmé ('enroulements'), and the mathematical branch of topology (the Möbius strip).

The language of ornament, taken from or modelled on the use of such figures by the composer and poet in their own writings, becomes prominent in the configuration of the different types of hesitation uncovered by analysis. The thyrsus, a figure borrowed from *La Musique et les Lettres*, provides in the *Trois poèmes* the necessary stepping stone between poem and song from which to survey the different scenarios where two impulses pull in different directions at once. In the figures of the *pli* and the *éventail* independent and intermediary poetic and musical rhythm is plotted and articulated. Amongst other things, the fan takes us further towards a notion of intermediary rhythm that is not regular and homogenized but flexible enough to express irregularity and syncopation. It is also shown how the fan can become a highly productive metaphor for the overlap, combining stasis at its pinion with the potential opening and closing movement of its panels, which hide the *plis*.

By its very status as both part of an artwork or text and also supplementary to it, ornament is a natural vehicle for the conceptual expression of the intermediary. As ornamental figures appear woven through the book they are both integral and supplementary to the analyses. The fact that they are historically grounded, taken from a currency of period aesthetic language by Mallarmé and Debussy, but also ahistorical, they overstep the limitations and context of a particular period, adds to their strength as methodological tool. Their presence as a third term constantly pulls the discussion away from settling into a simple dialectic of comparison. Rather than the intermediary being left expressed through series of opposites (meaning and non-meaning, convergence and divergence, similarity and difference, unity and multiplicity, for example), ornament creates a state suspended between the two, a hesitation beyond the binarism, composed of both its elements but also catching the elements that escape it. All of the figures capture this shimmering, or hovering, in one form or another. In this way they perform and model the intermediary in one move, exemplifying the tension between the particular relationship concerned and a more general, abstracted theory of the inter-art relation.

The culmination of this ornamental figuration is reached with the arabesque, whose arrival is prepared by the interwoven emergence and disappearance of the thyrsus and arabesque in the earlier chapters. Transported from the field of the decorative arts and architecture, the form of the arabesque expresses the flow, dips, curves, twisting, ruptures, and pulls between the linear and the florid in the acoustic dramas of *Un coup de Dés* and *Jeux*. In the arabesque their welding and divisive structural rhythms are typified. By bringing these extraordinary works together I have hoped to go some way towards reinventing the shape of meaning in the stories of fragmentation and spatialization, which they bring to a climax. In addition, the aim has been to outline the qualities that allow these works (and, by extension, modernist works by other artists) to escape fixity and hence to be considered 'modern' to this day.

The figures do their work on the higher of two conceptual, analytical levels. A certain blurring of the distinction between listening and reading occurs in the lower-level structures (such as surges, recessions, stases, violent ruptures, and so on) revealed in each art by the analyses. The figures reintroduce the analytical material at a higher structural level through concepts that allow the blurring to re-form into moments and perspectives of clarity. They also allow for the intermittent clarity and lack of clarity inherent in these structural moments that knit together improbable states. Emergent from these contrastive analyses is a particular poetics of hesitation, built up through a picture of shared structural rhythm and expressed in figures akin to the 'apertures', 'translucencies', and 'sluice gates' of Steiner's imagery (see the Introduction).

Song creates a different set of test conditions for the intermediary. Instead of non-verbal music it deals with music that sets words, in order to develop the profile of the poetics of hesitation from a different viewpoint. In song the voice sits precariously on a peculiarly intense intermediary edge between music and language. It offers a musical delivery of speech. In addition, the voice has its own interplay with the accompaniment, which runs alongside the direct intrusion of the poem and music into one another's domains.

As we know from 'le Livre', Mallarmé's 'mentale poursuite' (see Chapter 1, section 1.8) referred to 'rapports' that he believed to exist between all branches of knowledge. It is tempting to muse upon how far he was right, and upon whether the language of the intermediary I am proposing might form part of a future metalanguage that will be able to negotiate between all disciplines. (Clearly this is not to suggest that Mallarmé had all the answers—indeed by using a mixture of sources for the figures I have avoided this possibility—but rather to reflect that ornament was one kind of aesthetic metalanguage in circulation at that time.)

The foundation of ornament, and of arabesque in particular, upon patterns observable in nature—a cultural feature that was noted in Chapter 3 (section 3.4)—suggests that arts have a common basis in the objects and natural phenomena that fill the artist's world. As Focillon writes: 'La nature elle aussi crée des formes, elle imprime dans les objets dont elle est faite et aux forces dont elle les anime des figures et des symétries, si bien que l'on s'est complu quelquefois à voir en elle l'œuvre d'un Dieu artiste, d'un Hermès caché, inventeur des combinaisons.'[1]

Recently chaos theory has been used to examine the behaviour of certain systems, such as the weather and earthquakes, for example, and yielded results that suggest an underlying principle of ordered chaos, a principle that has much in common with the (dis-)organized complexity of *Un coup de Dés*. Such theory notices in the laws of nature a precarious, symmetry-breaking, unstable equilibrium. Perhaps Focillon's 'figures' and 'symétries' could be conceived of in a similar way. John Barrow illustrates 'chaos' by making a distinction between organized and disorganized complexity.[2] As the grains of sand fall in an hourglass, a pile builds in a cone shape until it reaches a critical state of equilibrium, a balance between order and disorder. One more grain of sand added could cause an avalanche. This state is called 'self-organizing critical complexity', a term that harnesses the interface between organization and disorganization. In this state, which is reminiscent of the mobilely static figures I have pulled together here (*éclat* and *explosante fixe*, for example), the structure of potential chaos can be described. We hear a version of this in jazz. Jazz is based on the mixture of tightly imposed structural order with a bending of the musical rules behind it. These are the transferable patterns of (dis-)organization that we take pleasure in hearing, reading, seeing, and experiencing.

What emerges in the Glossary at the end of this book in the shape of a series of figures, then, is an initial contribution to a metanarrative of the intermediary. These figures stand out from the book in the form of a connective tissue that holds together the elements of the intermediary discussed and taken into account during the course of the discussion. Putting the figures in glossary form goes some way towards demonstrating that a particular instance of inter-art relationship far exceeds the sum of its parts. That is to say, although this study has been confined to one such relationship, its implications are much broader. As it stands, this list is intended as a kind of guide or short cut to the instantiation of the intermediary of the Mallarmé–Debussy relationship. However, the figures have already shown themselves to be transferable from their own realm of discourse and signification to have structural meaning in the context of music and/or poetry. As their definitions in the Glossary suggest, each plots a set of coordinates that can be picked up and put down elsewhere or 'in between'. Those coordinates can shrink, expand, or be tipped in a certain direction in accordance with the special demands of the new location. Of course, I cannot claim that this glossary of figures is the key to the whole 'intermediary'. Clearly this study is limited by its reference

[1] *La Vie des formes*, 4–5.
[2] *The Artful Universe: The Cosmic Source of Human Creativity*, 2nd edn. (London: Penguin, 1997).

to only one kind of poetics of hesitation. What has been shown, though, is that these figures have a structural power that reaches beyond their immediate surroundings. It must be left to future work to decide whether or not the figures are structural tools powerful enough to be taken to a separate area of the music–poetry interface in this growing interdisciplinary field to do useful work there. The forking, twisting temporality of the arabesque, for example, could well be applied to other instances of spiralling acoustic and poetic dramas. Similarly, the static mobility that ties the fan to this particular instance of overlap need not be permanently binding. It could be used as a key to open out rhythms of tension and release in a different intermediary intersection. It would also be a useful starting point for further avenues of exploration into a critical language for the rhythm of poetry, which Nowottny calls for in *The Language Poets Use* (see Chapter 1, n. 58).

At these early stages of the interdisciplinary investigation the new avenues of exploration opened up can be taken in many directions. It has not been within the scope of this thesis to test the flexibility of some of these areas, such as ornament or topology, more generally as a site of the intermediary, but this would be an exciting route for future study in the field to take.

What is clear is the value, potential, and excitement for both literary and musical studies of 'thinking between'. Sounding for structural rhythms, either in the figures used here or in some similarly derived, if adopted as part of a battery of critical tools, could continue to produce fruitful readings between music and literature so that 'intermediacy' can usefully supplement and enrich the individual studies of each. It is hoped that this book will provide ways into other areas of overlap, both earlier and later, where the issues of text in music and of musical rewritings of text raise pressing and uncomfortable questions. In the latter part of the twentieth century musical 'translations' of literary 'narratives' were still very much alive. Luciano Berio has explored the relation between word and music by rewriting passages of Joyce, Brecht, and Proust, among others, for soprano and orchestra in *Epifanie* (1959–61, revised in 1965). Elliott Carter's use of 'Vents', the poem by Saint-John Perse about winds sweeping across and changing America, as the formal inspiration for the restless and multiple-layered music of his *Concerto for Orchestra* (1969) is just one other possible example among many.

Steiner (1969) writes in *After Babel*: 'It is . . . not astonishing that we lack an adequate critical vocabulary in which to analyse or even to paraphrase rigorously the phenomenology of interaction between the language of the word and that of music.'[3] This study has begun to develop tools for addressing this gap in the critical vocabulary by reinjecting music into the literary sphere and by applying literary concepts to music. The figures of the intermediary powerfully generate access to the works themselves while also articulating the

[3] 445.

common ground they share. They show that the interdisciplinary discussion can have analytical clarity and not succumb to the potential methodological flaw recognized by Roger Fowler: 'Interdisciplinarity in practice often founders on the fact that two disciplines are merely juxtaposed; work at their interface, which should be exciting, can become embarrassingly vague'.[4] The non-literal complexity of the figures allows them to function in a flexible, non-reductive manner. They hold great promise for comparative study.

[4] In *Modern Critical Terms* (London: Routledge, 1987), 218.

GLOSSARY

arabesque strongly inhabits time as its twisting form bifurcates and conjoins in three-dimensional space. It is a figure that holds together in filigree light, dancing flurries, and curlicues with a robust, linear telos. It is an enactment of the way motifs of text and music weave in and out of the texture, disappearing and then re-emerging, maintaining the appearance of movement on several planes at once.

éclat signifies an instant of violent rupture in a linear surface. It is an instant of eruption or atemporality heard or read occurring against a surrounding continuity. Its length and the degree of its violence will vary according to the emotional context of the work in question. Both the *éclat* and the *explosante fixe* are isolated enough in occurrence to remain agents of disorder and discontinuity when in dialogue with structural logics of forward progression.

enroulement describes the conflicting kinetic movements that are produced from, and fill, moments of discontinuity. They are transitory coilings and windings through time-space manufactured by the collision and intersection of two different vectors in the text or music.

éventail signifies with its *battement* a pulsating, rhythmic articulation of space poised in organized complexity. The pushes and retreats of the open, beating fan couple silence and sound, and mobility and stasis. Its movement holds antithetical states in tension both in the text and in music.

explosante fixe describes a phenomenon of mobile stasis. In these instances various textual or musical lines appear to be momentarily caught in a texture of opposing forces applied by the simultaneous movement and inertia found in passages of ostinato and oscillation.

Möbius strip is the term derived from topology for a surface whose torsion, when defined by a temporal event, allows depth to be perceived in space. As an intermediary figure it gives an abstract reading model for particular spatio-temporal hesitations and paradoxes that we encounter in music and text. It defines a very precise spatio-temporal curve, punctuated by the temporal paradox of its torsion, which is perceived as a horizon, but can never be reached, by an ant walking along the strip. This point on the strip describes reading or hearing two possible outcomes or interpretations, neither of which is settled upon, knitted together at a particular point.

pli describes heard or read gestures that are both opening and closural by its concealing and revealing motion. The figure contains the two movements in their simultaneous relation, neither excluded from one another nor united.

thyrsus symbolizes a counterpoint of two different impulses within the text or music. The rod or baton is the strand of unity running through the work, a telos of repetition and familiarity, against which improvisatory elements of open invention and variation can play.

BIBLIOGRAPHY

PRIMARY PRINTED SOURCES

Works by Mallarmé

(a) Collected editions

Œuvres complètes, ed. Henri Mondor and G. Jean-Aubry, Bibliothèque de la Pléiade (Paris: Gallimard, 1945).

Œuvres complètes, i, ed. Bertrand Marchal, Bibliothèque de la Pléiade (Paris: Gallimard, 1998).

Igitur, Divagations, Un coup de dés, ed. Yves Bonnefoy (Paris: Gallimard, 1976).

Correspondance complète, ed. Henri Mondor and Jean-Pierre Richard (vol. i), Henri Mondor and Lloyd James Austin (vols. ii–xi), 11 vols. (Paris: Gallimard, 1959–85).

Correspondance complète (1862–1871), suivi[e] de Lettres sur la poésie (1872–1898), avec des lettres inédites, ed. Bertrand Marchal and Yves Bonnefoy (Paris: Gallimard, 1995).

(b) Individual editions

Un coup de Dés jamais n'abolira le Hasard, ed. Mitsou Ronat (Paris: Change errant, 1980).

Le 'Livre' de Mallarmé, ed. Jacques Scherer, 2nd edn. (Paris: Gallimard, 1977).

Works by Debussy

Pelléas et Mélisande, rev. edn. (Paris: Durand, 1966).

Monsieur Croche et autres écrits, 2nd edn. (Paris: Gallimard, 1971).

Trois poèmes de Stéphane Mallarmé (Leipzig: Edition Peters, 1972).

Prélude à l'Après-midi d'un faune (London: Dover Publications, 1983).

La Mer (London: Eulenberg, 1983).

Images, Jeux and The Martyrdom of St. Sebastian in Full Score (New York: Dover Publications, 1992).

Correspondance (1884–1918), ed. François Lesure (Paris: Collections Savoirs, 1993).

Édition critique des œuvres complètes de Claude Debussy, ed. François Lesure et al. (Paris: Durand & Costallat, in progress).

OTHER PRIMARY WORKS

BAUDELAIRE, CHARLES, *Œuvres complètes*, ed. Claude Pichois, Bibliothèque de la Pléiade, 2 vols. (Paris: Gallimard, 1975–6).

—— *Petits Poèmes en prose*, ed. Henri Lemaître (Paris: Classiques Garnier, 1980).

—— *Les Fleurs du mal*, ed. Enid Starkie (Oxford: Blackwell, 1980).

—— *Critique d'art suivi de critique musicale*, ed. Claude Pichois and Claire Brunet (Paris: Gallimard, 1992).

GAUTIER, THÉOPHILE, *Émaux et camées*, ed. Adolphe Boschot (Paris: Éditions Garnier, 1954).

GHIL, RENÉ, *Traité du verbe* (Paris: Giraud, 1886).

HUYSMANS, JORIS K., *A rebours*, ed. Jean Borie (Arles: Actes Sud, 1992).

JOYCE, JAMES, *Finnegans Wake* (London: Flamingo, 1994).

POE, EDGAR A., *Tales of the Grotesque and Arabesque, With Other Stories* (London: G. Newnes, 1903).

—— *Great Short Works of Edgar Allan Poe*, ed. Gary R. Thompson (New York: Harper & Row, 1970).

RONSARD, PIERRE DE, *Les Amours* (Paris: Flammarion, 1981).

ROUSSEAU, JEAN-JACQUES, *Écrits sur la musique, la langue et le théâtre*, ed. Bernard Gagnebin and Marcel Raymond, Bibliothèque de la Pléiade (Paris: Gallimard, 1995).

STENDHAL, *Œuvres intimes*, ed. V. del Litto, Bibliothèque de la Pléiade, 2 vols. (Paris: Gallimard, 1981–2).

STEVENS, WALLACE, *Opus Posthumous: Poems, Plays, Prose*, ed. Milton J. Bates (New York: Vintage Books, 1989).

—— *The Collected Poems*, ed. Milton J. Bates (New York: Vintage Books, 1990).

VALÉRY, PAUL, *Introduction à la poétique*, 6th edn. (Paris: Gallimard, 1938).

—— *Écrits divers sur Stéphane Mallarmé* (Paris: Gallimard, 1950).

—— *Cahiers*, 29 vols. (Paris: CNRS, 1957–61).

—— *Œuvres*, ed. Jean Hytier, Bibliothèque de la Pléiade, 2 vols. (Paris: Gallimard, 1957–60).

VERLAINE, PAUL, *Œuvres complètes*, ed. Y. G. Le Dantec and Jacques Borel, Bibliothèque de la Pléiade (Paris: Gallimard, 1962).

WILDE, OSCAR, *The Picture of Dorian Gray*, ed. Peter Faulkner (London: Everyman, 1993).

CRITICAL AND BIOGRAPHICAL WORKS ON MALLARMÉ

ABASTADO, CLAUDE, *Expérience et théórie de la création poétique chez Mallarmé* (Paris: Minard, 1970).

—— 'Le "Livre" de Mallarmé: Un autoportrait mythique', *Romantisme*, 44 (1984), 65–81.

AUSTIN, LLOYD J., 'Mallarmé and the *Prose pour des Esseintes*', *Forum for Modern Language Studies*, 2 (1966), 197–213.

—— *Essais sur Mallarmé*, ed. Malcolm Bowie (Manchester: Manchester University Press, 1995).

BERNARD, SUZANNE, *Mallarmé et la musique* (Paris: Nizet, 1959).

BERSANI, LEO, *The Death of Stéphane Mallarmé* (Cambridge: Cambridge University Press, 1982).

BLANCHOT, MAURICE, *L'Espace littéraire* (Paris: Gallimard, 1955).

BLOOM, HAROLD (ed.), *Stéphane Mallarmé* (New York: Chelsea House Publishers, 1987).

BOWIE, MALCOLM, *Mallarmé and the Art of Being Difficult* (Cambridge: Cambridge University Press, 1978).

—— 'Genius at Nightfall: Mallarmé's "Quand l'ombre menaça de la fatale loi . . ." ', in C. Prendergast (ed.), *Nineteenth-Century French Poetry: Introductions to Close Reading* (Cambridge: Cambridge University Press, 1990), 225–42.

—— FAIRLIE, ALISON, and FINCH, ALISON (eds.), *Baudelaire, Mallarmé, Valéry: New Essays in Honour of Lloyd Austin* (Cambridge: Cambridge University Press, 1982).

BREATNACH, MARY, *Boulez and Mallarmé: A Study in Poetic Influence* (Aldershot: Scolar, 1996).

BURT, ELLEN, 'Mallarmé's "Sonnet en yx": The Ambiguities of Speculation', *Yale French Studies*, 54 (1977), 55–82.

CAMPION, PIERRE, *Mallarmé: Poésie et philosophie* (Paris: Presses Universitaires de France, 1994).

CARRON, JEAN-CLAUDE, '*Sainte* de Mallarmé: Poétique et musiques', *Kentucky Romance Quarterly*, 26 (1979), 133–41.

CHAUSSERIE-LAPRÉE, JEAN-PIERRE, 'L'Architecture secrète de l'"Ouverture ancienne"', *Europe*, 54 (Apr.–May 1976) 74–103.

CHISHOLM, A. R., *Mallarmé's L'Après-midi d'un faune: An Exegetical and Critical Study* (Melbourne: Melbourne University Press, 1958).

—— *Mallarmé's Grand Œuvre* (Manchester: Manchester University Press, 1962).

—— Mallarmé and the Riddle of the Ptyx', *AUMLA* 40 (1973), 246–8.

COHN, ROBERT G., *Mallarmé's 'Un coup de Dés': An Exegesis*, Yale French Studies (New Haven: Yale University Press, 1949).

—— *Towards the Poems of Mallarmé* (Berkeley and Los Angeles: University of California Press, 1965).

—— *Mallarmé's Masterwork: New Findings* (The Hague: Mouton and Co., 1966).

DAVIES, GARDNER, *Mallarmé et le drame solaire* (Paris: Corti, 1959).

—— *Mallarmé et le rêve d'*'*Hérodiade*' (Paris: Corti, 1978).

—— *Vers une explication rationnelle du 'Coup de Dés: essai d'exégèse mallarméenne'*, rev. edn. (Paris: José Corti, 1992).

DERRIDA, JACQUES, *La Dissémination* (Paris: Seuil, 1972).

FLORENCE, PENNY, *Mallarmé, Manet and Redon: Visual and Aural Signs and the Generation of Meaning* (Cambridge: Cambridge University Press, 1986).

GUYAUX, ANDRÉ (ed.), *Stéphane Mallarmé: Colloque de la Sorbonne* (Paris: Presses de l'Université de Paris-Sorbonne, 1998).

KILLICK, RACHEL, 'Mallarmé's Rooms: The Poet's Place in "La Musique et les Lettres"', *French Studies*, 51/2 (1997), 155–68.

KRISTEVA, JULIA, *La Révolution du langage poétique: L'Avant-garde à la fin du XIXe siècle: Lautréamont et Mallarmé* (Paris: Seuil, 1974).

LA CHARITÉ, VIRGINIA, *The Dynamics of Space: Mallarmé's 'Un coup de dés jamais n'abolira le hasard'* (Lexington, Ky.: French Forum, 1987).

LLOYD, ROSEMARY, *Mallarmé: 'Poésies'* (London: Grant & Cutler, 1984).

Mallarmé 1842–1898: Un destin d'écriture (Gallimard/Réunion des Musées Nationaux, 1998).

MARCHAL, BERNARD, *Lecture de Mallarmé* (Paris: José Corti, 1985).

—— *La Religion de Mallarmé* (Paris: José Corti, 1988).

—— (ed.), *Stéphane Mallarmé: Mémoire de la critique* (Paris: Presses de l'Université de Paris-Sorbonne, 1998).

MICHAUD, GUY, *Mallarmé*, 2nd edn. (Paris: Hatier, 1971).

MILLAN, GORDON, *Mallarmé: A Throw of the Dice: The Life of Stéphane Mallarmé* (London: Secker & Warburg, 1994).

MONDOR, HENRI, *Vie de Mallarmé*, 14th edn. (Paris: Gallimard, 1941).

MONDOR, HENRI, 'Stéphane Mallarmé et Paul Claudel: *Correspondance*', *Cahiers Paul Claudel*, 14 vols. (Paris: Gallimard, 1959–95), i. 40–55.

NOULET, ÉMILIE, *L'Œuvre poétique de Stéphane Mallarmé* (Paris: Droz, 1940).

PEARSON, ROGER, *Unfolding Mallarmé: The Development of a Poetic Art* (Oxford: Clarendon Press, 1996).

La Quinzaine littéraire, 749 (1998).

RICHARD, JEAN-PIERRE, *L'Univers imaginaire de Mallarmé* (Paris: Seuil, 1961).

ROBB, GRAHAM, *Unlocking Mallarmé* (New Haven: Yale University Press, 1996).

ROULET, CLAUDE, *Élucidation du poème de Stéphane Mallarmé: Un coup de dés jamais n'abolira le hasard* (Neuchâtel: Aux Ides et Calendes, 1943).

SARTRE, JEAN-PAUL, *Mallarmé: La Lucidité et sa face d'ombre* (Paris: Gallimard, 1986).

SCEPI, HENRI (ed.), *Mallarmé et la prose* (Poitiers: URF Langues Littératures, 1998).

SCOTT, DAVID, 'Mallarmé and the Octosyllabic Sonnet', *French Studies*, 31 (1977), 149–63.

SHAW, MARY L., *Performance in the Texts of Mallarmé: The Passage from Art to Ritual* (Philadelphia: The Pennsylvania State University Press, 1993).

TEMPLE, MICHAEL (ed.), *Meetings with Mallarmé in Contemporary French Culture* (Exeter: University of Exeter Press, 1998).

WATSON, LAWRENCE, 'Some Further Thoughts on Mallarmé's "Sonnet en -yx"', *French Studies Bulletin*, 27 (Summer 1988), 13–16.

CRITICAL, BIOGRAPHICAL, AND REFERENCE WORKS ON DEBUSSY

ABRAVANEL, CLAUDE, *Claude Debussy: A Bibliography* (Detroit: Detroit Studies, 1974).

AUSTIN, WILLIAM, *Music in the Twentieth Century: From Debussy through Stravinsky* (New York: Dent, 1966).

—— *Prelude to the Afternoon of a Faun* (New York: Norton Critical Scores, 1970).

BARRAQUÉ, JEAN, *Debussy* (Paris: Seuil, 1962).

—— '*La Mer* de Debussy, ou la naissance des formes ouvertes', *Analyse musicale*, 12 (1988), 15–62.

BERGERON, KATHERINE, 'The Echo, the Cry, the Death of Lovers', *Nineteenth-Century Music*, 18/2 (1994), 136–51.

BERMAN, LAURENCE, 'The Evolution of Tonal Thinking in the Works of Claude Debussy' Ph.D. thesis (Harvard, 1965).

—— '*Prelude to the Afternoon of a Faun* and *Jeux*: Debussy's Summer Rites', *Nineteenth-Century Music*, 3/3 (1980), 225–38.

BOUCOURECHLIEV, ANDRÉ, *Debussy: La Révolution subtile* (Paris: Fayard, 1998).

BRISCOE, JAMES R., *Claude Debussy: A Guide to Research* (New York: Garland Publications, 1990).

—— *Debussy in Performance* (New Haven: Yale University Press, 1999).

BRUSSEL, ROBERT, 'Claude Debussy et Paul Dukas', *La Revue musicale*, 7 (1926), 101–5.

COBB, MARGARET G., *The Poetic Debussy*, 2nd edn. (Rochester, Minn.: University of Rochester Press, 1994).

COX, DAVID, *Debussy: Orchestral Music* (London: BBC Music Guide, 1974).

DAWES, FRANK, *Debussy Piano Music* (London: Cox & Wyman, 1969).

EIMERT, HERBERT, 'Debussy's *Jeux*', *Die Reihe*, 5 (1959), 3–20.

FRANZ, CHARLES, F., '*Fin de siècle* Art and Debussy's Music: New Paths for Analysis and Interpretation', Ph.D. thesis (State University of New Jersey, 1997).

GRAYSON, DAVID, *The Genesis of Debussy's 'Pelléas et Mélisande'* (Ann Arbor, 1986).

HOLLOWAY, ROBIN, *Debussy and Wagner* (London: Eulenberg Books, 1979).

HOWAT, ROY, *Debussy in Proportion: A Musical Analysis* (Cambridge: Cambridge University Press, 1983).

JAMEUX, DOMINIQUE, 'Mallarmé: Debussy, Boulez', *Silences*, 4 (1987), 191–201.

JANKÉLÉVITCH, VLADIMIR, *La Vie et la mort dans la musique de Debussy* (Neuchâtel: La Baconnière, 1968).

JAROCINSKI, STEFAN, *Debussy, Impressionism and Symbolism*, trans. Rollo Myers (London: Eulenberg Books, 1976).

LANGHAM SMITH, RICHARD (ed.), *Debussy Studies* (Cambridge: Cambridge University Press, 1997).

LESURE, FRANÇOIS, *Claude Debussy avant 'Pelléas', ou les années symbolistes* (Paris, 1992).

—— *Claude Debussy* (Paris, 1994).

LOCKSPEISER, EDWARD, *Debussy: His Life and Mind*, 2 vols. (London: Cassell & Co., Ltd., 1962–5).

MARTIN-LAU, PHILLIPE (ed.), *Centenaires de* Pelléas (Orléans: Paradigme, 2001).

NICHOLS, ROGER, *Debussy* (Oxford: Oxford University Press, 1973).

—— *Debussy Remembered* (London: Faber & Faber, 1992).

—— *The Life of Debussy* (Cambridge: Cambridge University Press, 1998).

ORLEDGE, ROBERT, *Debussy and the Theatre* (Cambridge: Cambridge University Press, 1982).

—— 'The Genesis of Debussy's *Jeux*', *Musical Times*, 128 (1987), 68–73.

PARKS, ROGER, *The Music of Claude Debussy* (New Haven: Yale University Press, 1989).

PASLER, JANN, 'Debussy, *Jeux*: Playing with Time and Form', *Nineteenth-Century Music*, 6/1 (1982), 60–75.

ROBERTS, PAUL, *Images: The Piano Music of Claude Debussy* (Portland, Ore.: Amadeus Press, 1996).

SOURIS, ANDRÉ, 'Debussy et Stravinsky', *Revue belge de la musicologie*, 1–4 (1962), 45–56.

TREZISE, SIMON, *Debussy: La Mer* (Cambridge: Cambridge University Press, 1994).

VALLAS, LÉON, *Claude Debussy et son temps* (Paris, Albin Michel, 1958).

WARBURTON, THOMAS, 'Bitonal Miniatures by Debussy from 1913', *Cahiers Debussy*, 6 (1982), 5–15.

WENK, ARTHUR, *Claude Debussy and the Poets* (Berkeley and Los Angeles: University of California Press, 1976).

WHITTALL, ARNOLD, 'Tonality and the Whole-Tone Scale in the Music of Debussy', *Music Review*, 36 (1975), 261–71.

OTHER CRITICAL WORKS

On music

ABBATE, CAROLYN, *Unsung Voices: Opera and Musical Narrative in the Nineteenth Century* (Princeton: Princeton University Press, 1991).

AGAWU, KOFI, *Playing with Signs: A Semiotic Interpretation of Classical Music* (Princeton: Princeton University Press, 1991).

BERRY, WALLACE, *Musical Structure and Performance* (New Haven: Yale University Press, 1989).

BOULEZ, PIERRE, *Relevés d'apprenti* (Paris: Seuil, 1966).

—— *On Music Today*, 2nd edn. (London: Faber & Faber, 1975).

—— *Par volonté et par hasard* (Paris: Seuil, 1975).

—— *Orientations* (London: Faber & Faber, 1986).

—— *Jalons (pour une décennie)* (Paris: Christian Bourgois, 1989).

—— *Points de repère* (Paris: Christian Bourgois, 1995).

BRENDEL, ALFRED, *Music Sounded Out* (London: Robson Books, 1990).

BUJIC, BOJAN, *Music in European Thought* (Cambridge: Cambridge University Press, 1988).

BUTLER, CHRISTOPHER, *Early Modernism: Literature, Music and Painting in Europe 1900–1916* (Oxford: Clarendon Press, 1994).

CONE, EDWARD T., *The Composer's Voice: Sound and Poetry* (New York: Columbia University Press, 1957).

DAHLHAUS, CARL, *Nineteenth-Century Music*, trans. J. Bradford Robinson (Berkeley and Los Angeles: University of California Press, 1989).

GRIFFITHS, PAUL, *Modern Music: A Concise History from Debussy to Boulez*, 2nd edn. (London: Thames & Hudson, 1990).

HANSLICK, EDWARD, 'On the Musically Beautiful', in Edward Lippman (ed.), *Musical Aesthetics: A Historical Reader*, trans. Guy Payzant, 3 vols. (New York: Pendragon Press, 1986–8), ii. 265–307.

HERTZ, DAVID, *The Tuning of the Word: Musico-Literary Poetics of the Symbolist Movement* (Carbondale: Southern Illinois University Press, 1987).

HINDEMITH, PAUL, *The Craft of Musical Composition*, 4th edn. (Mainz, 1970).

HODGE, JOANNA, 'Aesthetic Decomposition: Music, Identity, and Time', in Michael Krausz (ed.), *The Interpretation of Music: Philosophical Essays* (Oxford: Clarendon Press, 1993).

KERMAN, JOSEPH, 'How We Got into Analysis, and How to Get Out', *Critical Inquiry*, 7/2 (1980), 311–31.

KIVY, PETER, *Sound and Semblance: Reflections on Musical Repetition* (Princeton: Princeton University Press, 1984).

KRAMER, JONATHAN, 'Multiple and Non-linear Time', *Perspectives of New Music*, 11/2 (1973), 122–45.

—— 'Moment Form in Twentieth-Century Music', *Musical Quarterly*, 64/2 (1978), 177–94.

—— *The Time of Music* (New York: Schirmer Books, 1988).

KRAMER, LAWRENCE, *Music and Poetry: The Nineteenth Century and After* (Berkeley and Los Angeles: University of California Press, 1984).

—— *Music as Cultural Practice, 1800–1900* (Berkeley and Los Angeles: University of California Press, 1990).

—— *Classical Music and Postmodern Knowledge* (Berkeley and Los Angeles: University of California Press, 1995).

KRAUSZ, MICHAEL (ed.), *The Interpretation of Music: Philosophical Essays* (Oxford: Clarendon Press, 1993).

LANG, PAUL H., *Musicology and Performance* (New Haven: Yale University Press, 1997).

LANGER, SUSANNE, *Philosophy in a New Key* (Cambridge, Mass.: Harvard University Press, 1942).

—— *Feeling and Form* (New York: Scribner's, 1953).

LIPPMAN, EDWARD (ed.), *Musical Aesthetics: A Historical Reader*, trans. Guy Payzant, 3 vols. (New York: Pendragon Press, 1986–8).

MCCLARY, SUSAN, *Feminine Endings: Music, Gender and Sexuality* (Minneapolis: University of Minnesota Press, 1991).

MAGEE, BRYAN, *Aspects of Wagner*, 2nd edn. (Oxford: Oxford University Press, 1988).

MITCHELL, DONALD, *The Language of Modern Music*, rev. edn. (London: Faber & Faber, 1993).

MORGAN, ROBERT, 'Musical Time/Musical Space', *Critical Inquiry*, 6 (1980), 527–38.

NATTIEZ, JEAN-JACQUES, *Fondements d'une sémiologie de la musique* (Paris: Union Générale d'Éditions, 1975).

—— *De la sémiologie à la musique* (Université du Québec à Montréal: Les Cahiers du Département d'Études Littéraires, 1988).

NEUBAUER, JOHN, *The Emancipation of Music from Language: Departure from Mimesis in Eighteenth-Century Aesthetics* (New Haven: Yale University Press, 1986).

PADDISON, MAX, *Adorno's Aesthetics of Music* (Cambridge: Cambridge University Press, 1993).

POPLE, ANTHONY, *Theory, Analysis and Meaning in Music* (Cambridge: Cambridge University Press, 1994).

ROSEN, CHARLES, *Schoenberg* (London: Fontana/Collins, 1975).

—— *Sonata Forms* (New York: Norton, 1980).

—— *The Romantic Generation* (London: Harper Collins, 1996).

—— *The Classical Style: Haydn, Mozart, Beethoven*, 3rd edn. (London: Faber & Faber, 1997).

SCHINDLER, ANTON, *Beethoven As I Knew Him* (London: Dover, 1996).

SCHOENBERG, ARNOLD, *Style and Idea: The Selected Writings of Arnold Schoenberg* (Berkeley and Los Angeles: University of California Press, 1984).

SCHUMANN, ROBERT, *Gesammelte Schrifte über Musik und Musiker*, 2 vols. (Leipzig: Breitkopf & Härtel, 1914).

SCRUTON, ROGER, *The Aesthetics of Music* (Oxford: Oxford University Press, 1997).

SEBEOK, THOMAS A. (ed.), *A Perfusion of Signs* (Bloomington, IN: Indiana University Press, 1977).

STRAUS, JOSEPH N., *Remaking the Past: Musical Modernism and the Influence of the Tonal Tradition* (Cambridge, Mass.: Harvard University Press, 1990).

TOVEY, DONALD, *A Companion to Beethoven's Pianoforte Sonatas*, rev. edn. (London: Associated Boards of the Royal Schools of Music, 1998).

WAGNER, RICHARD, 'Opera and Drama', in Edward Lippman (ed.), *Musical Aesthetics: A Historical Reader*, trans. Guy Payzant, 3 vols. (New York: Pendragon Press, 1986–8), ii. 215–60.

On literature

ABRAMS, MEYER H., *The Mirror and the Lamp: Romantic Theory and the Critical Tradition* (New York: Oxford University Press, 1951).

BARTHES, ROLAND, *Le Degré zéro de l'écriture* (1953), suivi de *Nouveaux Essais critiques*, 'Points' (Paris: Seuil, 1972).

—— *S/Z* (Paris: Seuil, 1970).

BARTHES, ROLAND, *Le Plaisir du texte* (Paris: Seuil, 1973).
—— *Image, Music, Text*, trans. Stephen Heath (New York: Hill & Wang, 1977).
—— *L'Obvie et l'obtus* (Paris: Seuil, 1982).
—— *Le Bruissement de la langue*, 2nd edn. (Paris: Seuil, 1984).
—— *Œuvres complètes*, ed. Éric Marty, 2 vols. (Paris: Seuil, 1994).
BENNETT, TONY, *Outside Literature* (London: Routledge, 1990).
BOWIE, MALCOLM (ed.), 'Freud, Lacan and the Critique of Culture', Paragraph, 14/1 (1991).
—— *Psychoanalysis and the Future of Theory* (Oxford: Blackwell, 1993).
BURKE, SEÁN, *Authorship from Plato to the Postmodern: A Reader* (Edinburgh: Edinburgh University Press, 1995).
CULLER, JONATHAN, *Structuralist Poetics* (London: Routledge and Kegan Paul, 1975).
—— *The Pursuit of Signs: Semiotics, Literature, Deconstruction* (London: Routledge & Kegan Paul, 1981).
—— *Barthes*, 2nd edn. (London: Fontana Modern Masters, 1991).
DE MAN, PAUL, *Allegories of Reading* (New Haven: Yale University Press, 1979).
DERRIDA, JACQUES, *De la grammatologie* (Paris: Minuit, 1967).
—— *La Dissémination* (Paris: Seuil, 1972).
—— *L'Écriture et la différence* (Paris: Seuil, 1979).
—— 'Structure, Sign and Play in the Discourse of the Human Sciences' in David Lodge (ed.), *Modern Criticism and Theory: A Reader* (New York: Longman, 1988), 108–23.
EAGLETON, TERRY, *Literary Theory*, 2nd edn. (Oxford: Blackwell, 1996).
ECO, UMBERTO, *The Open Work*, trans. Anna Cancogni (London: Hutchinson, 1989).
FOUCAULT, MICHEL, *Les Mots et les choses* (Paris: Gallimard, 1966).
—— 'Compte rendu de la séance', *Bulletin de la Société Française de Philosophie*, 63 (1969), 75–94.
—— *L'Archéologie du savoir* (Paris: Gallimard, 1969).
FREEMAN, MICHAEL et al. (eds.), *The Process of Art: Studies in Nineteenth-Century French Literature, Music and Painting in Honour of Alan Raitt* (Oxford: Clarendon Press, 1998).
GANS, ERIC, 'The Poem as Hypothesis of Origin: Lamartine's "Le Lac" ', in Christopher Prendergast (ed.), *Nineteenth-Century French Poetry: Introductions to Close Reading* (Cambridge: Cambridge University Press, 1990), 29–47.
GENETTE, GÉRARD, *Figures I* (Paris: Seuil, 1966).
GORDON, RAE BETH, *Ornament, Fantasy and Desire in Nineteenth-Century French Literature* (Princeton: Princeton University Press, 1992).
HOBSON, MARIAN, *Jacques Derrida: Opening Lines* (London: Routledge, 1998).
HOLUB, ROBERT, *Reception Theory: A Critical Introduction* (London: Methuen, 1984).
ISER, WOLFGANG, *The Act of Reading: A Theory of Aesthetic Response* (London: Routledge & Kegan Paul, 1978).
JAKOBSON, ROMAN, 'Linguistics and Poetics' and 'The Metaphoric and Metonymic Poles', in David Lodge (ed.), *Modern Criticism and Theory. A Reader* (New York: Longman, 1988), 32–61.
JAUSS, HANS R., *Towards an Aesthetics of Reception* (Brighton: Harvester, 1982).
JEFFERSON, ANN, *Reading Realism in Stendhal* (Cambridge: Cambridge University Press, 1988).
JOHNSON, BARBARA, *Défigurations du langage poétique: La Seconde Révolution baudelairienne* (Paris: Flammarion, 1979).

—— *The Critical Difference: Essays in the Contemporary Rhetoric of Reading* (Baltimore: Johns Hopkins University Press, 1980).

KERMODE, FRANK, *The Sense of an Ending: Studies in the Theory of Fiction* (Oxford: Oxford University Press, 1966).

KRISTEVA, JULIA, 'The Ethics of Linguistics', in David Lodge (ed.), *Modern Criticism and Theory: A Reader* (New York: Longman, 1988), 230–9.

LEHMANN, A. G., *The Symbolist Aesthetic in France 1885–95* (Oxford: Blackwell, 1950).

LODGE, DAVID (ed.), *Modern Criticism and Theory: A Reader* (New York: Longman, 1988).

MICHAUD, GUY, *Message poétique du symbolisme*, 3 vols. (Paris: Nizet, 1947).

NOWOTTNY, WINIFRED, *The Language Poets Use* (London: The Athlone Press, 1962).

PIMENTEL, LUZ A., *Metaphoric Narration: The Paranarrative Dimensions in 'A la recherche de temps perdu'* (Toronto: University of Toronto Press, 1990).

POULET, GEORGES, *La Distance intérieure (Études sur le temps humain, II)* (Paris: Plon, 1952).

—— *La Conscience critique* (Paris: José Corti, 1971).

POUND, EZRA, *Literary Essays of Ezra Pound*, ed. T. S. Eliot (London: Faber & Faber, 1954).

PRENDERGAST, CHRISTOPHER (ed.), *Nineteenth-Century French Poetry: Introductions to Close Reading* (Cambridge: Cambridge University Press, 1990).

RIFATERRE, MICHEL, *The Semiotics of Poetry* (Bloomington: Indiana University Press, 1978).

ROUBAUD, JACQUES, *La Vieillesse d'Alexandre* (Paris: Maspero, 1978).

SCOTT, CLIVE, *The Riches of Rhyme* (Oxford: Clarendon, 1988).

—— *Vers Libre: The Emergence of Free Verse in France 1886–1914* (Oxford: Clarendon, 1990).

—— *The Poetics of French Verse* (Oxford: Clarendon, 1998).

SCOTT, DAVID, *Sonnet Theory and Practice in Nineteenth-Century France: Sonnets on the Sonnet* (Hull: University of Hull, 1977).

—— *Pictorialist Poetics: Poetry and the Visual Arts in Nineteenth-Century France* (Cambridge: Cambridge University Press, 1988).

—— 'The Poetics of the Rebus: Word, Image and the Dynamics of Reading in the Poster of the 1920s', *Word and Image*, 13/3 (1997), 270–8.

SMITH, BARBARA HERNSTEIN, *Poetic Closure* (Chicago: University of Chicago Press, 1968).

WEINBERG, BERNARD, *The Limits of Symbolism* (Chicago: University of Chicago Press, 1966).

WELLEK, RENÉ, *Concepts of Criticism* (New Haven: Yale University Press, 1963).

On music and literature

ADORNO, THEODOR, *Philosophy of Modern Music*, trans. Anne G. Mitchell and Wesley V. Bloomster (New York: The Seabury Press, 1973).

—— *Notes to Literature*, ed. L. D. Kritzman and R. Wolin, trans. Shierry Weber Nicholsen, European Perspectives, 2 vols. (New York: Columbia University, 1992).

—— *Quasi una fantasia: Essays on Modern Music*, trans. Rodney Livingstone (London: Verso, 1992).

BERNHART, WALTER et al. (eds.), *Word and Music Studies: Defining the Field* (Amsterdam: Rodopi, 1999).

BERNHART, WALTER and WOLF, WERNER (eds.), *Word and Music Studies: Essays on the Song Cycle and Defining the Field* (Amsterdam: Rodopi, 2001).

BERNSTEIN, SUSAN, *Virtuosity of the Nineteenth Century: Performing Music and Language in Heine, Liszt and Baudelaire* (Stanford, Calif.: Stanford University Press, 1998).

CUPERS, JEAN-LOUIS, et al. (eds.), *Musico-Poetics in Perspective: Calvin S. Brown in Memoriam* (Amsterdam: Rodopi, 2000).

HOLLANDER, JOHN, *Untuning the Sky: Ideas of Music in English Poetry* (Princeton: Princeton University Press, 1961).

LODATO, SUZANNE, et al. (eds.), *Word and Music Studies: Essays in Honour of Steven Paul Scher and on Cultural Identity and the Musical Stage* (Amsterdam: Rodopi, 2002).

NIETZSCHE, FRIEDRICH, 'On Music and Words', in Carl Dahlhaus (ed.), *Between Romanticism and Modernism: Four Studies in the Music of the Later Nineteenth Century*, trans. Mary Whittall (Berkeley and Los Angeles: University of California Press, 1980).

—— *The Birth of Tragedy and The Case of Wagner*, trans. Walter A. Kaufman (New York: Vintage Books, 1967).

RUWET, NICOLAS, *Langage, musique, poésie*, 2nd edn. (Paris: Seuil, 1972).

SCHER, STEVEN P., *Music and Text: Critical Inquiries* (Cambridge: Cambridge University Press, 1992).

STEINER, WENDY, *The Sign in Music and Literature* (Austin: University of Texas Press, 1981).

WINN, JAMES A., *Unsuspected Eloquence* (New York: Yale University Press, 1981).

Other works consulted

BARROW, JOHN, *The Artful Universe: The Cosmic Source of Human Creativity*, 2nd edn. (London: Penguin, 1997).

BRAQUEMOND, FÉLIX, *Du dessin et de la couleur* (Paris: Charpentier, 1885).

BRYSON, NORMAN, *Visual Theory: Painting and Interpretation* (Cambridge: Cambridge University Press, 1991).

CASSIRER, ERNST, *The Philosophy of Symbolic Form* (New Haven: Yale University Press, 1953).

DICKIE, GEORGE, *Aesthetics: An Introduction* (Indianapolis: The Bobbs-Merrill Company, 1971).

FOCILLON, HENRI, *La Vie des formes*, rev. edn. (Paris: Alcan, 1939).

FOWLER, ROGER, *Modern Critical Terms* (London: Routledge, 1987).

GOMBRICH, ERNST, *Art and Illusion: A Study in the Psychology of Pictorial Representation*, 5th edn. (Oxford: Oxford University Press, 1983).

GRANON-LAFONT, JEANNE, *La Topologie ordinaire de Jacques Lacan* (Paris: Point Hors Ligne, 1985).

GUILLEMOT, MAURICE, *Villégiatures d'artistes* (Paris: Flammarion, 1898).

HOFSTADTER, DOUGLAS R., *Gödel, Escher, Bach: An Eternal Golden Braid* (Brighton: Harvester Press, 1979).

JOHNSON-LAIRD, PHILIP N., *The Computer and the Mind* (Glasgow: Fontana Press, 1988).

PETERSON, IVARS, *The Mathematical Tourist: Snapshots of Modern Mathematics*, 2nd edn. (New York: W. H. Freeman, 1998).

PRASOLOV, VIKTOR, *Intuitive Topology* (Providence, RI: American Mathematical Society, 1995).

RUSKIN, JOHN, *Modern Painters* (London: G. Bell, 1927).

SCHOPENHAUER, ARTHUR, *The World as Will and Idea*, trans. R. B. Haldane, 3rd edn. (London, 1891).

SHATTUCK, ROGER, *The Banquet Years*, 3rd edn. (London: Faber & Faber, 1958).

STEINER, GEORGE, *After Babel*, 2nd edn. (Oxford: Oxford University Press, 1992).

WIEDMANN, AUGUST K., *Romantic Roots in Modern Art, Romanticism and Expressionism: A Study in Comparative Aesthetics* (London: Gresham Books/Unwin, 1979).

WORNUM, RALPH, *Analysis of Ornament: The Characteristics of Style* (London: Chapman & Hall, 1873).

INDEX

This index makes no attempt to reference topics such as the relationship of music and poetry, silence, syntax, and so on, which are discussed too widely in the book to make indexing them useful to the reader. In the case of certain important topics such as discontinuity, hesitation, temporality, and rhythm, which also occur very frequently, only the most important discussions are indexed. Concepts and tools specific to verse and music analysis are indexed only where they are applied to, or illuminate, both music and poetry, not where they occur in their individual analytical contexts.